Fighting Modern Slavery and Human Trafficking

Over the last two decades, fighting modern slavery and human trafficking has become a *cause célèbre*. Yet large numbers of researchers, non-governmental organizations, trade unions, workers, and others who would seem like natural allies in the fight against modern slavery and trafficking are hugely skeptical of these movements. They object to how the problems are framed, and are skeptical of the "new abolitionist" movement. Why? This book tackles key controversies surrounding the anti-slavery and anti-trafficking movements head on. Champions and skeptics explore the fissures and fault lines that surround efforts to fight modern slavery and human trafficking today. These include: whether efforts to fight modern slavery displace or crowd out support for labor and migrant rights; whether and to what extent efforts to fight modern slavery mask, naturalize, and distract from racial, gendered, and economic inequality; and whether contemporary anti-slavery and anti-trafficking crusaders' use of history are accurate and appropriate.

Genevieve LeBaron is Professor of Politics at the University of Sheffield and an award-winning expert on the contemporary business of forced labor. She is the author of *Combatting Modern Slavery: Why Labour Governance Is Failing and What We Can Do About It* (Polity, 2020), among other books and articles. Her research has been featured widely in the media, including *The New York Times*, the BBC, *Forbes*, and the *Financial Times*. She was elected to the College of the Royal Society of Canada in 2020.

Jessica R. Pliley is Associate Professor of Women's and Gender History at Texas State University and holds a PhD from the Ohio State University. She is the author of *Policing Sexuality: The Mann Act and the Making of the FBI* (Harvard, 2014) and *Global Anti-Vice Activism* (Cambridge University Press, 2016). Her work has appeared in the *Journal of Women's History*, the *Journal of the Gilded Age and Progressive Era*, the *Journal of the History of Sexuality*, and several anthologies.

David W. Blight is Sterling Professor of American History at Yale University. He is the author of Pulitzer Prize-winning *Frederick Douglass: Prophet of Freedom* (2018, Simon & Schuster), among other books, book chapters, and articles. He was elected to the American Academy of Arts and Sciences in 2012.

Slaveries since Emancipation

General Editors

Randall Miller, *St. Joseph's University*
Zoe Trodd, *University of Nottingham*

Slaveries since Emancipation publishes scholarship that links slavery's past to its present, consciously scanning history for lessons of relevance to contemporary abolitionism and that directly engages current issues of interest to activists by contextualizing them historically.

Also in this series:

Fighting Modern Slavery and Human Trafficking

History and Contemporary Policy

Edited by

GENEVIEVE LEBARON
University of Sheffield

JESSICA R. PLILEY
Texas State University

DAVID W. BLIGHT
Yale University

CAMBRIDGE
UNIVERSITY PRESS

CAMBRIDGE
UNIVERSITY PRESS

University Printing House, Cambridge CB2 8BS, United Kingdom

One Liberty Plaza, 20th Floor, New York, NY 10006, USA

477 Williamstown Road, Port Melbourne, VIC 3207, Australia

314–321, 3rd Floor, Plot 3, Splendor Forum, Jasola District Centre,
New Delhi – 110025, India

79 Anson Road, #06–04/06, Singapore 079906

Cambridge University Press is part of the University of Cambridge.

It furthers the University's mission by disseminating knowledge in the pursuit of
education, learning, and research at the highest international levels of excellence.

www.cambridge.org
Information on this title: www.cambridge.org/9781108830621
DOI: 10.1017/9781108902519

First published 2021

A catalogue record for this publication is available from the British Library.

Library of Congress Cataloging-in-Publication Data
NAMES: LeBaron, Genevieve, editor. | Pliley, Jessica R., 1977– editor. | Blight, David
W., editor.
TITLE: Fighting modern slavery and human trafficking : history and contemporary
policy / edited by Genevieve LeBaron, University of Sheffield, Jessica R. Pliley, Texas
State University, San Marcos, David W. Blight, Yale University, Connecticut.
DESCRIPTION: Cambridge, United Kingdom ; New York, NY : Cambridge University
Press, 2021. | Series: Slaveries since emancipation | Includes bibliographical references
and index.
IDENTIFIERS: LCCN 2020040220 | ISBN 9781108830621 (hardback) | ISBN
9781108822404 (paperback) | ISBN 9781108902519 (ebook)
SUBJECTS: LCSH: Slavery – History – 21st century. | Human trafficking – History – 21st
century.
CLASSIFICATION: LCC HT867 .F54 2021 | DDC 306.3/620905–dc23
LC record available at https://lccn.loc.gov/2020040220

ISBN 978-1-108-83062-1 Hardback
ISBN 978-1-108-82240-4 Paperback

Contents

Figures

Tables

Contributors

Kevin Bales (PhD, social science, London School of Economics; CMG; FRSA) is Professor of Contemporary Slavery and Research Director of the Rights Lab, University of Nottingham. He is a member of the Gilder Lehrman Center's Modern Slavery Working Group at Yale University. He co-founded the nongovernmental organization (NGO) Free the Slaves. His research focuses on contemporary slavery. His 1999 book *Disposable People: New Slavery in the Global Economy* has been published in twelve languages. Other titles include *Ending Slavery: How We Free Today's Slaves* (2007) (Grawemeyer Award), *The Slave Next Door: Modern Slavery in the United States* (with Ron Soodalter, 2009), and *Blood and Earth* (2016), also published in Chinese and Japanese, awarded the Green Prize for Sustainable Literature 2017. The Association of British Universities named his work one of "100 World-Changing Discoveries."

David W. Blight (PhD, history, Wisconsin) is Sterling Professor of American History at Yale University and Director of Yale's Gilder Lehrman Center for the Study of Slavery, Resistance, and Abolition. He is the author of Pulitzer Prize–winning *Frederick Douglass: Prophet of Freedom* (2018), *American Oracle: The Civil War in the Civil Rights Era* (2013), and *A Slave No More: Two Men Who Escaped to Freedom, Including Their Own Narratives of Emancipation* (2007), among other books, book chapters, and articles. He was elected to the American Academy of Arts and Sciences in 2012.

Luis C. deBaca (JD, University of Michigan) is Senior Fellow of Modern Slavery at the Gilder Lehrman Center for the Study of Slavery, Resistance, and Abolition and Visiting Lecturer in Law at Yale Law School. His research and teaching examine the development of US antislavery laws in the wake of emancipation, the development of modern supply chain transparency laws, and the problem of forced labor in the built environment. As US Ambassador at Large to Monitor and Combat Trafficking in Persons, he led US bilateral and multilateral diplomacy and coordinated US government activities against contemporary forms of slavery. Among other official positions, he served as the US Justice Department's Involuntary Servitude and Slavery Coordinator. He played a key role in the drafting of the US Trafficking Victims Protection Act of 2000 and subsequent reauthorizations.

Janie Chuang (JD, Harvard Law School) is Professor of Law at American University Washington College of Law and a member of the Gilder Lehrman Center's Modern Slavery Working Group at Yale University. She teaches and writes in the areas of international law, human trafficking, and labor migration. Professor Chuang's articles have appeared in the *American Journal of International Law*, the *University of Pennsylvania Law Review*, the *UCLA Law Review*, and the *North Carolina Law Review*, and have been cited in *The Washington Post, The Wall Street Journal, The New York Times,* and the *Guardian,* among others. Drawing on her expertise on human trafficking issues, Chuang has served as an adviser to the United Nations, the International Labour Organization, and the Organization on Security and Cooperation in Europe.

Grace Peña Delgado (PhD, history, UCLA) is Associate Professor of History at the University of California, Santa Cruz (UCSC). She is also a member of the Gilder Lehrman Center's Modern Slavery Working Group at Yale University. Delgado is the author of *Making the Chinese Mexican: Global Migration, Localism, and Exclusion in the US-Mexico Borderlands* (2012) and a forthcoming work on sexuality and border control, *Freedom of Movement: Intercourse, States, and Intimacies at the U.S.-Mexico Border.* She is also the coauthor of *Latino Immigrants in the United States* (2011). She is the author of several articles and book chapters, and her piece in the *Western Historical Quarterly,* "Border Control and Sexual Policing," received numerous best article awards. In addition to her research, Delgado received UCSC's top teaching award conferred by its Academic Senate.

Anna Mae Duane (PhD, English, Fordham University) is Associate Professor of English at the University of Connecticut and a member of the Gilder Lehrman Center's Modern Slavery Working Group at Yale University. Her research focuses on how children experienced slavery in the eighteenth- and nineteenth-century United States. She is the author, editor, or coeditor of six books, including *Child Slavery before and after Emancipation: An Argument for Child-Centered Slavery Studies* (2017) and *Who Writes for Black Children?: African American Children's Literature before 1900* (2017). Her most recent book is *Educated for Freedom: The Incredible Story of Two Fugitive Schoolboys Who Grew up to Change a Nation* (2020). Her work has been supported by Fulbright and National Endowment for the Humanities (NEH) grants.

Lauren Eglen (MA, race and resistance, University of Leeds) is a PhD student in the Department of American and Canadian Studies at the University of Nottingham, UK, and a research fellow in survivor narratives with the Rights Lab at the University of Nottingham. Her research focuses on women's activism and print culture in the US Black Freedom Struggle, and her work with the Rights Lab includes expanding a database of modern slavery survivor narratives.

Alison Gardner (PhD, politics, University of Nottingham) is Associate Director for Communities and Society at the University of Nottingham's Rights Lab. Her work focuses on place- and community-based responses to modern slavery and includes publications in the *Journal of Human Rights Practice*, *Anti-Trafficking Review*, and the *Journal of Human Trafficking*. Gardner holds a Nottingham Research Fellowship and is coinvestigator on a Global Challenges Research Fund Global Engagements Network Grant to investigate the social determinants underpinning exploitation. She has career experience and expertise in local government and public policy.

Penelope Kyritsis (BA, postcolonial legal studies, Brown University) is Director of Strategic Research at the Worker Rights Consortium, an independent labor rights monitor that investigates working conditions in garment factories across major apparel-exporting countries. Her research areas include forced labor, corporate accountability, and worker-centered strategies for combatting labor abuse. She coauthored *Confronting Root Causes: Forced Labour in Global Supply Chains* (2018) and coedited *Domestic Workers Speak: A Global Fight for Rights and Recognition* (2017).

Genevieve LeBaron (PhD, political science, York University) is Professor of Politics at the University of Sheffield, UK. She is co-chair of the Gilder

Lehrman Center's Modern Slavery Working Group at Yale University. Her research investigates the political economy and business of forced labor and effectiveness of initiatives to combat it. She is the author of *Combatting Modern Slavery: Why Labour Governance Is Failing and What We Can Do About It* (2020) and editor of *Researching Forced Labour in the Global Economy: Methodological Challenges and Advances* (2018), among other books, and has published in leading political science and international relations journals.

Erica R. Meiners (PhD, education, Simon Fraser University) is the Bernard J. Brommel Distinguished Research Professor at Northeastern Illinois University. A writer, educator, and prison abolitionist, her current work includes a coedited anthology *The Long Term: Resisting Life Sentences, Working Towards Freedom* (2018), and *The Feminist and the Sex Offender* (2020). She has published articles in a range of journals, including *Meridians, Women's Studies Quarterly, Radical Teacher, American Quarterly, Captive Genders*, and *In These Times*.

Andrea Nicholson (PhD, American and Canadian studies, University of Nottingham) is a Nottingham Research Fellow in the School of Politics and International Relations and in the Rights Lab at the University of Nottingham, UK. Her research focuses on the narratives and antislavery ideas of survivors of slavery and other forms of extreme human exploitation, working closely with survivors and NGOs. She has provided consultancy to international governmental bodies, including the UN Special Rapporteur for Contemporary Forms of Slavery. She has published articles on survivors' own definitions of slavery, the support needs of survivors of slavery, the value of survivor narratives to the antislavery agenda, and international law and antislavery politics in the nineteenth century.

Gunther Peck (PhD, history, Yale University) holds a joint appointment in the History Department and the Sanford School of Public Policy at Duke University. He is a member of the Gilder Lehrman Center's Modern Slavery Working Group at Yale University. His research focuses on the intertwined histories of human trafficking, race relations, and antislavery. In his first book, *Reinventing Free Labor: Padrones and Immigrant Workers in the North American West, 1885–1930* (2000), Peck explored how and why immigrant workers in the West lost their ability to quit and to move during the half century after the end of Reconstruction. One of the first scholars to historicize the origins of modern slavery, Peck has recently completed a second book which explores the complex relationship between human trafficking and white supremacy and the twined historical resistance to both. Entitled *Race Traffic: Radical Antislavery and the Long Resistance to White Supremacy, 1660–1860*, the book is forthcoming from the Omohundro Institute with the University of North Carolina Press.

Jessica R. Pliley (PhD, history, Ohio State University) is Associate Professor of Women's and Gender History at Texas State University. She is co-chair of the Gilder Lehrman Center's Modern Slavery Working Group at Yale University. Her current research explores the long history of anti-trafficking movement from the late nineteenth century to the early twenty-first century. She is the author of *Policing Sexuality: The Mann Act and the Making of the FBI* (2014) and *Global Anti-Vice Activism: Fighting Drink, Drugs, and 'Immorality'* (2016). Her work has appeared in the *Journal of Women's History*, the *Journal of the Gilded Age and Progressive Era*, and the *Journal of the History of Sexuality*.

Jennifer (JJ) Rosenbaum (JD, Harvard Law School) is Executive Director of Global Labor Justice- International Labor Rights Forum (GLJ-ILRF). GLJ-ILRF is a strategy hub supporting transnational collaboration among worker and migrant organizations to expand labor rights and new forms of bargaining on global value chains and international labor migration corridors. Rosenbaum was a Robina Fellow at Yale Law School's Orville H. Schell Jr. Center for International Human Rights and is a member of the Gilder Lehrman Center's Modern Slavery Working Group at Yale University. She is a lecturer in law on international labor migration at Harvard Law School.

Elena Shih (PhD, sociology, UCLA) is Manning Assistant Professor of American Studies and Ethnic Studies at Brown University and director of a human trafficking research cluster through Brown's Center for the Study of Slavery and Justice. A former faculty fellow (2016) at the Gilder Lehrman Center for the Study of Slavery, Resistance, and Abolition, Shih is also a member of the Gilder Lehrman Center's Modern Slavery Working Group at Yale University. Her forthcoming book *Manufacturing Freedom: Trafficking Rescue, Rehabilitation, and the Slave Free Good* is a global ethnography of market-based efforts to combat trafficking in China, Thailand, and the United States. Her research brings sex worker rights and racial justice frameworks into the transnational movement to combat human trafficking.

Zoe Trodd (PhD, American studies, Harvard University) is Professor and Director of the Rights Lab at the University of Nottingham. She is a member of the Gilder Lehrman Center's Modern Slavery Working Group at Yale University. Her research focuses on modern slavery and strategies to end it, including the role of survivors' leadership and ideas in today's global antislavery movement. Her books about historical and contemporary slavery and antislavery movements include *To Plead Our Own Cause: Personal Stories by Today's Slaves* (2008), *Modern Slavery* (2009), *The Tribunal: Responses to John Brown and the Harpers Ferry Raid* (2012), and *Picturing Frederick Douglass* (2015).

Preface

David W. Blight

Men tilled the soil long before they wrote books, and would never
have written books if they had not tilled the soil. All the present rests
upon all the past.[1]

How humbling it is to contemplate the weight of what Frederick Douglass
called "all the past" in any present. The past is indeed infinite and no
matter how hard we try we can only know parts of it. But search and know
we must. Such a quest is among the highest of human callings. In its
storehouses of human folly and tragedy as well as human imagination
and progress, history itself can be overwhelming, what James Baldwin
once called a "terrifying deity ... to which no sacrifice in human suffering
is too great."[2]

This depends of course on our essential conceptions of the nature of
history. If we seek only evidence for a triumphal narrative in order to
bolster the present and win power in contemporary affairs, then history
may be only a loving and delivering deity, and easily satisfied or manipulated. We please the gods and they please us back. But those gods will
prove false in the end. Trained, serious approaches to the past that help us
cope with the darknesses that history unfolds about human character need
clearer-eyed vision and moral backbone. All witnesses and scribes of the
story of slavery and other forms of human exploitation and their

[1] Frederick Douglass, "Address before the Tennessee Colored Agricultural and Mechanical
Association," September 18, 1873, Nashville, Tennessee, in Howard Brotz, ed., *African-
American Social & Political Thought, 1850–1920* (New York: Routledge, 1992),
284–297.
[2] James Baldwin, "The Crusade of Indignation," Nation, July 7, 1956, in Baldwin, *Collected
Essays* (New York: Library of American, 1998), 613.

abolitions understand that knowledge of these experiences of inhumanity across time is painful in its truths, while liberating and inspiring in its realization. This book of cutting-edge essays on what research and strategies have had the most efficacy in the struggle against modern slavery is a tribute to that dual inheritance of all social scientific and historical inquiry. Telling the story is our way through the darkness. History may or may not be a god at all. But we surely learn not to test and abuse it with our petty needs, our unchecked prejudices, or our powers of denial.[3]

In the same 1873 oration to an agricultural convention of African American freedmen when Douglass spoke of the apparent infinity of the connection of past and present, he also left this caution: "I shall attempt no solution of the origins of evil in the world. Whether it came by the fall of Adam or the fall of anybody else, I neither know or care ... It is enough to know that we have it and it is in abundance, and that the best use we can make of it is to resist and destroy it as far as we can."[4] Such might be the charge for scholars and activists alike who seek to abolish forms of modern slavery from our contemporary world. It is surely the aim of the scholar-activists in this volume. We have a challenge equally as daunting as that faced by the abolitionists of the nineteenth century who set standards of moral and political activism which are difficult to match.

In Eric Hobsbaum's *The Age of Extremes*, his history of the "Short Twentieth Century," (1914–1991), published in 1994, he opens with epigraphs from twelve eminent thinkers, artists, or scientists. Each was asked what they believed was the most compelling or lasting legacy of the twentieth century through which they had lived. The most prevalent answer in the group was the scale of violence, war, massacre, or genocide. Others named the emancipation of women, astonishing advances in science, electronics, the destruction of ideals, and one said that however

---

[3] Among the growing works on the links between historical and contemporary forms of slavery and abolition, see especially Elizabeth Swanson and James Brewer Stewart, eds., *Human Bondage and Abolition: New Histories of Past and Present Slaveries* (Cambridge, UK: Cambridge University Press, 2018). I have personally found the introductory essay, as well as essays by David Richardson, James Sidbury, Allison Gorsuch, Kerry Ward, Anna Mae Duane, and Jessica R. Pliley, extremely helpful in my own evolving understanding, as a nineteenth-century historian, of the complex phenomenon of modern slavery. All of these scholars have been fellows and conference participants at the Gilder Lehrman Center as well. The leadership of Randall Miller and Zoe Trodd as general editors of this Cambridge series has been pivotal for the growth of this field.

[4] Frederick Douglass, "Agriculture and Black Progress: An Address Delivered in Nashville, Tennessee," September 18, 1873, in *The Frederick Douglass Papers*, vol. IV, ed. John W. Blassingame and John R. McKivigan (New Haven: Yale University Press, 1991), 391.

devastating the results of history, humankind had learned that it can always "start all over again." Primo Levi said that too many "survivors" did not return or "returned wordless." One, anthropologist, Julio Caro Baroja, worried about the "contradiction" of having experienced a full life cycle despite the "terrible events" of the century.[5] Survivors' guilt, or better a sense of humane responsibility, has been a deep source of many reforms and social movements.

Hobsbaum wrote just after the end of the Cold War and the Soviet era. He named "globalization" as one of the three most significant transformations the world had realized by the 1990s, with its heretofore "unimaginable acceleration of communication and transport," and its identification of the "globe" as the "primary operational unit" of capital and labor. His other two most salient transformations were that the world was no longer "Eurocentric" because of changing geopolitics and mass consumer culture, and that, in his view most disturbing of all, the ties between past and present in world cultures were steadily disintegrating in the face of the "a-social individualism" at the heart of world capitalism. Capitalism, Hobsbaum believed, had become a "permanent and continuous revolutionizing force" that severed social bonds between tradition and modern growth, opening whole new realms of exploitation and wealth.[6] Hobsbaum's criteria and conclusions are all debatable, but they serve as a poignant starting point to understand why and how human trafficking and modern slavery emerged by the twenty-first century as a major world crisis.

As the twenty-first century arrived, and now after its first two decades, the world Hobsbaum surveyed has transformed again. Today's world faces at the very least a series of new challenges it has only begun to collectively fight: rising ethnic and religious terrorism; the fragmentation of post-World War II alliances; a resurgent nationalism in forms some thought the end of the Cold War had thwarted; a growing global crisis of refugees from famine and civil wars; an emergent authoritarianism in all parts of the earth, including the United States; a widely recognized but as yet dangerously unaddressed existential problem of climate change; huge chasms of economic inequality between the global North and South; and now a once-in-a-century viral pandemic that may kill millions and throw our economies into a spiraling depression of unpredictable dimensions.

---

[5] Eric Hobsbaum, *The Age of Extremes: A History of the World, 1914–1991* (New York: Pantheon, 1994), 1–2.
[6] Ibid., 14–17.

This list of twenty-first century rolling crises are, of course, all inter-related. In late April 2020, the International Labour Organization announced that an estimated 1.6 billion workers in the world were newly vulnerable to exploitation and potential enslavement due to collapsing economies in the Covid-19 pandemic. A week later, on May 1, 2020, the *New York Times* reported in a front-page story that such a number may be closer to 2 billion workers. Two million garment workers in the already fragile economy of Bangladesh were among the recently fired and newly vulnerable to extreme poverty.[7] The significant traction gained in the quest to intercept and stop sex trafficking and to create ethical supply chains in the even larger labor trafficking across the world faces a new scale of challenge as this book goes to press.

In the past two decades billions of dollars have been spent, hundreds of NGOS have launched crusades, foundations have created task forces, governments have tried to act, and many academics in universities and lawyers in political institutions have devoted their careers to the fight against the systems of human trafficking and labor slavery tied to production supply lines that have emerged in this new world order. Indeed, a new abolition movement has appeared in this century; its participants are a motley assortment of litigators, prime ministers, researchers and field workers, big data scientists, activist nuns and entrepreneurs, religious and secular reformers, scholars in many disciplines, filmmakers, journalists, and many slavery survivors telling their own stories.

At the Gilder Lehrman Center for the Study of Slavery, Resistance, and Abolition at Yale University (GLC) we assembled an international working group on modern slavery in 2016–2019, with generous funding from the Robina Foundation. That group's two co-chairs, Genevieve LeBaron and Jessica R. Pliley, are also the intrepid organizers and architects of this book. Each of them has held one of our full-year fellowships in modern slavery and written books at Yale during their residence. They mingle the instincts and methods of a political scientist and a historian. Further, over the past eight years or so the GLC has also hosted two major international conferences on modern slavery, including one in 2018 built around this working group of writers and scholars. This book is a product of that conference as well as of the energy and intellectual sizzle of our long weekend meetings of the working group.

The essays in this volume contain and enrich all the tensions and divisions in this field. These authors do not all agree on the best methods

---

[7] *New York Times*, May 1, 2020.

for fighting modern forms of slavery, but they have respectfully assembled together in New Haven, Connecticut, at least five times and in a literary sense in this book of original pieces. The work is a tribute to the best traditions in scholarship. The volume contains a good deal of ambivalence and certainty, passion and activism, and at its heart rests some of the most important research and field work ever done on the vast story of twenty-first century enslavement of vulnerable and disposable people. This is scholarship with great moral consequences.

As the editors' Introduction carefully indicates, the authors include both "sceptics" and "champions" of today's antislavery crusade, and they represent many disciplines: history, political science, sociology, law, business management, and anthropology. All of them are among the new era's abolitionists, and they have all walked the walk of archival, participant observation, court room, or field work engagement in order to talk the talk. But as was the case in the nineteenth century in British and American abolitionism, they differ in strategy, in vision, and in method-ology. They sometimes argue fruitfully about how best to use and under-stand history as a guide to this new era. Disagreements endure over the numbers debate about modern slavery. And they do not always find common ground on just who benefits most from antislavery activism. They do not differ, however, on the overall goal, as painfully difficult as it is, of ridding the world of the scourge of modern slavery in this century if not in our lifetimes. They all seek solutions to this global dilemma through what we scholars know how to do best – create knowledge and teach it to the world in our demonstrations of evidence and in our stories.

The greatest story ever told by a former slave sings psalm-like in Frederick Douglass's autobiographies. His story has much to inform today's new abolition movement. In *My Bondage and My Freedom* (1855), Douglass wrote of his time under many kinds of owners and overseers. He experienced savage brutality from some, but even while rented out to a good master, Douglass said he learned that "the kindness of the slavemaster only gilds the chain of slavery, and detracts nothing from its weight and power." Brutality could benumb his desires at times for liberation. But even while only a teenager, he said, he had "ascertained ... the natural and inborn right of every member of the human family" to personal freedom. Even when losing hope the desire to breathe free "only needed a favorable breeze to fan it into a flame." Such might be said of countless entrapped fishermen on shrimp boats in the South China Sea, or on tea or cocoa plantations in India and Africa, in garment factories or brick kilns on several continents, in mica mines or brothels in South Asia, or in various stops on supply chains for making surgical gloves or various kinds of electronic devices. They lack what Douglass so lyrically described in remembering his own enslavement. "The thought of only being a creature of the present and the past troubled me," he wrote, "and I longed to have a future – a future with hope in it. To be shut up entirely to the past and present is abhorrent to the human mind; it is to the soul – whose life and happiness is unceasing progress – what the prison is to the body . . . a hell of horrors."[8] The natural rights tradition is not dead in the twenty-first century unless we allow it to die.

Today's millions of enslaved people across the globe need their own favorable breezes to fan their hope of release from conditions that bind them down economically and physically. They too need futures. The authors in this book are devoting themselves to the intellectual, organizational, legal, and moral work to bring that about.

---

[8] Frederick Douglass, *My Bondage and My Freedom* (1855; rpr. New Haven: Yale University Press, 2014), 218.

Acknowledgments

This book comes from the Gilder Lehrman Center's Modern Slavery Working Group at Yale University, initiated and hosted by the Gilder Lehrman Center for the Study of Slavery, Resistance, and Abolition (GLC), which is a unit of The Whitney and Betty MacMillan Center for International and Area Studies at Yale University.

Founded in 2016 by the Center's Director David W. Blight, and Working Group Co-Chairs Genevieve LeBaron and Jessica R. Pliley, the Gilder Lehrman Center's Modern Slavery Working Group at Yale University provides a platform for interaction for a diverse group of top scholars researching Modern Slavery and Trafficking to come together and explore opportunities of intellectual exchange and collaboration. Group members are experts on different dimensions of contemporary slavery and trafficking who share a commitment to big-picture thinking, rigorous scholarship, public engagement, and to carving out the policy relevance of their work. The group is multidisciplinary and includes historians, social scientists, lawyers, and scholars of the arts and humanities. Support for the Working Group came from a generous grant from the Robina Foundation to the GLC.

The Group's members are David W. Blight, Genevieve LeBaron, Jessica R. Pliley, Kevin Bales, Andrew Crane, Janie Chuang, Anna Mae Duane, Gunther Peck, Grace Peña Delgado, Joel Quirk, J. J. Rosenbaum, Elena Shih, and Zoe Trodd. We are grateful to all of the Group members for their participation, collaboration, and contributions, for being willing to challenge and encourage each other, and for continuing to work together across intellectual and political differences.

We are grateful to the fantastic staff at the GLC who have supported our Group, including by organizing meetings and events, booking travel, recording and editing podcasts and films, and helping us to get our research out into the world. Special thanks go to Michelle Zacks, Melissa McGrath, Tom Thurston, David Spatz, and Daniel Vieira.

Thanks are due to our wonderful editors at Cambridge University Press, Cecelia Cancellaro and Debbie Gershenowitz, and their teams, especially Rachel Blaifeder. As well, we are grateful to the series editors for the Slavery since Emancipation series for their support. Charline Sempéré was a terrific help in pulling together the final manuscript.

Draft chapters of this book have been presented at universities around the world, including at Yale; we are grateful to all who took part in those discussions and helped us to improve our work. We are especially grateful to fellow panelists and audience members who attended the GLC's 20th Annual International Conference, entitled *Fighting Modern Slavery: What Works?*, at Yale University, which was organized and hosted by our Group. Thanks to the scholars, journalists, activists, and advocates who joined us as keynotes and speakers, including Martina Vandenberg, Tim Bartley, Lyndsey Beutin, Eileen Boris, Austin Choi-Fitzpatrick, Amb. Luis C. deBaca, Laura Germino, Kieran Guilbert, Elizabeth Hinton, Todd Landman, Tracey L. Meares, Neha Misra, Krishna Patel, and Cathy Zimmerman. All of these colleagues, as well as the audience members, gave us valuable feedback on the chapters within this book and this book project as a whole.

Not only has the GLC provided a home for our Working Group, but several of us have also been fortunate enough to hold funded fellowships at the GLC, which helped to make our individual scholarship and publications possible. The GLC has long been a hugely important hub and support for scholarship on slavery, and in recent years, has been influential in shaping and nurturing scholarship on contemporary slavery, forced labor, and human trafficking.

Beyond the GLC, other departments and colleagues at Yale have also supported and collaborated with our group. Colleagues at the Yale Law School, Yale School of Management, and Yale's Program of Ethnicity, Race, and Migration have been wonderful collaborators and cosponsors of Group events and activities. As well, librarians and staff within several of Yale's libraries and the Yale Digital Humanities Lab have assisted us along the way.

We are profoundly grateful to David W. Blight, who leads the GLC and whose vision and ambition have propelled this volume and our Group from the start. David is a mentor and friend to many in our group. He is a public intellectual, meticulous and ambitious scholar, accessible writer, and brilliant storyteller; in other words, a powerful model of the scholar and activist that many of us would like to be. This Group and book simply wouldn't have happened without him. And without his encouragement and generosity, we wouldn't be the scholars we are today.

Genevieve LeBaron and Jessica R. Pliley

Abbreviations

CIW	Coalition of Immokalee Workers
GEMS	Global Estimates of Modern Slavery
GLC	Gilder Lehrman Center for the Study of Slavery, Resistance, and Abolition at Yale University
GSI	Global Slavery Index
ILO	International Labour Organization
IOM	International Organization for Migration
SDG	Sustainable Development Goals
TIP Report	Trafficking in Persons Report
TVPA	US Trafficking Victims Protection Act of 2000
UN	United Nations
US	United States
USAID	United States Agency for International Development
UK	United Kingdom

Introduction

Fighting Modern Slavery from Past to Present

Genevieve LeBaron and Jessica R. Pliley

Over the last two decades, fighting modern slavery and human trafficking has become a cause célèbre. Policies to fight modern slavery are championed by right- and left-wing governments. Multinational corporations host panels about fighting modern slavery at the World Economic Forum, United Nations (UN) summits, and rock music festivals. A motley civil society coalition of antislavery activists, students, churches, and conservative anti-feminist organizations have banded together to eradicate slavery with an arsenal ranging from "slave raids" to awareness-raising campaigns. This coalition has spent billions of dollars on projects that promise to end slavery in our lifetime.

But for just as long as there has been a movement to fight modern slavery and human trafficking, others have struggled with and against these efforts. Rarely do workers themselves, nor the migrants' rights organizations, trade unions, and legal empowerment organizations who have long advocated for them sit on modern slavery panels at Davos or celebrate antislavery day. Researchers and scholars are often hesitant to position themselves as part of the modern slavery and trafficking cause, given concerns about the lack of rigor that often characterizes scholarship in this field or worries that governments will use their data for devious political purposes. Even some victims of human trafficking and modern slavery staunchly refuse to be identified with these designations. While corporations and big foundations hold award ceremonies to celebrate antislavery crusaders, the "modern abolitionist movement" has been met with concern and suspicion from some of the very people who would seem to be its most natural champions.

Sceptics caution that not only does the antislavery movement distort the nature of the problem, its causes, and effective solutions, but also that efforts to fight human trafficking and modern slavery can create "collateral damage," harming and endangering the very people that the movement claims to save.[1] They caution that: governments are disguising restrictive immigration policies and border tightening as anti-trafficking efforts, and waging trade wars where they claim to be fighting modern slavery; corporations are using antislavery efforts as a fig leaf to cover up endemic labor exploitation in global supply chains; and antislavery and anti-trafficking efforts impose faulty solutions and create new obstacles for vulnerable workers, who are rarely consulted about plans to "rescue" them and intervene in their lives and are sometimes left worse off because of these well-intentioned efforts. In addition to these real-world problems, sceptics have raised alarm bells about the research and scholarship attached to the antislavery movement, which they see as relying on poor quality estimates and data that value awareness-raising potential over scholarly integrity – ultimately, many scholars see large swathes of anti slavery research as an obstacle to develop accurate understandings of the problem and evidence-based policy to combat it.

Some antislavery sceptics are no doubt politicians, businesses, and others who have a vested interest in downplaying the problem and discrediting the movement. But others are scholars, activists, advocates, and other people who care profoundly about migrant, worker, and human rights, equality and justice, and worry that modern slavery and human trafficking framings of the problem won't deliver the solutions that are so badly needed.[2] This latter group of antislavery sceptics has spent the last two decades fighting modern slavery and human trafficking in two senses. First, they have continued to research and fight for better social protections, mobility, remuneration, and rights for workers at the bottom end of the labor market, who have become increasingly vulnerable to forced labor, human trafficking, and overlapping forms of exploitation amidst globalization. And second, sceptics have in parallel contested antislavery

---

[1] GAATW, *Collateral Damage: The Impact of Anti-Trafficking Measures on Human Rights Around the World* (Bangkok: GAATW, 2007), www.gaatw.org/Collateral%20Damage_Final/CollateralDamage_Frontpageswithcover.pdf; Julia O'Connell Davidson, *Modern Slavery: The Margins of Freedom* (London: Palgrave, 2015); see also chapters in this volume by Shih, Rosenbaum, & Kyritsis.

[2] The uncomfortable alignment between these two groups of sceptics (who are radically opposed in political terms, but cross over on their resistance to 'modern day slavery' framings) is something that deserves further consideration.

and anti-trafficking politics, activism, and framings of the problem, which they generally see as doing more harm than good when it comes to advancing the causes they hold dear.

We have gathered together antislavery champions and sceptics within this book to explore the fissures and fault-lines that surround efforts to fight modern slavery and human trafficking in the contemporary economy. The social scientists, historians, and humanities and legal scholars assembled here benchmark and reflect on what is working in contemporary struggles to fight modern slavery and human trafficking. They reflect on government, business, and activist initiatives, combining contemporary empirics and analysis with rich historical insights to explore the fight against slavery and trafficking, bridging the past and present. Contributors also consider what *isn't* working, shining a spotlight on the ineffectiveness, unintended consequences, and perverse effects of efforts to fight modern slavery and human trafficking, and linking these to historical tensions and dynamics surrounding abolitionism and struggles to end slavery.

The contributors to our book have vastly different understandings of modern slavery and human trafficking, academic disciplinary orientations, theoretical frames and politics. Too often, these differences impede interaction amongst scholars; debates remain siloed in separate academic journals and corners of the internet, with little to no engagement between those who see things differently. The lead authors of this book's chapters have spent the last four years together as members of the Gilder Lehrman Center's Modern Slavery Working Group at Yale University,[3] engaging in conversations about key controversies in the field, amongst other things. This book draws together their disparate views, tackling the controversies in our field head on, with the hope that this volume will move the literature forward by consolidating and illuminating key fault-lines and debates within our field.

Countless controversies surfaced within our group, including how to define modern slavery, human trafficking, and forced labor; whether and how we should seek to count and measure their prevalence; the effectiveness of prevailing solutions to modern slavery, from law-and-order policing and criminalization to corporate social responsibility (CSR); whether or not historic comparisons made by contemporary activists and scholars are appropriate and accurate; and the agency and appropriate role for workers, migrants, survivors, non-governmental organizations (NGOs), businesses, and the state in combatting slavery and

---

[3] See description in the Acknowledgments.

trafficking. Several of these controversies are explored in this introduction and throughout the book. Three stand out.

The first is whether efforts to fight modern slavery and human trafficking displace or crowd out support for labor rights and migrant rights, and undermine the funding, political traction, and legitimacy of organizations that have long advocated for them – like trade unions and worker-driven movements. Sceptics claim that antislavery and anti-trafficking politics rarely give workers a meaningful role in articulating the nature of the problem and devising solutions, but rather patronize these workers by imposing solutions without their consultation or consent – solutions which do not always lead to improvements for victims and can cutoff crucial sources of income without adequate alternatives.[4] Further, they point out that anti-trafficking and antislavery policy has long been tightly intertwined with restrictive mobility regimes, migration control, and harsh forms of policing and incarceration.[5] Nevertheless, those fighting modern slavery and human trafficking see an urgent need to rescue workers who are tricked and trapped, and have defended sensationalism as an important means of elevating antislavery efforts in a competitive marketplace of causes.[6] Questions arise within this context about the appropriate role for governments, activists, businesses, and citizens in fighting modern slavery and human trafficking and bringing about better lives and livelihoods for victims.

The second key controversy is whether and to what extent efforts to fight modern slavery and human trafficking mask, naturalize, and distract from the unequal fabric of our global economy along lines of race, gender, and wealth. Sceptics claim that contemporary antislavery and anti-trafficking projects and political forces can give cover to racist, colonial, anti-immigrant, anti-sex, and misogynist politics and policies that can

---

[4] See chapters by Shih, Rosenbaum, & Kyritsis; Peña Delgado, this volume; Giulia Garofalo Geymonat and P. G. Macioti, eds. *Sex Workers Speak: Who Listens?* (London: openDemocracy, 2016); Elena Shih, "The Anti-trafficking Rehabilitation Complex: Commodity Activism and Slave-free Goods," *Beyond Trafficking and Slavery*, openDemocracy, August 19, 2015, accessed May 18, 2020, www.opendemocracy.net/en/beyond-trafficking-and-slavery/antitrafficking-rehabilitation-complex-commodity-activism-and-slavefree-goo/.

[5] See chapters by Peña Delgado; Chuang, this volume.

[6] See, for instance, the openDemocracy debate on awareness campaigns convened by Elena Shih and Joel Quirk, "Introduction: Do the Hidden Costs Outweigh the Practical Benefits of Human Trafficking Awareness Campaigns?," *Beyond Trafficking and Slavery*, openDemocracy, June 20, 2019, accessed May 18, 2020, www.opendemocracy.net/en/beyond-trafficking-and-slavery/introduction-do-hidden-costs-outweigh-practical-benefits-of-huma/.

make life worse for already vulnerable people.[7] However, antislavery scholars and activists frequently claim that race and gender are no longer relevant when it comes to contemporary forms of slavery compared to historic slave systems. As Kevin Bales put it, "In the past, ethnic and racial differences were used to explain and excuse slavery" but "in the new slavery race means little."[8] Several chapters in this volume argue that antislavery scholars and activists can profoundly misunderstand the role of race, colonialism, and patriarchy in shaping slavery and trafficking, both historically and today. They see a tendency within antislavery scholarship and movements to overlook how racism, western superiority, and anti-feminist politics intertwine with abolitionism. Sceptics claim that this controversy isn't simply academic; rather, these blind spots cause scholars and activists to overlook key causes and sites of vulnerability to unfreedom in contemporary society – from carceral facilities to borders and deportation facilities – and elide the suffering of women, people of color, indigenous peoples, and migrants. These blind spots weaken the solutions proposed to fight modern slavery and mean antislavery efforts rarely recognize the need to tackle root causes, like inequalities along racial and gendered lines, or between the global North and South, as a key part of ending forced labor.[9]

The final controversy, which interlocks with the previous two, surrounds the use and understanding of history by contemporary abolitionists. Contemporary antislavery and anti-trafficking crusaders – from Ivanka Trump to Boris Johnson – frequently invoke histories of slavery and the heroic efforts to combat it led by powerful white men like William Wilberforce and Abraham Lincoln. No doubt, these invocations aim to inspire and ignite antislavery efforts by positioning contemporary activism as part of a valiant multi-century struggle for freedom. But historians within this book raise alarm bells about the misuse of history and how it can be distorted by contemporary antislavery efforts.[10] In their view, not only are many historical claims made by the new abolitionist movement partial and inaccurate, but they also tend to gloss over the historic dynamics of racism, colonialism, and patriarchy that shaped the classification

---

[7] See chapters by Pliley; Peck; Duane & Meiners, this volume.
[8] Kevin Bales, *Disposable People: New Slavery in the Global Economy* (Berkeley: University of California Press, 2004), 10.
[9] For analysis of the tendency to overlook root causes, see Genevieve LeBaron, Neil Howard, Cameron Thibos, and Penelope Kyritsis, *Confronting Root Causes: Forced Labour in Global Supply Chains* (Sheffield: SPERI & University of Sheffield, 2018).
[10] See chapters by Pliley; Duane & Meiners; Peck, this volume.

and representation of enslaved peoples and quests to liberate them. Contributors identify a linked tendency to overstate the heroisms of western democracy and white abolitionists and understate the agency of enslaved peoples, giving rise to considerable blind spots and misplaced credit and blame in the use of historical narrative and metaphors.[11] Contributors also stress the importance of social forces – from community activists to labor organizers to survivors – who made important contributions to historic antislavery movements but are often glossed over by contemporary abolitionists.[12]

As we explore within this introduction and book, these controversies are important for scholarly reasons, but also because they shape people's lives in the real world. At the heart of the book, and a core challenge confronting contemporary abolitionist movements, lies the question of whose interests are being served by contemporary antislavery and anti-trafficking struggles. Are efforts to fight modern slavery and human trafficking genuinely creating better lives and fairer and more equitable economy for millions of people vulnerable to forced labor, for victims, and for survivors? Or are antislavery and anti-trafficking struggles rather enriching NGOs, bolstering the credibility and legitimacy of already rich corporations, assuaging the guilt of consumers, and providing a useful cause for governments to champion as they seek to distract voters from the soaring inequality and exploitation within their labor markets and coercive immigration policies?

1.1 DEFINITIONS AND POLITICS: WHO IS FIGHTING FOR WHAT? AND WHY DOES IT MATTER?

In 2000, the issue of human trafficking and modern slavery was legislated at the international level as the United Nations adopted the 2000 Convention Against Transnational Crime to include the Protocol to Prevent, Suppress and Punish Trafficking in Persons, Especially Women and Children (UN Trafficking Protocol). That same year the United States (US) Congress passed the Trafficking Victims Protection Act (TVPA) to address trafficking within the US and establish a global system of benchmarking on antislavery progress led by the US State Department through its annual Trafficking in Persons Report (TIP Reports). The definition offered for trafficking in the UN Trafficking Protocol and the TVPA illuminates the varied and vexed nature of definitions of trafficking and slavery.

---

[11] See chapters by Peck; Pliley; Shih, Rosenbaum, & Kyritsis, this volume.
[12] See chapters by Bales & Gardner; Trodd, Nicholson, & Eglen; Peck, this volume.

The UN Trafficking Protocol considers "trafficking in persons" to mean the "recruitment, transportation, transfer, harboring or receipt of persons," by means of threats, force, fraud, coercion, "for the purposes of exploitation. Exploitation shall include, at minimum, the exploitation of the prostitution of others or other forms of sexual exploitation, forced labor or services, slavery or practices similar to slavery," including the prostitution of anyone under the age of eighteen.[13] This unwieldy definition emphasizes trafficking as a process that combines acts, means, and purpose.[14] As a process, trafficking in this understanding encompasses a huge variety of circumstances that may or may not be comparable. As a product of intense international negotiation, aspects of the Protocol were left intentionally vague or undefined (such as, what constitutes sexual exploitation). The Protocol has come to embrace the idea of "trafficking as modern slavery" even as it papered over significant political and epistemic divisions among activists concerned with forced vs. voluntary prostitution, confusions about the distinction between smuggling and trafficking, and conflicts between the human rights approach and criminal justice approach.[15] The UN trafficking protocol's definition of trafficking is summarized in Table 1.1.

Forced labor is defined through the International Labour Organization's (ILO) 1930 Forced Labor Convention, which reads: "'Forced or compulsory labor' shall mean all work or service which is exacted under menace of any penalty for its non-performance and for which the worker concerned does not offer himself voluntarily." This definition is widely recognized to encompass practices like debt bondage, serfdom, human trafficking, and slavery. But it excludes certain forms of state-imposed forced labor, such as some forms of prison labor and military conscription.[16]

---

[13] See Article 3, "Protocol to Prevent, Suppress and Punish Trafficking in Persons Especially Women and Children, supplement in the United Nations Convention against Transnational Organized Crime," accessed October 13, 2017, www.ohchr.org/EN/Prof essionalInterest/Pages/ProtocolTraffickingInPersons.aspx.

[14] Jo Doezema, *Sex Slaves and Discourse Masters: The Construction of Trafficking* (London: Zed Books, 2010); Gillian Wylie, *The International Politics of Human Trafficking* (London: Palgrave MacMillan, 2016); Jennifer K. Lobasz, *Constructing Human Trafficking: Evangelicals, Feminists, and an Unexpected Alliance* (Switzerland: Palgrave MacMillan, 2019).

[15] Prabha Kotiswaran, *Revisiting the Law and Governance of Trafficking, Forced Labor and Modern Slavery* (New York: Cambridge University Press, 2017).

[16] See ILO 1930 Forced Labour Convention (No. 29); ILO, *ILO Global Estimate of Forced Labour: Results and Methodology* (Geneva: International Labour Organization, 2012), 19–22.

TABLE 1.1 *Overview of UN trafficking protocol*

Act	Means	Purpose	
Recruitment	Threat or use of force	Exploitation, including	
Transport	Coercion	Prostitution of others	
Harboring	Abduction	Sexual exploitation	
Receipt of persons	Fraud	Forced labor	**Trafficking**
	Deception	Slavery or similar practices	
	Abuse of power or vulnerability	Removal of organs	
	Giving payments or benefits	Other types of exploitation	

Source: The authors.

The contributions to this book use – and are informed by – different terminology and definitions, which relate to and reflect the variegated ways that authors approach and view the subject matter. We welcome this diversity, since it helps to illustrate different viewpoints and positions within the debates we explore within the book.

1.1.1 The Politics of Definitions

While such definitions may seem straightforward, their interpretation and application have been contentious; tugs-of-war over trafficking and slavery terminology reflect fundamental political differences. For instance, debates over the how far the concept of forced labor should extend reveal fundamentally different conceptions of capitalism and freedom. Though the ILO definition of forced labor stresses that financial, physical, and psychological coercion can cause involuntary labor, the ILO's Committee of Experts have made it clear that economic coercion – including the threat of immanent destitution or starvation – is not a valid form of compulsion rendering labor involuntary.[17] Several scholars have claimed that this interpretation excludes a profoundly important – if not the most

[17] Committee of Experts on the Application of Conventions and Recommendations, "General Survey concerning the Forced Labour Convention, 1930 (No. 29)," and "The Abolition of Forced Labour Convention 1957 (No. 105)," (Geneva: International Labour Organization, 2007), 20–21.

important – source of compulsion into involuntary labor in contemporary capitalism, which is the lack of viable economic alternatives. As scholars like Jens Lerche have argued, those who exclude the role of economic coercion from definitions of forced labor overlook the profound unfreedom that characterizes capitalist labor markets, and reinforce fanciful ideological suppositions that capitalism offers opportunities and freedom to everyone living within it.[18]

Another important example of the political differences anchoring definitional debates are how the divisive politics of prostitution that had split feminists in the Global North since the 1980s shaped discussions of trafficking. Historically, and in many parts of the contemporary world, prostitution has been a legal if disreputable form of labor. In the 1990s, anti-prostitution abolitionists argued that prostitution constituted a form of violence against women that within patriarchal societies illustrated women's enslaved status.[19] "The sex trade is a form of contemporary slavery and all indication predict its growth and expansion into the twenty-first century," proclaimed American anti-prostitution abolitionist Donna Hughes in 1999.[20] In this view, all prostitution is slavery. Countering such a position stood many sex workers' rights organizations that sought to distinguish between voluntary and forced prostitution. Typical of this position was the Global Alliance Against the Traffic in Women (GAATW) that in 1994 warned against "disregarding the will of adult persons engaged in prostitution" and called for anti-trafficking policies to be "based on respect for human rights, specifically the right of all persons to self-determination."[21] Yet, sex workers' rights activists could not marshal the levels of international influence as anti-prostitution abolitionists, who by the 1995 Beijing World Conference on Women could take credit for Hillary Clinton declaring that sex trafficking is "a violation of human rights when women and girls are sold into the slavery

---

[18] Jens Lerche, "A Global Alliance Against Forced Labour? Unfree Labour, Neoliberal Globalization, and the International Labour Organization," *Journal of Agrarian Change* 7, no. 4 (2007): 425–452.

[19] Alice M. Miller, "Sexuality, Violence against Women, and Human Rights: Women Make Demands and Ladies Get Protection," *Health and Human Rights* 7, no. 2 (2004): 16–47.

[20] Quoted in Sanja Milivojevic and Sharon Pickering, "Trafficking In People, 20 Years On: Sex, Migration and Crime in the Global Anti-Trafficking Discourse and the Rise of the 'Global Trafficking Complex'," *Current Issues in Criminal Justice* 25, no. 2 (2018): 585–604, 587.

[21] Quoted in Jo Doezema, "Forced to Choose: Beyond the Voluntary v. Forced Prostitution Dichotomy," in *Global Sex Workers: Rights, Resistance, and Redefinition*, eds. Kamala Kempadoo and Jo Doezema (New York: Routledge, 1998), 37.

of prostitution for human greed."[22] Activists from both camps met at Vienna to negotiate the UN Trafficking Protocol's definition of trafficking, and the ultimate definition attempts to take a neutral stance in the fight about prostitution. It offers no clarity over the meaning of "the exploitation of the prostitution of others or other forms of sexual exploitation" because as the GAATW noted "the government delegates to the negotiations could not agree on a common meaning."[23] Consequently the question of whether all prostitution is a form of modern slavery, or just forced prostitution, continues to divide antislavery activists today.[24]

Also passed in 2000, the US Trafficking Victims Protection Act (TVPA) complements the UN Trafficking Protocol by establishing US domestic policy. But it also establishes a sanctions regime authorizing the US to withdraw financial assistance from countries the US deems as falling behind in the fight against slavery.[25] The TVPA offered this definition for "severe forms of trafficking in persons": "(a) sex trafficking in which a commercial sex act is induced by force, fraud, or coercion, or in which the person induced to perform such act has not attained 18 years of age; or (b) the recruitment, harboring, transportation, provision, or obtaining of a person for labor or services, through the use of force, fraud or coercion for the purpose of subjection to involuntary servitude, peonage, debt bondage, or slavery."[26] The TVPA echoes the UN Protocol's emphasis on trafficking as a process and it sought to balance the demands of anti-prostitution abolitionists and activists who worried about extreme labor exploitation. Yet, as law professor Janie Chuang has noted, both of these definitions opened the door to "exploitation creep" wherein all labor exploitation is "recast as trafficking" and "all trafficking is labeled as slavery."[27]

---

[22] Quoted in Elizabeth Bernstein, *Brokered Subjects: Sex, Trafficking & the Politics of Freedom* (Chicago: University of Chicago Press, 2018), 10.

[23] Quoted in Julia O'Connell Davidson and Bridget Anderson, "The Trouble with 'Trafficking'," in *Trafficking and Women's Rights*, ed. Christien L. van den Anker and Jeroen Doomernik (New York: Palgrave MacMillan, 2006), 11–26, 14.

[24] Emily Bazelon, "Why Amnesty International is Calling for Decriminalizing Sex Work," *New York Times* May 25, 2016; Letters to the Editor, "Re: Prostitution," *New York Times*, May 20, 2016.

[25] Janie A. Chuang, "The United States as Global Sheriff: Using Unilateral Sanctions to Combat Human Trafficking," *Michigan Journal of International Law* 27, no. 2 (2006): 437–494.

[26] US Department of State, *Trafficking in Persons Report* (Washington, DC: Government Printing Office, July 2001), 2.

[27] Janie A. Chuang, "Exploitation Creep and the Unmaking of Human Trafficking Law," *The American Journal of International Law* 108 (2014): 609–649, 611.

Though the TVPA and UN Protocol seem to give equal attention to the issues of sex trafficking and labor trafficking, in reality sex trafficking (and anti-prostitution policies) has long dominated global anti-trafficking agendas and TVPA enforcement. And the ways in which sex trafficking is depicted by NGOs and the media underscore how conceptions of consent, coercion, and agency shape accounts of these practices. For instance, many NGOs' narratives that portray victims of modern slavery and trafficking as passive and vulnerable victims of sex trafficking have fed into simplistic and sensationalistic narratives about modern slavery and trafficking that are then reproduced by journalists. Media representations of trafficking frequently highlight the ignorance and innocence of migrant women, emphasizing the role deceit plays in recruiting them as victims. Media representations of modern slavery and trafficking tend to conflate all forms of slavery under the "trafficking" umbrella and then use images of sexual exploitation to raise awareness, thereby erasing awareness of forced labor. Such awareness raising activities can suggest that trafficking and modern slavery is the result of "bad men" doing bad things rather than the result of structural problems in the global economy.[28] These narratives are profoundly gendered;[29] sex trafficking victims are imagined as female and labor trafficking victims are imagined as male, thereby distorting the actual gender breakdown of forced labor (see Table 1.2).

1.1.2 Scholarly Attempts to Clarify Definitions

Though the TVPA and the UN Trafficking Protocol offered legal definitions of trafficking, their unwieldiness has prompted scholars and activists to develop their own definitions, even as the terms "human trafficking," "trafficking in persons," and "modern slavery" have frequently been used interchangeably. In his enormously influential book, *Disposable People* (1999), Kevin Bales defines modern slavery as, "the total control of one person by another for the purpose of economic exploitation."[30] Seeking to develop even greater clarity and a harmonized, contemporary definition of slavery, experts recently developed the Bellagio-Harvard Guidelines on the Legal Parameters of Slavery. These Guidelines start from the 1926 League

---

[28] Kimberly Kay Hoang and Rhacel Salazar Parreñas, eds., *Human Trafficking Reconsidered: Rethinking the Problem, Envisioning New Solutions* (New York: IDEBATE Press, 2014), 4.

[29] Eileen Boris, *Making the Woman Worker: Precarious Labor and the Fight for Global Standards, 1919–2019* (New York: Oxford University Press, 2019).

[30] Bales, *Disposable People*, 6.

TABLE 1.2 *Breakdown of modern slavery*

		Forced Labor	Forced Sexual Exploitation + Sexual Exploitation of Children	State-Imposed Forced Labor	Total Forced Labor	Forced Marriage	Modern Slavery
Male	No.	6766	29	2411	9206	2442	11648
	Percentage	42.35	0.7	59.37	36.45	15.82	28.9
Female	No.	9209	4787	1650	15646	13000	28645
	Percentage	57.65	99.3	40.63	61.95	84.18	71.09

Source: ILO et al., *Global Estimates of Modern Slavery: Forced Labour and Forced Marriage* (ILO: Geneva, 2017) 18.

of Nations Slavery Convention, which defined slavery as "the status or condition of a person over whom any or all of the powers attaching to the right of ownership are exercised."[31] According to the Bellagio group, the 1926 definition remains relevant today, even though it is couched in a seemingly obsolete property paradigm – because, after all, actual *ownership* of another human being is currently illegal the world over.[32] According to the guidelines, "Possession is foundational to an understanding of the legal definition of slavery," in that it presupposes "control over a person by another such as a person might control a thing."[33] The Bellagio-Harvard Guidelines offer a clear definition of slavery while echoing Bales's emphasis on control and profitability. Consequently, modern slavery has emerged as the dominant concept under which sex trafficking, forced labor, and a number of other practices exist, though the precise definitions scholars use continue to be contested.

A wide range of practices sit under the umbrella of modern slavery and trafficking. These practices include sex trafficking, the sexual exploitation of people under the age of eighteen, bonded labor (debt bondage), forced labor, domestic servitude, child soldiering, forced child labor, hereditary or descent-based bondage, state-imposed forced labor, forced prison labor, and forced marriage.[34] The recent addition of forced marriage caused consternation among some sceptics, who noted that the inclusion of forced marriage occurred with no negotiations, convention, nor long-term study. Some experts have asked whether including forced marriage amounts to comparing apples to oranges.[35] Others point to the ways that adding forced marriage dilutes the term "slavery."[36] Other scholars have

---

[31] See the Bellagio-Harvard Guideline on the Legal Parameters of Slavery, Research Network on the Legal Parameters of Slavery, accessed October 13, 2017, http://glc .yale.edu/sites/default/files/pdf/the_bellagio-_harvard_guidelines_on_the_legal_parame ters_of_slavery.pdf.

[32] Jean Allain, "Contemporary Slavery in Its Definition in the Law," in *Contemporary Slavery: Popular Rhetoric and Political Practice*, eds. Annie Bunting and Joel Quirk (Vancouver: University of British Columbia Press, 2017), 36–37, 39.

[33] See the Bellagio-Harvard Guideline, guideline 3.

[34] See US Department of State, Trafficking in Persons Report (June 2017), 17, and the ILO et al., *Global Estimates of Modern Slavery: Forced Labour and Forced Marriage* (Geneva: ILO, 2017).

[35] Daniel Mügge, "40.3 Million Slaves? Four Reasons to Question the New Global Estimates of Modern Slavery," *Beyond Trafficking and Slavery*, openDemocracy, October 17, 2017, www.opendemocracy.net/en/beyond-trafficking-and-slavery/403- million-slaves-four-reasons-to-question-new-global-estimates-of-moder/.

[36] See Orlando Patterson and Xiaolin Zhuo, "Modern Trafficking, Slavery, and Other Forms of Servitude," *Annual Review of Sociology* 44 (July 2018): 407–439, 410.

welcomed the expanded concept of modern slavery for the way that it can bring attention to practices long subject to legal prohibition, yet that continue to thrive; but even then, they warn that this "risks diluting attention and effort, and potentially deflecting attention from the worst forms of exploitation that are more difficult for States to address."[37]

The scholars featured in this volume agree on the difficulty in defining "slavery," with each offering their own variegated approach to the issue. Some embrace the Bellagio-Harvard definition, which then prompts them to accept the process-oriented framework offered by the TVPA and the UN Protocol.[38] Others see slavery as existing on a spectrum of worker exploitation that also includes practices such as wage theft, unsafe workplaces, gendered and racialized precarity, and captive migrant workforces. Rather than seeing slavery as a distinct process, in this view, it is a logical outcome of racial capitalism.[39] Still other considers the development of definitions of "slavery" as a type of knowledge production that sheds light on the political economy. From this perspective, the process of definition making is as important as the definition offered.[40] The lack of a common definition of "slavery" reflects the ways that individual scholars address the controversies of the relationship between modern slavery and labor and migrant rights, the question of whether the modern slavery discourse naturalizes inequalities in the global economy, and the mis(use) of history.

The question of how to use the past to fight slavery and trafficking today has emerged as more and more historians of slavery, trafficking, and abolition have turned their attentions to the contemporary fight against modern slavery and trafficking. The phrase "modern slavery" and its ability to conjure imagery of "historical slavery" invites historical discussion, debate, and analysis. Additionally, the abolitionist campaigns against slavery of the late eighteenth and nineteenth centuries, which constituted the first human rights campaigns, were racked by internal divisions, but succeeded in changing the course of human history regardless. These past struggles provide fertile ground for those looking for a usable past in the antislavery movement today. Historians writing about the past with an eye to contemporary

---

[37] Anne T. Gallagher, "Two Cheers for the Trafficking Protocol," *Anti-Trafficking Review* 4 (2015), 10.

[38] See chapters by Bales & Gardner; Trodd, Nicholson, & Eglen this volume.

[39] See chapters by Shih, Rosenbaum, & Kyritsis; LeBaron, this volume.

[40] See chapters by Peck; Duane and Meiners; and Pliley, this volume.

antislavery campaigns use the past to offer legitimate warnings about the power (and limits) of the state, provide tactical insight into current antislavery organizing, and give us inspirational stories of sacrifice, success, and empowerment.[41]

A key theme explored within the volume is the extent to which contemporary abolitionist challenges differ from or bear similarities to those confronted by abolitionists in earlier eras of history. As historians within the volume note, the abolitionist movement against the transatlantic slave trade and slavery in the Americas grew to become one of the most dynamic human rights campaigns in global history.[42] The fight against sex trafficking, emerging out of the 1880s, was similarly global in scope and ambitions, yet had a more limited reach.[43] Examining these different abolitionist movements to understand the methods deployed, tactics embraced, and challenges faced by activists, government, and industry is helpful in illuminating the challenges and decisions that contemporary abolitionists face today. By analyzing what has worked, and what works today, in the fights against slavery and human trafficking contributors to this volume draw lessons and inspiration from the past and bring it to bear on efforts to fight modern slavery and human trafficking in the present day.

[41] See Alison Bryst and Austin Choi-Fitzpatrick, eds. *From Human Trafficking to Human Rights: Reframing Contemporary Slavery* (Philadelphia, Pennsylvania: University of Pennsylvania Press, 2012); Anna Mae Duane, *Child Slavery before and after Emancipation: An Argument for Child-Centered Slavery Studies* (New York: Cambridge University Press, 2017); Jessica R. Pliley, *Policing Sexuality: The Mann Act and the Making of the FBI* (Cambridge, Massachusetts and London: Harvard University Press, 2014); Joel Quirk and Genevieve LeBaron, *On History: Beyond Trafficking and Slavery Short Course*, Vol. 4. (London: OpenDemocracy, 2015); and Elizabeth Swanson and James Brewer Stewart, *Human Bondage and Abolition: New Histories of Past and Present Slaveries* (New York: Cambridge University Press, 2018).

[42] James Brewer Stewart, *Holy Warriors: The Abolitionists and American Slavery* (New York: Hill and Wang, 1996); Seymour Drescher, *Abolition: A History of Slavery and Antislavery* (Cambridge: Cambridge University Press, 2009); Joel Quirk, *The Antislavery Project: From the Slave Trade to Human Trafficking* (Philadelphia: University of Pennsylvania, 2011); and Manisha Sinha, *The Slave's Cause: A History of Abolition* (New Haven: Yale University Press, 2017).

[43] The literature on the history of trafficking is growing rapidly. See, for instance Edward Bristow, *Prostitution and Prejudice: The Jewish Fight Against White Slavery, 1870–1939* (New York: Schocken Books, 1982); Donna J. Guy, *Sex in Danger in Buenos Aires: Prostitution, Family, and Nation in Argentina* (Lincoln: University of Nebraska Press, 1990); Stephanie Limoncelli, *The Politics of Trafficking: The First International Movement to Combat the Sexual Exploitation of Women* (Stanford: Stanford University Press, 2010); and Pliley, *Policing Sexuality.*

1.1.3 The New Abolitionists: Abolitionist Genealogies

Just as definitions of "modern slavery," and "human trafficking" remain imprecise and contested, similar imprecision surrounds contemporary activists' claims to be "New Abolitionists." The story of the demise of legal slavery, as Seymour Drescher notes, "remains a model of comparative achievement for all who seek to expand the range of human rights,"[44] and consequently, the story of the abolitionist fight against slavery remains a powerful legacy that activists fighting against a range of social injustices turn to for inspiration. Assertions of a new abolitionist movement have regularly appeared since the Civil War, with labor leaders, feminists, and Black freedom activists all tapping into the abolitionist legacy and claiming the mantle of "New Abolitionists." For example, in 1876, when two anti-prostitution activists from England visited the US to launch a "new abolitionist" movement that opposed legal, regulated prostitution, they met with the former editor of the abolitionist newspaper *Anti-Slavery Sentinel*, Aaron Macy Powell, who was so inspired by tales of a new form of slavery – sex slavery – that he launched the New York Committee for the Prevention of the State Regulation of Vice (later the American Purity Alliance).[45] Similarly, in 1884, labor leaders in the Knights of Labor resurrected earlier calls to abolish wage slavery, but in the post-Civil War context pulled on the rhetorical and moral power of the abolitionist movement to justify their fight against labor exploitation. Leading Black intellectual, W. E. B. Du Bois regularly used the phrase "New Abolition Movement" to describe the activism of the National Association for the Advancement of Colored People in the early twentieth century.[46] In each of these examples, the legacy of the original campaign to abolish chattel slavery is used to different effect.

Each invocation of the legacy of abolitionism produced distinct branches in the complicated genealogy of abolitionism that continues to shape both campaigns against trafficking and modern slavery and the ways activists use historical analogy. These branches include the anti-regulated prostitution and anti-trafficking form of abolitionism that emerged in the 1870s and culminated in the global anti-sex trafficking movement of the interwar period; the anti-prostitution feminist abolitionism of the 1980s and beyond that came to dominate the anti-trafficking movement of the 1990s (in alliance with Christian conservatives); and the

---

[44] Drescher, *Abolition*, 462.   [45] Pliley, *Policing Sexuality*, 19–20.
[46] Sinha, *The Slave's Cause*, 590–591.

anti-prison abolitionists that draw upon the work of W. E. B. Du Bois to argue that as long as racialized mass incarceration structures American society, the fight for Black freedom that spurred the original abolitionists is not finished. All forms of abolition draw on the history of slavery, anti-slavery, and abolition in their campaigns, and they pull on the past in different ways.

Abolitionism that opposed legal licensing of prostitution and sex trafficking emerged in the cold of the English winter of 1869, initially as a feminist movement that sought to abolish government regulation of prostitution, as was common at the time in Europe. Josephine Butler launched this feminist abolitionist movement – the Ladies' National Association for the Repeal of the Contagious Diseases Acts – to overturn the UK Contagious Diseases Acts of 1864, 1866, and 1869 (CD Acts) that required the arrest, forced medical examination, and incarceration of women who police suspected of selling sex in port towns covered by the acts. Inspired by her father who instilled in her a "horror of slavery and all arbitrary power," Butler opposed the way the CD Acts granted the police with arbitrary power, institutionalized the sexual double standard by targeting women and not men in its attempts to control the spread of sexually transmitted infections, treated women, and especially prostitutes, as a distinct class with fewer rights than men, purported to make prostitution benign for male customers, and gave implicit state license to prostitution.[47] Butler believed that through regulated prostitution "man in this nineteenth century has made woman his degraded slave."[48] For Butler, abolition meant eradicating legal licensed brothels, eliminating third-party profiteering from prostitution, and resisting any law that treated prostitutes as a distinct class because she remained sensitive to the arbitrary power of police to assign the label of "prostitute" to any, but especially poor, women. In 1875 British abolitionists expanded beyond the British Isles to form the British, Continental, and General Federation for the Abolition of Government Regulation of Prostitution (later renamed the International Abolitionist Federation) to fight legal, state-regulated prostitution. Among its American members listed in its first annual report were many acclaimed white antebellum abolitionists, including William Lloyd Garrison, Mary Livermore, Lucretia Mott,

---

[47] Judith R. Walkowitz, *Prostitution and Victorian Society: Women, Class, and the State* (Cambridge: Cambridge University Press, 1980), 93, quote on 115.

[48] Josephine E. Butler, *An Autobiographical Memoir*, eds. George W. and Lucy A. Johnson (Bristol: J. W. Arrowsmith, 1909), 133.

Wendell Philips, Sam Sewall, and Lucy Stone.[49] The British activists celebrated their connections to American antebellum abolitionists and frequently deployed the term "new abolitionist" to describe their women's rights campaign.

Later on, the campaign against white slavery, understood to be "the procurement, by force, deceit, or drugs, of a white woman or girl against her will, for prostitution,"[50] blossomed into a transatlantic and later global human rights campaign against sex trafficking. Though feminist abolitionists and paternalist abolitionists frequently fought over their tactics, analyses of prostitution and state power, and leadership of the anti-trafficking movement, they successfully lobbied countries to sign five international conventions on the traffic in women between 1904 and 1949; each adopting a progressively more abolitionist perspective.[51] The consequences of this early form of anti-regulation and trafficking abolition was, as Kamala Kempadoo has argued "stronger anti-prostitution ideologies, infantilizing rescue missions to save women and girls deemed 'innocent victims,' greater police surveillance of the sex trade, new policies and programs to catch traffickers, new legislation to catch 'pimps' and clients of prostitutes, more border controls to prevent 'aliens' from entering wealthy areas of the world, a greater number of detentions and deportations of so-called illegal migrants, and a generalized panic about the idea of human trafficking that is causing anxiety especially amongst young women seeking to travel abroad or to migrate."[52] Significantly, because paternalist abolitionists dominated the anti-trafficking movement of the first half of the twentieth century, the appropriation of the antebellum abolitionist legacy included the erasure of the sexual violence of chattel slavery. The prostitution of white women and girls – "slavery not for labor but for lust" – became seen as a greater human rights

---

[49] Marion Horan, "Trafficking in Danger: Working-Class Women and Narratives of Sexual Danger in English and the United States Anti-Prostitution Campaigns, 1875–1914," PhD diss. (Binghamton: State University of New York, 2006), 38.

[50] Jo Doezema, "Loose Women or Lost Women? The Re-emergence of the Myth of White Slavery in Contemporary Discourses of Trafficking in Women," *Gender Issues* 18, no. 1 (Winter 2000): 23–50, 25.

[51] The conventions are: the 1910 International Congress for the Suppression of the White Slave Traffic, the 1921 International Convention for the Suppression of the Traffic in Women and Children, 1933 International Convention for the Suppression of the Traffic in Women of Full Age, and the 1949 Convention for the Suppression of the Traffic in Persons and of the Exploitation of the Prostitution of Others.

[52] Kamala Kempadoo, "The Modern-Day White (Wo)Man's Burden Trends in Anti-Trafficking and Anti-Slavery Campaigns," *Journal of Human Trafficking* no. 1 (2015): 8–20, 12.

tragedy.[53] This color-blind analysis of prostitution and trafficking ultimately upheld white supremacist ideas both of chattel slavery and of the value (or lack thereof) of Black suffering. Sadly, this historical erasure continues to characterize anti-trafficking abolitionism of the late twentieth century.[54]

In their efforts to document and theorize patriarchy, American feminists of the 1970s turned their attention to prostitution. Initially, feminists in the National Organization for Women (NOW) worked alongside women who sold sex to produce a critique of the ways that police undermined the safety, security, and sanity of women (and men) who sold sex, and by 1973, NOW endorsed decriminalization of prostitution.[55] Yet, by the end of the decade an analysis of prostitution would emerge that reframed all prostitution as sex slavery that needed to be fought with a new abolitionist movement. In 1979, Kathleen Barry published *Female Sexual Slavery*, offering a theoretical framework that connected the practices of prostitution, forced marriage, incest, pornography, sex tourism, kidnapping, and domestic servitude, and later in the 1980s pushed to harness the power of the state to criminalizing the purchasing of sex and to achieve, quoting the 1926 Slavery Convention, "the complete abolition of slavery in all its forms."[56]

Committed to abolishing prostitution, Barry turned to the UN, getting female sexual slavery onto the agenda of the World Conference of Women in Copenhagen (1980), Nairobi (1985), and Beijing (1995). To aid in these efforts, Barry helped to form the Coalition Against Trafficking in Women (CATW) in 1990 to lobby the UN for international action against sex trafficking. The CATW embraced Barry's analysis that all prostitution constituted violence against women and consequently anyone who helped

---

[53] Alfred S. Dyer, "The European Slave Trade in English Girls," (London: Dyer Brothers, Amen Corner, 1880), 6.

[54] Cheryl Nelson Butler, "The Racial Roots of Human Trafficking," *UCLA Law Review* 62 (2015): 1464–1515; Jasmine Phillips, "Black Girls and the (Im)Possibilities of a Victim Trope: The Intersectional Failures of Legal and Advocacy Interventions in the Commercial Sexual Exploitation of Minors in the United States," *UCLA Law Review* 62 (2015): 1642–1675.

[55] Stephanie Gilmore, "Strange Bedfellows: Building Feminist Coalitions around Sex Work in the 1970s," in *No Permanent Waves: Recasting Histories of U.S. Feminism*, ed. Nancy A. Hewitt (New Brunswick: Rutgers University Press, 2010), 246–272; Valerie Jenness, *Making it Work: The Prostitutes' Rights Movement in Perspective* (New York: Aldine de Gruyter, 1993); and Melinda Chateauvert, *Sex Workers Unite: A History of the Movement from Stonewall to SlutWalk* (Boston: Beacon Books, 2013).

[56] Kathleen Barry, *The Prostitution of Sexuality: The Global Exploitation of Women* (New York: New York University Press, 1991), 371.

a woman move from one place to another to sell sex was a trafficker.[57] The CATW tried to get the US to take an anti-prostitution position in the negotiations over the UN Trafficking Protocol, and after teaming up with conservative Christians in the Bush administration, the CATW sought to make the abolition of prostitution part of the war on terror.[58] In addition to its work in the UN, CATW lobbied all levels of US government and targeted countries with liberal prostitution policies, like Germany, Sweden, and the Netherlands.[59] Yet, the CATW has not been successful in its lobbying efforts. It opposed placing sex trafficking with labor trafficking under the same umbrella of "trafficking in persons" within the TVPA.

Like most self-identified abolitionists, Barry and other anti-prostitution abolitionists use the past in creative and convenient ways. As we just saw, Barry pulled on the 1926 Slavery Convention to suggest that the fight against the prostitution of women and girls is part of the unfinished business of fighting slavery. Like other forms of abolitionism, the prostitution abolitionists "depends on the history of Black people in the Americas to speak about conditions of forced labor, and similarly reproduces the uneasy, often exploitative historical relationship between white feminist and Black emancipation movements."[60] More commonly, anti-prostitution feminist abolitionism draws on the campaigns against white slavery. In pulling on these campaigns – which erased the presence of women of color in sexual marketplaces while reconstituting understandings of chattel slavery as an economic system rather than a sexual system based on reproductive violence – when advocating for stricter anti-prostitution laws, anti-prostitution abolitionists developed what Elizabeth Bernstein calls "carceral feminism" – turning to the state's carceral apparatus to achieve gender justice – as their "preferred political remedies" in the 1990s and 2000s.[61] The turn toward law-and order-solutions – recall that the UN Trafficking Protocol is part of the Organized

---

[57] Doezema, *Sex Slaves and Discourse Masters*, 28.   [58] Ibid., 129–131.

[59] Lobasz, *Constructing Human Trafficking*, 142.

[60] Kamala Kempadoo, "Abolition, Criminal Justice, and Transnational Feminism: Twenty-first-century Perspectives on Human Trafficking," in *Trafficking and Prostitution Reconsidered: New Perspectives on Migration, Sex Work, and Human Rights*, 2nd edition, ed. Kamala Kempadoo with Jyoti Sanghere and Bandana Pattanaik (Boulder, CO: Paradigm, 2012), xv.

[61] Elizabeth Bernstein, "Militarized Humanitarianism Meets Carceral Feminism: The Politics of Sex Rights, and Freedom in Contemporary Anti-Trafficking Campaigns," *Signs* 36, no. 1 (2010): 45–71, 54.

Crime Protocol – sets contemporary anti-trafficking feminists and modern slavery abolitionists in opposition to anti-prison abolitionists.

The prison abolitionist movement has little in common with the anti-regulated prostitution, anti-trafficking, and anti-modern slavery movement except for a shared invocation of the legacy of antebellum abolition. Even the way that anti-carceral activists frame their understanding of antebellum abolition differs dramatically from the ways other activists have invoked the abolitionist legacies. Put simply, prison abolitionists seek to eliminate the caging of human beings and the use of the prison industrial complex – "the apparatus of surveillance, policing, and incarceration the state increasingly employs to solve the problems caused by social inequality, stifle politics resistance by oppressed communities, and serve the interests of corporations that profit from prisons and police forces" – to control poor communities and uphold racial capitalism.[62] Responding to the dramatic growth of the number of incarcerated people in America, the overrepresentation of people of color within prison populations, and the prisoners' rights movement that declares, "We are not Slaves!," prison abolitionists – as activists and a body of critical literature – offer a resounding critique of the ongoing subjugation of people of color and the role of criminal punishment in maintaining racial capitalism.[63]

Though prison abolitionists offering varying definitions of abolition and people who identify as prison abolitionists are involved in a diverse set of reform projects, prison abolitionists consistently articulate a historical understanding that roots mass incarceration and the prison industrial complex in chattel slavery in the United States.[64] They pull on W. E. B. Du Bois's understanding of abolition as a process that required not only emancipation and the ballot but also education, land reform, freedom to contract, and the right to bear arms; in short, full equality. As Du Bois argues in the seminal *Black Reconstruction* the tragedy of

---

[62] Dorothy E. Roberts, "Abolition Constitutionalism," *Harvard Law Review* 133, no. 1 (November 2019):1–121, 6.

[63] Robert T. Chase, *We Are Not Slaves: State Violence, Coerced Labor, and Prisoners' Rights in Postwar America* (Chapel Hill: University of North Carolina Press, 2020); William J. Stuntz, *The Collapse of American Criminal Justice* (Cambridge: Harvard University Press, 2011); Elizabeth Hinton, *From the War on Poverty to the War on Crime: The Making of Mass Incarceration in America* (Cambridge: Harvard University Press, 2016); Michelle Alexander, *The New Jim Crow: Mass Incarceration in the Age of Colorblindness* (New Press, 2010); and Roberts, "Abolition Constitutionalism," 4.

[64] Roberts, "Abolition Constitutionalism," 7; Kim Gilmore, "Slavery and Prison: Understanding the Connections," *Social Justice* 27, no. 3 (2000): 195–205.

abolition is that it remained unrealized in the South, as white Southerners blocked Black aspirations. Prison abolitionists take up Du Bois's observation that in the post-Civil War South, penal institutions and criminal law emerged as key sites for controlling Black labor and denying Black freedom. Similarly, prison abolitionists also adopt Du Bois's analysis that abolition, in the words of legal scholar Allegra McLoed, "required the creation of new democratic forms in which the institutions and ideas previously implicated in slavery would be remade to incorporate those persons formerly enslaved and to enable a different future for all members of the polity."[65] Prison abolitionists take up Du Bois's framework to point to both the continuity of anti-Black racism in carceral systems (that extract Black labor and suffering) and the more positive abolitionism to call for the remaking of our collective communities in ways and forms that allow for more substantive forms of justice. While prison abolitionists ground their analysis of the present by arguing for a strong thread of continuity with the past, they also look to the future as the space where the unfinished revolution of Reconstruction can be completed. For prison abolitionists, their work constitutes "the unfinished struggles of the past."[66]

The fact that various abolitionists draw their moral and historical authority by declaring themselves to be "new abolitionists" should come as no surprise because the antebellum abolitionist movement was, as David Brion Davis recalled, a "*willed* achievement, a century's moral achievement that may have no parallel."[67] The desire to lay claim to that moral achievement remains powerful. When they pull on the past, abolitionists – regardless of what type – are describing a historical process and producing a historical narrative. The stories that modern slavery abolitionists tell matter because as they tell stories of Harriet Tubman or Frederick Douglass or William Wilberforce they are producing a historical narrative for a political purpose. In that production all kinds of erasure and elision can occur, as is explored by several chapters within this volume. Historical claims are inherently political and not equal. Michel-Rolph Trouillot notes, "The production of historical narratives involves the uneven contribution of competing groups and individuals who have unequal access to the means of such production."[68]

---

[65] Allegra M. McLeod, "Prison Abolition and Grounded Justice," *UCLA Law Review* 62 (2016): 1156–1239, 1162.

[66] Roberts, "Abolition Constitutionalism," 49.

[67] David Brion Davis, *Inhuman Bondage: The Rise and Fall of Slavery in the New World* (New York: Oxford University Press, 2006), 331.

[68] Michel-Rolph Trouillot, *Silencing the Past: Power and Production of History* (Boston: Beacon Press, 1995), xxiii.

The historians in this volume see much potential in the way that modern slavery abolitionists turn to the past for inspiration. By drawing attention to the unfinished business of freedom, abolitionists are producing historical narratives that can aid in unmasking the chronic structural inequalities in global capitalism, can draw attention to the potential collateral damage of policies that ignore the ways that race, ethnicity, gender, and sexuality shape vulnerability, and that can inspire new activists to imagine new forms of freedom, like the ones that undergird the United Nations' Sustainable Development Goals (SDGs).

I.2 ARE EFFORTS TO FIGHT MODERN SLAVERY WORKING?

As governments race to achieve SDG 8.7 of ending child labor by 2025 and forced labor by 2030, many scholars, policy-makers, and commentators are pausing to ask "what works?" when it comes to fighting modern slavery. Of the sizable resources spent on CSR initiatives and civil society projects, NGO and activist antislavery activities, and enacting new government policies over the last three decades, what is actually leading to concrete change in terms of addressing forced labor on the ground? Is this flurry of activity achieving reductions in the prevalence and severity of severe labor exploitation and human trafficking?

As more and more resources are poured into initiatives that seek to make progress toward SDG 8.7, it is an important moment to be asking these questions. Alliance 8.7 (the global partnership committed to achieving SDG 8.7, coordinated by the International Labour Organization (ILO)), has even supported United Nations University to set up a global knowledge platform to explore "what works to eradicate forced labor, modern slavery, human trafficking and child labor, an aim set out in Target 8.7 of the UN Sustainable Development Goals."[69] Benchmarking the effectiveness of ongoing efforts is a critical endeavor, and one that is taken up in this book. For instance, chapters explore the effectiveness of popular initiatives to combat modern slavery and human trafficking in supply chains, such as ethical certification schemes and worker-led initiatives,[70] as well as international conventions.[71]

But at the same time, we argue that the answer to the question "what works?" is far less straightforward than it is typically made out to be.

[69] See "Homepage," Alliance 8.7, accessed February 10, 2020, https://Delta87.org.
[70] See chapters by LeBaron and Shih, Rosenbaum, & Kyritsis, this volume.
[71] See chapter by Chuang, this volume.

Whether efforts to fight modern slavery and human trafficking appear to be *working* depends on how you understand and measure the problem and solutions. As mentioned earlier, different people see the problem and goals of antislavery movements in very different ways. For some, ending modern slavery means paying off the businesses that illegally exploit victims of forced labor to "buy their freedom," and then finding workers jobs in sweatshops that they have technically consented to. For others, ending modern slavery means abolishing restrictive border regimes, carceral facilities, and monopoly corporations that infuse the economy with the forms of inequality and vulnerability that lead to forced labor in the first place. For some activists, ending modern slavery means abolishing all forms of sex work; for others, it means ensuring that sex workers are given labor protections and rights so they can no longer be subjected to violence with virtual impunity. Some antislavery activists see criminalization and policing as the answer, while others see it as a form of state violence that reinforces the very forms of racial inequality that leave people of color more vulnerable to exploitation and abuse.[72] In short, the question of "what works?" is not neutral or objective. No doubt, individual initiatives and policies can be evaluated according to their stated purposes and aims. But these are marked by exceedingly different definitions of the problem and visions of success.

1.2.1 The Prospects and Perils of Quantification

One key barrier to assessing progress is the lack of high-quality baseline estimates, which could allow researchers to analyze whether forced labor is growing or shrinking. Forced labor, modern slavery, and human trafficking are notoriously difficult to estimate, but over the last decade progress has been made toward measuring prevalence. In 2018, the International Conference of Labour Statisticians published *Guidelines Concerning the Measurement of Forced Labour*, which the ILO is currently developing into a standard methodology for estimating forced labor. This will help to harmonize definitions and data collection across sectors and countries, which will strengthen the evidence base on prevalence of forced labor. Signs of progress are visible on the Delta 8.7 website, where United Nations agencies and governments are beginning to release data for researchers and the media to analyze. But we are still a way off from having good quality, consistently measured, time-series data that

---

[72] See chapters by Duane & Meiners and Peña Delgado, this volume.

could give a firm answer to the question of whether prevalence is rising or falling at the global, sectoral, and country levels.

Existing estimates of modern slavery are controversial and continue to be fraught with methodological problems. The Global Slavery Index (GSI) compiled annually by the Walk Free Foundation provides a "country by country ranking of the number of people in modern slavery, as well as an analysis of the actions governments are taking to respond, and the factors that make people vulnerable."[73] Since the first version of the GSI was published in 2013, it has attracted methodological criticism, some of which is discussed in Gunther Peck's contribution to this volume. Critiques of the GSI range from claims that it uses poor quality and limited source data, inappropriate extrapolation, and flawed and partial definition of modern slavery, to the claim that GSI portrays modern slavery as a national problem, obfuscating global and historical drivers like multinational corporations and their sourcing practices or histories of colonial plunder. As it has developed over the last seven years, the GSI has increased transparency around its methodology and made strides toward addressing some of these critiques. However, it is far from providing a solid basis for assessing whether the prevalence of forced labor is going up or down, in part because its estimation techniques have only recently stabilized. Critics of the GSI are quick to point out that the global estimate of modern slavery ballooned from 29.8 million people in modern slavery in 2013 to 40.3 million in 2018 (which they often see as an attempt to inflate the scale of the problem); however, the growth can mostly be explained by changes in approach to counting.

In addition to the GSI, the ILO has published estimates of forced labor since 2012, focusing on regional and global estimates and shying away from national estimates which they see as currently undesirable given data limitations, potential for bias, and political sensitivities. However, in 2017, the ILO joined forces with the Walk Free Foundation and International Organization for Migration to produce a notably different Global Estimate of Modern Slavery compared to earlier estimates. One key difference between the ILO's 2017 estimate and previous versions is that the 2017 one estimated *modern slavery;* rather than just forced labor, this meant that it also included forced marriage. This has been hugely controversial given debates around consent (and how this is assumed and captured by researchers), the methodology used to calculate forced

[73] "About The Index," Global Slavery Index, accessed May 13, 2020, www.globalslaveryin dex.org/about/the-index/.

marriage (which the authors acknowledge is admittedly weak), and some researchers' sense that given that forced labor and forced marriage are "apples and oranges," it is irresponsible and misleading to aggregate them within the same estimate.[74] As well, unlike forced labor, forced marriage doesn't flow from an international instrument adopted through multilateral process and stakeholder consultation as is typical of ILO processes; rather, it was simply included. For these and other reasons, some scholars and activists see the new global estimate as a step backwards rather than forwards when it comes to having an accurate understanding of the prevalence of severe labor exploitation.

Having reliable estimates for the prevalence of forced labor that could demonstrate change over time could be a useful tool in assessing the effectiveness of prevailing attempts to fight modern slavery and human trafficking. But efforts to quantify the problem will always be a lightning rod for methodological criticism because they reveal important political choices by researchers, which in turn will shape policy responses. As macro-economic statistics expert and professor Daniel Mügge puts it, recent global estimates of forced labor "will guide international policy for years to come, which is why we need to start taking their data limitations seriously."[75] The ILO, International Organization for Migration, UNICEF, and Organization for Economic Cooperation and Development acknowledged recently that "measuring child labour, forced labour and human trafficking in global supply chains remains a significant challenge."[76]

Dozens of thorny questions lurk behind prevalence numbers. Here, we'll name just three. First, one of the trickiest tasks that researchers face is where and how to draw the line on forced labor. As described above, most definitions of forced labor – including the ILO's definition – tend to exclude labor that is involuntary due to economic coercion, such as the legitimate threat of starvation or destitution. This means that workers in dismal and exploitative conditions, who are stuck in their jobs because they lack any other option to secure their subsistence, are not encompassed within standard definitions of forced labor. A second issue researchers face is that it is challenging to isolate labor situations that *do* meet the bar of forced labor from those that do not. The boundary between forced labor and other forms of exploitation is not fixed or obvious, but rather is porous, tricky to demarcate, and highly contingent

---

[74] Mügge, "40.3 Million Slaves?"   [75] Ibid.
[76] ILO, OECD, IOM, UNICEF, *Ending Child Labour, Forced Labour and Human Trafficking in Global Supply Chains* (Geneva: ILO), 5.

since empirical research suggests many workers move in between situations of "forced labor" and other forms of exploitation in relatively short periods of time, multiple times in their lives.[77] Finally, classification of people into prevalence figures reveal difficult decisions researchers make with respect to workers' agency and perceptions of their own working conditions, since not all workers in forced labor conditions identify with such characterizations of their work.

Given these and many other challenges, some researchers have asked whether quantifying forced labor is appropriate or useful at all.[78] Among their concerns, scholars claim that quantification: isn't possible to achieve for a complex social phenomenon like modern slavery, and measures will always be imperfect compared to those of disease or environmental damage; can misplace causality and blame for the problem, such as by framing forced labor as a national issue when its determinants also lie in the global economy;[79] is driven by philanthrocapitalists, who are reconfiguring the anti-trafficking and antislavery movement and policymaking in adverse ways;[80] obscures important distinctions between coerced people, whose labor is in many senses unfree, elevating some forms of unfreedom in importance over others;[81] and siphons away resources that could be better spent solving the problem rather than measuring it. Ultimately, as Gunther Peck notes in his chapter within this volume, "new and better estimates will not solve the political challenges that activists and policymakers face in fighting human trafficking."

Others have vigorously defended the need for numbers. Public health researchers focused on human trafficking and labor exploitation noted, for instance, that evaluating the effectiveness of interventions and prevention measures requires robust evidence.[82] Other scholars have claimed that

---

[77] For a longer discussion of these challenges, see Genevieve LeBaron, ed. *Researching Forced Labour in the Global Economy: Methodological Challenges and Advances* (Oxford: Oxford University Press, 2018).

[78] Anne T. Gallagher, "What's Wrong with the Global Slavery Index?," *Anti-Trafficking Review* 8 (2017): 90–112.

[79] Siobhan McGrath and Fabiola Mieres, "Mapping the Politics of National Rankings in the Movement against 'Modern Slavery'," in *Beyond Trafficking and Slavery*, openDemocracy, December 4, 2014, www.opendemocracy.net/en/beyond-trafficking-and-slavery/mapping-politics-of-national-rankings-in-movement-again/.

[80] Janie A. Chuang, "Giving as Governance? Philanthrocapitalism and Modern-Day Slavery Abolitionism," *UCLA Law Review* 62, no. 4 (2016): 1516–1556.

[81] See chapter by Peck, this volume.

[82] Ligia Kiss and Cathy Zimmerman, "Human Trafficking and Labor Exploitation: Toward Identifying, Implementing, and Evaluating Effective Responses," *PLoS Medicine* 16, no. 1 (2019): https://doi.org/10.1371/journal.pmed.1002740.

without being able to quantify the problem, it won't receive the attention, resources, or policy responses it deserves. Reliable measurements of modern slavery are crucial, they urge, and academics and organizations need to join together to collaborate to achieve these. As Kevin Bales puts it, "the ongoing lack of transparency and data sharing in the study of slavery is not just a threat to good science – it prevents comparable analyses that might reduce suffering and the extreme human cost of slavery."[83]

As David W. Blight notes in his foreword to the book, these contemporary debates about numbers echo debates among historians about the scale, prevalence, and value of the slave trade and slave economies that have characterized earlier eras of capitalist development. It is striking how many similarities there are between historic and contemporary debates about numbers, not least because the core challenge they represent to corporate interests and governments remains in the wake of legal emancipation.

1.2.2 Trends in Research

Some scholars have jumped to contribute to the expanding evidence base to assess what's working when it comes to fighting modern slavery and human trafficking. But others reject the very premise of the question. They are critical of the notion that modern slavery can be "fought" through targeted interventions, flagging the need for structural reforms that address root causes. Sceptics are also critical of the assumption that slavery and trafficking can be "fought" by the same actors hardwiring the economy to produce systematic vulnerability to these forms of exploitation, like corporations and governments.[84]

Debates over the appropriate and ideal form for research on forced labor and human trafficking are kicking off within our field. Academic research on modern slavery spans over a dozen disciplines – from health science to politics – and the full epistemological, theoretical, and methodological spectrums that characterize inquiry within those disciplines. Research methods and data hide and illuminate certain dimensions of our complex social world – none are all-encompassing. Like all research,

---

[83] Kevin Bales, "Unlocking the Statistics of Slavery," *Chance* 32, no. 1 (2019): 18–26.

[84] See, for instance Genevieve LeBaron and Nicola Phillips, "States and the Political Economy of Unfree Labour," *New Political Economy* 24, no. 1 (2019): 1–21; Genevieve LeBaron, *Combatting Modern Slavery: Why Labour Governance Is Failing and What We Can Do About It* (Cambridge: Polity, 2020).

different types of research on modern slavery and human trafficking foreground different phenomena, politics, and perspectives. Understanding that academics come from different disciplinary, epistemological, and theoretical places is important in understanding why they collect different types of data (or indeed, feel that data shouldn't be collected at all) and in making sense of their participation (or not) in efforts to fight modern slavery and human trafficking.

1.3 THIS BOOK'S CONTRIBUTION

Shortly before we sent this book to press, in spring 2020, United Kingdom (UK) Prime Minister Boris Johnson emphasized his newly elected Conservative government's commitment to fighting modern slavery. He promised that "those behind such crimes, these traders in human misery, must and will be ruthlessly hunted down and brought to justice."[85] Johnson's promise echoes those made by leaders around the world over recent decades and positions his government as part of the fight against modern slavery, human trafficking, and forced labor – a battle that unites US President Donald Trump, far-right political parties across Europe, as well as some left parties and regimes. Many conservative governments champion the cause of fighting modern slavery, just as they gut human rights and social protections, de-fund labor inspectorates, roll back hard-won laws and legal victories made by unions, champion stricter immigration laws, and give ever-greater power to businesses who perpetrate forced labor with virtual impunity. Given that the coalition to fight forced labor and human trafficking has attracted bipartisan support and strange bedfellows, the question of how to relate to such efforts is a complex and contradictory one for activists and scholars.[86]

While the antislavery movement is sometimes presented as a cohesive force pulling in the same direction, as this book shows, there are considerable tensions within it. These include tensions around who is fighting for what; whether some fights, goals, and solutions are undermining others; how to measure the problem, progress toward resolving it, and what success will ultimately look like; and the often unaccounted-for failures, perverse effects, and hidden costs associated with antislavery initiatives

---

[85] United Kingdom Government, *UK Government Modern Slavery Statement* (London: HM Government, 2020), 1.

[86] Melissa Gira Grant, "Beyond Strange Bedfellows: How the 'War on Trafficking' was Made to Unite the Left and the Right," *The Public Eye* (Summer 2018), 11–16, 23.

and policies. Rather than merely asking whether antislavery efforts are working, contributors to this book shine a light on *who* antislavery efforts are working *for* and examine how competing definitions of the problem lead to very different answers to the question of what works.

The book draws together leading scholars, who speak to controversies described above. As they explore these core challenges, our authors cover an impressive timespan, drawing lessons from and connections between the eighteenth, nineteenth, and twentieth centuries' slave trades and movements to combat these, and contemporary dynamics of modern slavery and human trafficking and movements to combat these. Exploring the continuities and discontinuities that animate slavery and labor exploitation, and struggles to combat these in the past and present, scholars within this book challenge contemporary misuses and distortions of history, including the ways in which contemporary antislavery struggles neglect racism and racial politics, colonialism, sexism, and misogyny. By bringing into focus the ways in which classification and representation of enslaved people has always been shaped by racial, colonial, and gendered patterns, this collection complicates the triumphant stories about the heroic defeat of slavery by historic abolition movements and western democracies. As well, the historians and social scientists within the book reflect together on how the world has changed since the widespread abolition of slavery in the nineteenth century, altering the terrain on which contemporary antislavery and anti-trafficking struggles are waged compared to previous eras in global capitalism.

As mentioned earlier, one key controversy that shapes efforts to fight modern slavery is the question of whether, and to what extent, contemporary antislavery activism aligns with conservative political agendas and naturalizes systemic problems. Grace Peña Delgado finds evidence for alignment between anti-human trafficking causes and conservative politics in her examination of Mexico in the early twenty-first century. She finds the rise of evangelical Christian power within the PAN Party and conservative political values were fundamental for support for anti-trafficking and modern slavery efforts. As Peña Delgado's work implies, Mexican feminists' embracing of trafficking as violence against women displaced earlier support for workers' rights as a way to ensure workers' freedom.

Contributors also speak to controversies surrounding the market and the role of corporations and business within the contemporary fight against forced labor and trafficking. As Genevieve LeBaron's chapter explores, businesses have championed a number of solutions to forced labor in supply chains, including CSR tools like social auditing and ethical certification schemes like Fairtrade and Rainforest Alliance. Yet, as she argues – relying on extensive fieldwork with tea workers at the base of global supply chains – while these certifications include standards that prohibit forced and child labor, as well as wage underpayment and violations, such standards are routinely not met by employers. Elina Shih, J. J. Rosenbaum, and Penelope Kyritsis also examine the role of markets and supply chains in anti-trafficking governance. They examine corporate-led efforts to fight modern slavery, contending that anti slavery efforts enable corporate greenwashing while displacing modes of global south labor organizing. Their chapter tracks how the anti slavery movement has become a powerful ally and legitimating factor of CSR efforts, which are in fact highly limited when it comes to advancing working conditions and addressing the issues that workers care most about. By contrast, they argue that worker-driven social responsibility initiatives are proving to be a more effective means of addressing forced labor, gender-based violence, and overlapping forms of exploitation and abuse. Kevin Bales and Alison Gardner also explore the role of business and present a more optimistic view. Exploring the vital role that corporate citizenship and ethical consumerism played in nineteenth century antislavery struggles, they note that businesses can proactively embrace antislavery campaigns, with important results.

The chapters by LeBaron, Shih, Rosenbaum, and Kyritsis, and Chuang raise important questions about whose perspective, voice, and agency dominate anti-slavery initiatives and their implementation. These questions are also powerfully tackled by Zoe Trodd, Andea Nicholson, and Lauren Elgen who argue that it is imperative we listen to survivors' own perspectives on the solutions to the problems they have faced. Presenting "a major new collection of contemporary slavery survivor narratives," and using these narratives to map out a perspective on which SDG targets are most effective in ending enslavement, this chapter argues for the importance of shaping policy around the visions of survivors themselves. Exploring the layered experiences of slavery, gender-based violence, and other challenges confronted by survivors, the authors argue that the SDGs cannot be achieved in isolation, but rather, there is a need for an intersectional and holistic approach. Picking up the question of whose interests are served by various forms and tools of antislavery and anti-trafficking governance, Janie Chuang's chapter investigates the UN Global Compact on Safe and Orderly Migration, asking whether it is a hindrance to efforts to combat human trafficking, or a powerful tool. Chuang argues that in the context of a long-standing governance deficit and vacuum of robust policies, laws and institutions for migrant workers, the compact is an important development. However, she cautions that competing interests are at play within the Compact and warns that it will be "incumbent upon rights advocates to closely scrutinize" implementation efforts.

A related controversy explored in the volume is who counts and is represented within the antislavery movement and struggle, and histories of it. Kevin Bales and Alison Gardner reflect on the vital role played by community organizations, religious organizations, and other grassroots groups in transforming public perceptions of slavery from an economic benefit into a moral scourge within early abolitionist movements. While the role of these organizations has sometimes been overlooked, this moral redefinition, they argue, was foundational in triggering the legislative action that abolished chattel slavery. Bales and Gardner argue for the critical role and importance of faith networks, business, and community organizations in fighting modern slavery today. Just as the volume contains important investigation of more traditional actors, such as governments and international organizations, so too does it highlight the role and stories of under-studied actors within the anti-trafficking and anti-slavery landscape.

Threaded throughout this volume are perspectives on the multifaceted controversy surrounding the use of historical analogy discussed throughout this introduction. Though critical of the limitations that employing historical analogy can impose on narrative and imagination, Duane and Meiners's chapter argues for an expansive transformative imaginary that can accommodate the nuanced history of slavery and slave resistance, while tracing the threads of continuity that not only help explain the persistence of racial capitalism but also hold the potential for unraveling such systems of oppression as the prison industrial complex and modern slavery and trafficking. Jessica R. Pliley is even more skeptical about simplistic invocations of abolitionist history, in her essay about knowledge production and international governance of anti-trafficking movement between World War I and World War II (1918–1939). She demonstrates through a study of the abolitionist movement against sex trafficking in the 1920s and 1930s that historic forms of abolitionism were deeply intertwined with anti-sex and anti-feminist agendas, fraught racialized politics, and the coercive use of state power to stop migration and police poor women. She cautions that contemporary abolitionist movements can echo the same paternalistic, white supremacist politics that shaped such movements historically. Gunther Peck's chapter similarly cautions against contemporary scholars' and activists' tendency to invoke simplistic analogies and claims about the past, homing in on claims that are made about the number of slaves today and that this number is greater than it was in earlier eras of capitalism. He reflects on how such claims can elide suffering, misrepresent the past, and disguise the power relations that shaped the collection of data about different types of slavery, servitude, trafficking, and exploitation in history.

Our aim in this volume is not to settle the controversies that pervade scholarship and activism on forced labor, modern slavery, and human trafficking. Rather, it is to bring these controversies into the open and offer multiple perspectives on them. Our hope is that by exploring history and the multiple, at times conflicting, origins and politics of efforts to fight modern slavery and human trafficking, we will deepen understandings of why these controversies exist and be able to navigate through them. As our field grows and matures, with new students, scholars, and non-academic researchers joining this cause, it's imperative that we have awareness and sensitivity to the fault-lines that characterize scholarship, activism, and advocacy in our field – and an understanding of the long histories that underpin these.

2

Counting Modern Slaves

Historicizing the Emancipatory Work of Numbers

Gunther Peck

2.1 INTRODUCTION

Numbers have been an essential feature of the modern movement to combat the complex problem called "modern slavery." Perhaps the most important number in that effort has been twenty-seven million, the estimate of how many people were toiling without recompense across the planet when Kevin Bales first published his important book *Disposable People: New Slavery in the Global Economy* in 1999. Since then, as Bales noted in 2012, the number has taken on "a life of its own."[1] His twenty-seven million estimate has proved vital to a great variety of people, from authorities in the US Department of State persuading countries to pass anti-trafficking legislation to self-heroizing abolitionists like Aaron Cohen, who cited the number as his starting point for a one-man crusade against the trafficking of underage girls in brothels across Asia and Africa.[2] As significant as the size of Bales's estimate has been the way activists and government actors alike have used the number to draw comparisons between the coercive phenomena known as "modern slavery" and the history of slavery in the Americas. David Batstone used the twenty-seven million number to foreground a shocking conclusion at the beginning of his 2007 bestseller *Not for Sale*: "More slaves live in bondage today than were bartered during four centuries of the

---

[1] Kevin Bales, *Disposable People: New Slavery in the Global Economy* (Berkeley: University of California Press, 2012), originally published 1999, 25.
[2] Aaron Cohen, *Slave Hunter: One Man's Global Quest to Free Victims of Human Trafficking* (New York: Simon & Schuster, 2009), xi.

transatlantic slave trade."[3] The number has been used by modern abolitionists to bolster an ethical claim of extraordinary power: that "modern slavery" is not only bigger in absolute terms than the historical slave trade out of Africa but a morally proportionate crime as well, one demanding the immediate attention of any citizen with a conscience. Getting the estimate right has been important not only for persuading those who doubt that modern slavery is indeed real but also for addressing the movement's critics. "There seems nothing to debate about slavery," writes Bales: "It must stop."

But if the twenty-seven million number has successfully highlighted the scale and severity of coercion in today's global economy, it has not in fact ended debate about modern slavery. What exactly separates a "modern slave" from people experiencing systematic exploitation or discrimination? And how can onlookers or authorities know it is modern slavery when so many trafficked people refuse the label of slave? Skeptics and defenders of the twenty-seven million number have noted it is an estimate rather than an actual census, since in no country was slavery officially legal in 1999. Indeed, contemporary abolitionists freely acknowledge the challenge that illegality generates, as no exact accounting is possible, in sharp contrast to the historical slave trade out of Africa. Writes Siddharth Kara, "data related to human trafficking are inherently imprecise due to the clandestine nature of the crimes and the broad overlap with smuggling and migration."[4] In his 2012 republication of *Disposable People*, Bales addressed some of these criticisms, conceding that "I am the first to admit that this is a rough and flawed estimate of a hidden and poorly defined crime."[5] Yet Bales defended his estimate as the best one yet made in the field of modern slavery. "It is the only estimate," he wrote in 2012, "that has had external and independent review and assessment."[6] Bales has recently revised his estimate upward to forty million people who are currently enslaved or working under threat of violence for no wages.

Unfortunately, new and better estimates will not solve the political challenges that activists and policy-makers face in fighting human trafficking, nor will they offer much guidance for migrant workers choosing between human traffickers or corrupt government authorities. To

---

[3] David Batstone, *Not for Sale: The Return of the Global Slave Trade and How We Can Fight It* (New York: Harper, 2007), 5.
[4] Siddhath Kara, *Sex Trafficking: Inside the Business of Modern Slavery* (New York: Columbia University Press, 2009), 264.
[5] Bales, *Disposable People*, 25.   [6] Ibid.

understand why, we need first to reflect on *how* activists, scholars, and government actors have used numbers over the past two decades. In both the past and the present, counting slaves has created an illusion of commensurability, the ahistoric and misleading fiction that very different kinds of coercion are summable and therefore interchangeable. In practice, that transactional premise has fueled not only antislavery sentiment but hierarchical evaluations of human suffering too, a calculus at odds with the universal moral claims deployed to abolish buying and selling people. Counting slaves has expressed not only the deepest moral values of abolitionists seeking to end slavery but also the mercantilist logic that originally generated a global slave trade from Africa more than four centuries ago, and which still informs global economic development today. The emancipatory work of numbers has been elusive not because today's traffickers are especially smart or because good people remain skeptical of modern slavery but because counting slaves has obscured crucial distinctions among coerced peoples, while frequently exempting states and corporations from responsibility for fomenting human trafficking. The quest for a single aggregate number of modern slaves, moreover, has preempted a more sustained and nuanced conversation about how history might better inform current efforts to abolish coercion throughout the global economy.

In this chapter, I explore how and why counting modern slaves has both clarified *and* paradoxically obscured the ethical importance of slavery and the varied forms of coercion associated with it. First, I explore in greater depth how and why the emancipatory work of numbers has been so elusive to contemporary activists and policy-makers. I then consider the work that counting slaves accomplished during key moments in the history of human trafficking. I begin not with the abolitionists of the late eighteenth century but with the crucial work that counting slaves and servants played in shaping the origins of race and global circuits of human trafficking during the seventeenth century. In the final section, I consider how historical abolitionists might help contemporary activists and researchers alike to rethink how they use numbers and history more generally in building a stronger global movement against the exploitation known as "modern slavery."

2.2 ELUSIVE GAINS: COUNTING THE COSTS OF ONE NUMBER

To understand the complex work that counting modern slaves has accomplished, we need first to analyze the broader context in which numbers about trafficking have been deployed – a global political economy in which numeracy is a requirement of both international policy engagement and global development work. "We live in a hyper-numeric world preoccupied with quantification," write the political scientists Peter Andreas and Kelly Greenhill, one in which "difficult to perceive phenomena are not perceived to be 'real' until they are quantified and given a number." But quantifying complex problems can also be remarkably difficult, Andreas and Greenhill note, as "death tolls, refugee flows, trafficking numbers, and smuggling estimates are commonly inflated, deflated, or simply fabricated, all in the service of political goals."[7] The challenge for researchers is twofold: accounting for the inaccuracies in the data that researchers rely upon and making their choices as transparent as possible, enabling advocates to see the ethical choices they make when compiling data.

Andreas and Greenhill provide a useful starting point for evaluating not only the accuracy of the data that modern abolitionists have compiled but also the ethical implications of their estimations. Efforts to count modern slaves have produced a mixture of candor, critique, and obfuscation. On the one hand, some researchers such as David Feingold have challenged what he describes as an "overreliance on numbers in trafficking research." "Trafficking numbers provide the false precision of quantification," writes Feingold, while "lacking any of the supports of statistical rigor."[8] On the other hand, Kevin Bales and others have been quite candid about the limitations of their estimates, even while demonstrating their utility to policy-makers and advocates. But other researchers have been less careful or self-critical when counting modern slaves. David Batstone is not alone among contemporary abolitionists in pairing a partial disclaimer about numerical estimates with bold assertions about the magnitude of the problem. When investigating sex trafficking among children in Thailand, for example, he acknowledged that the "precise number of parents who sell their children to traffickers in Southeast Asia cannot be easily assessed" but then promptly claimed that "close to 35 percent of the Vietnamese families living in Cambodia sell a daughter into the sex trade, while another 25 to 30 percent seriously consider the option."[9] Rather than considering the context of this data or

[7] Peter Andreas and Kelly M. Greenhill, "Introduction: The Politics of Numbers," in *Sex, Drugs, and Body Counts: The Politics of Numbers*, eds. Peter Andreas and Kelly M. Greenhill (Ithaca: Cornell University Press, 2012), 1, 6.

[8] David Feingold, "Trafficking in Numbers: The Social Construction of Human Trafficking Data," in Andreas and Greenhill, *Sex, Drugs, and Body Counts*, 47.

[9] Batstone, *Not For Sale*, 23.

its potential to blame victims for being trafficked, Batstone simply quoted more sources that amplified the aggregate number of modern slaves, even when of dubious integrity. Batstone cited President George W. Bush as an authority on modern slavery, for example, quoting his speech to the United Nations in 2003 in which he said that "each year eight hundred to nine hundred thousand human beings are bought, sold, or forced across the world's borders." In that same speech President Bush also called for an invasion of Iraq because it possessed weapons of mass destruction.[10] Ignoring evidence to the contrary as well as its political context, Batstone urged, like President Bush, action rather than reflection in prosecuting a contemporary "war" on modern slavery. "There are times to read history," Batstone wrote, "and there are times to make history."[11]

What to make of that recent history remains the subject of considerable controversy, for good reasons. Batstone's claims led David Feingold to single him out among contemporary abolitionists for using numbers to mislead, painting a broader portrait of abolitionist researchers putting politics ahead of evidence. "I believe it is quite clear," Feingold writes, "that global estimates of trafficking do not 'serve any serious policy purposes.' However, they do serve a socio-political purpose: to advocate for and justify the expenditure of resources."[12] Those sociopolitical purposes include not only funneling millions of dollars of US State Department aid to nongovernmental organizations (NGOs) around the globe that engage the 3Ps of anti-trafficking work – prosecution, protection, and prevention – but also counting modern slaves to justify particular aspects of American foreign policy.[13] To observe that "socio-political purposes" exist should not end scholarly critique, however, but generate a more expansive inquiry into the history of numbers and antislavery, one that might help contemporary actors rethink their efficacy and ethical purpose. The historical abolitionists were not averse to using empire and nation to achieve emancipation, after all, nor did they eschew spending the state's resources.[14] If we are to make history, we do in fact need to read the past and learn from the

---

[10] Ibid., 3.   [11] Ibid., 17.   [12] Feingold, "Trafficking in Numbers," 55.

[13] On the geopolitical context of US anti-trafficking policy, see Anthony M. DeStefano, *The War on Human Trafficking: U.S. Policy Assessed* (New Brunswick: Rutgers University Press, 2007).

[14] On the importance of empire to abolitionist arguments and politics, see Christopher Brown, *Moral Capital: Foundations of British Abolitionism* (Chapel Hill: The Omohundro Institute, 2006).

mistakes and accomplishments that both idealistic and opportunistic actors made when counting slaves.

2.2.1 Counting Servants and Slaves

We begin by using history to reconsider how the aggregate totals of "modern slaves" have been reached. We must acknowledge first that they would make little sense to the historical abolitionists or their adversaries. When contemporary abolitionists count modern slaves, they lump groups that metropolitan and colonial authorities during the seventeenth and eighteenth centuries labored hard to keep legally and culturally apart: slaves and indentured servants. To colonial and metropolitan authorities alike, sharp legal and political distinctions distinguished servants from slaves, even before notions of racial hierarchy were deployed to naturalize such differences by the late seventeenth century. Servants retained their names, could seek legal redress for crimes that their masters committed, and became, after a period of time, free subjects. No such rights existed for African slaves. Nor did the common fact of servants and slaves being trafficked and sold as bills of goods make them equally coerced. Defenders and opponents of slavery alike knew that being bought and sold were not the same things as being enslaved, along with your progeny, in perpetuity. To insist that all trafficked peoples across the planet were necessarily slaves, as the Trafficking Violence Protection Act and the UN Trafficking Protocol declare, collapses important historical distinctions among unfree laborers, differences that structured the historical evolution of both racial capitalism and resistance to it.[15]

Modifiers used to describe trafficking in project descriptions of US funded anti-trafficking initiatives							
	2002	2003	2004	2005	2006	2007	2008
"Human"	70%	71%	76%	61%	71%	76%	85%
"Child"	40%	33%	11%	12%	13%	22%	17%
"Sex"	9%	15%	5%	6%	10%	18%	23%
Total grantees	193	225	271	358	252	244	223

[15] I historicize the origins of white racial grammar in chapters 1 and 2 of my forthcoming book *Race Traffic: Radical Antislavery and the Long Fight against White Supremacy, 1660–1860* (Chapel Hill: The Omohundro Institute, forthcoming).

There are compelling ethical and historical reasons to link servants and slaves when combatting unfree labor across the planet today, not the least being the fact that indentured servitude and chattel slavery historically functioned as twined parts of a larger whole. The political remedy to that history of unequal bondage – the 13th Amendment – crucially included both servitude and slavery in 1865, after all.[16] But the 13th Amendment did not in fact conflate servitude and slavery. Lumping them in the present into the same category ignores awkward asymmetries among trafficked people and links past and present inconsistently. When David Batstone remarks that there are more modern slaves living today than in four centuries of the African slave trade, for example, he counts trafficked actors in the present as slaves but does not count their antecedents as slaves in the past. Indentured servants across the Americas, Russian serfs, and women without property rights in marriages across the planet, all toiled for no wages under threat of violence for centuries before 1865. Why not include them when using a single number to compare past to present? Doing so would upend the simple and misleading comparison between today's expansive category of "modern slaves" and the history of the slave trade out of Africa. Insisting that there are *more* enslaved people alive today than in the entire history of the African slave trade suggests that today's coercion is somehow worse, diminishing the severity of the African slave trade while fortifying a hierarchy of victimhood among historically trafficked peoples.[17]

---

[16] The inclusion of indentured servitude in the 13th Amendment has received less historical attention than it might have because it had already withered across North America due to judges' refusal to criminalize breaches of contract when servants ran away after 1820. Yet its abolition in 1865 put the United States on a different political footing from its antislavery rival Great Britain, which expanded indentured labor across its empire in the wake of slavery's abolition in 1833. The United States, by contrast, would prohibit the importation of workers under contract into its borders and territories. On the Foran Act of 1885, see Gunther Peck, *Reinventing Free Labor: Padrones and Immigrant Workers in the North American West, 1880–1930* (Cambridge: Cambridge University Press, 2000), 93–105.

[17] In the introduction to *Race Traffic*, I use the insights and aspirations of trafficked people to draw a distinction between the histories of human trafficking and of slavery. Trafficking describes the processes by which people become fungible property, bought and sold to owners who extract value from the bodies they have purchased. Slavery on the other hand describes a relationship of continuous theft in which one's body, labor, identity, skills, and progeny are stolen by others, with or without one's commodification. While obviously related historical processes, they have not been identical, with some trafficked people, like indentured servants or sailors, not being enslaved and many slaves never being trafficked or sold at auction.

The conflation of trafficking with enslavement in the present but not the past, then, has distorted how modern abolitionists see and learn from the histories of slavery and abolition. That is especially apparent in the way that writers like Batstone have summarized abolitionist accomplishments such as the 1808 abolition of the African slave trade. Batstone suggested that the slave trade's abolition spelled the death knell of slavery as an institution in the Americas, writing that the "legislation gave abolitionists an effective tool to hold slaveholders accountable for their inhumane activity."[18] But little historical evidence supports Batstone's claim that slavery was on the ropes after 1808. The American slaveholders who supported the abolition of the slave trade in 1808 would have been startled by Batstone's claim. Slavery did not "persist for decades" after the abolition of the African slave trade as Batstone put it but grew exponentially throughout the Antebellum Era, much of it fueled by an internal slave trade across the United States. As a political institution, slavery was hardly preindustrial, outmoded, or inefficient but the central economic engine of racial capitalism.[19] Slavery was eventually destroyed not because of the enlightened leadership of white legislators, moreover, but because *millions* of enslaved men and women used their mobility before and during the American Civil War to upend the moral, strategic, and political purposes of that bloody conflict. By running to northern states in spite of the Dred Scott decision and fleeing to Union lines during the war, enslaved people transformed a sectional conflict over the status of fugitive slaves and slavery in the territories into a war for the national liberation of Black people.[20]

To assess the historical efficacy of counting slaves, we need to consider when, where, and why English authorities began to put energy into counting them. Both metropolitan and colonial authorities across England's expanding empire during the seventeenth century spent a great deal of time discussing numbers in their letters to each other. Much of that correspondence involved broader discussions about the

---

[18] Batstone, *Not For Sale*, 5.

[19] Of many scholars noting the profitability of slavery and its intrinsic connections to the history of capitalism, see Marcus Rediker, *The Slave Ship: A Human History* (New York: Penguin Books, 2007); Cedric Robinson, *Black Marxism: The Making of the Black Radical Tradition* (London: Zed Books, 1983); and Walter Johnson, "To Remake the World; Slavery, Racial Capitalism, and Justice," *Boston Review*, Forum 1 (Spring 2017), 25.

[20] On the crucial role of African and African American peoples in shaping the history of abolition, see Manisha Sinha, *The Slave's Cause: A History of Abolition* (New Haven: Yale University Press, 2016).

value of moveable things, traffic that made mercantilism not only possible but profitable. Counting "things" mattered, not only because that is how English authorities gained financial value from trafficking people and goods across oceans but also as a measure of imperial authority itself. To count things, whether bales of tobacco, indentured servants from Ireland, or slaves from Africa, was to express and enact English sovereignty simultaneously.[21]

Counting trafficked people could indeed articulate emancipatory aspirations during the seventeenth century, but only in the rare contexts when trafficked people themselves protested their commodification and used their political rights to protest their mistreatment as English subjects, an opportunity not yet available to newly enslaved Africans. One such context involved an effort to create a census of indentured servants that would prevent them from being trafficked and kidnapped to the Americas. In 1670, a group of reformers in parliament passed the first anti-trafficking law in England's history, a response to petitions on behalf of the aggrieved families of indentured servants who protested the coercive ways their children were literally kidnapped, stolen, or "spirited" into America-bound ships, never to return to their families. The Spiriting Law prescribed the death penalty to anyone using force, fraud, or coercion in recruiting a prospective servant onto a transatlantic ship. Ostensibly a victory for the rights of trafficked people, the 1670 law created a servant registry or a census, conducted on every America-bound ship, that included the names of every indentured servant. A key requirement of the new law was that every servant swear, under oath, that they had not been coerced into traveling to the Americas. After 1670, consent thus became a formal requirement of the transatlantic traffic in servants, a partial but important reform on behalf of any indentured servant sailing from an English port.[22]

But a closer look at how the new law was enforced after 1670 highlights the challenge that trafficked servants and their advocates confronted in trying to transform the behavior of English ship captains. Rather than protecting indentured servants from so-called spirits, the servant registry

---

[21] For an excellent reappraisal of mercantilism that stresses contemporary resonances, see Philip J. Stern and Carl Wennerlind, eds., *Mercantilism Reimagined: Political Economy in Early Modern Britain and Its Empire* (New York: Oxford University Press, 2014).

[22] Calendar of State Papers (London, 1873), preface, xxix, 233. See also a description of the Spiriting Law as passed in Barbados in 1670. "Six Acts of Barbados Passed in 1670," CO 30/1, August 11, 1670, 75–83, Colonial State Papers, Public Records Office, British National Archives, Kew, London.

was deployed by ship captains and their recruiting agents to create the appearance of consent. Servants were compelled to sign the registry, whether or not they had assented to the voyage. Even craftier, ship captains used the servant registry to protect themselves from servants' subsequent legal challenges. Passed as an emancipatory measure to protect trafficked servants, the spiriting law in practice indemnified ship captains from any liability generated by hiring unethical men to fill their holds with human cargo, the standard practice of recruitment before and after the law's passage. The Spiriting Law of 1670 not only expressed and contained political conflicts at the heart of the servant trade but also preempted questions about coercion within England's imperial navy. One reason that King Charles II enthusiastically supported the Spiriting Law was that it burnished his antislavery credentials, even as he dragged his feet in financing the ransom payments for English sailors held captive in North Africa, expanded impressment among English sailors, and put them to work protecting England's growing management of the African slave trade.[23]

If the Spiriting Law of 1670 serves as a cautionary tale about the difficulties of getting industry and state actors to perform genuinely emancipatory work, it also highlights the centrality of race to numeracy and to mercantile power. White grammar, in particular, emerged dramatically in metropolitan and colonial correspondence during the second half of the seventeenth century as a way of calculating the value of trafficked bodies who could build new plantations of tobacco and sugar in the Americas. At its inception, white grammar did not comprise a set of fully realized rights and privileges for English subjects but rather served as a signpost of having been trafficked. To be white was to be bought and sold, a trafficked thing like "a Black," who could be sent to a plantation for work in the Americas. "Whites" were often transported convicts, "the sweepings of Bridewell," London's largest prison, men and women not entitled to consideration about inhumane treatment that "Christian servants" might expect at the hands of common masters. In 1664, for example, Barbadian planters presented a proposal to the Committee of

---

[23] Peck, *Race Traffic*, "Royalist Antislavery," in chapter 1. For more on the mischievous uses of antislavery by Charles II, see Holly Brewer, "Slavery and Sedition in Britain and its Empire," unpublished paper presented at the Triangle Global History Seminar, April 23, 2015.

Council for Foreign Plantations that described trafficked convicts and African slaves all as "servants," but had them "classed under two heads, Blacks and whites." Known as "perpetual servants," rather than slaves, Africans were described as "Blacks, bought by way of trade," who were "sold about 20 l. a head." "Whites" in turn, who had been in "divers ways gathered up in England" and a "few from Ireland and Scotland," were "transported at the rate of 6 l. per head" and "exchanged for commodities at different rates according to their condition or trade." All servants, Black and white, were fungible commodities according to the planters: The difference between them amounted to 14 l. per head, or a ratio of two and a half to one and a reflection of white servants' temporary status and Blacks' "perpetual service."[24]

But if whites, like Blacks, were commodities to be counted and taxed, they were also "things" which might unite in opposition to colonial and metropolitan authorities during the late seventeenth century. The language of whiteness and Blackness would in time make it easier for English authorities in Barbados and elsewhere to make distinctions between the work and political status of African slaves and indentured servants from England, Scotland, and Ireland. But those political distinctions had not yet been naturalized in the minds of the colonial and metropolitan elites who first deployed racial grammar, nor in the actions of trafficked actors in the New World, who resisted being raced, commodified, and compelled to work simultaneously. Fears of servant-slave cooperation rippled across every English colony that imported them during the late seventeenth century, a potential conspiracy that ironically relied on race for its articulation. When London authorities raised an important tax on colonial sugar plantations in 1685, for example, authorities in Barbados protested that "we have been obliged to discharge our hired servants, who were a great safety to the island, since they formed most part of the Militia and curbed our negroes and white servants . . . . being the sweepings of the jails."[25] The striking distinction that colonial

---

[24] "Certain propositions for the better accommodating the Foreigne Plantations with servants reported from the Committee to the Council of Foreigne Plantations," 1664, Barbados, CO 324/1, 275–276, Colonial State Papers, Public Records Office, British National Archives, Kew, London. On the modernity of slavery and its weak legal foundations within English common law, see Christopher Tomlins, *Freedom Bound: Law, Labor, and Civic Identity in Colonizing America* (Cambridge: Cambridge University Press, 2010), 418.

[25] Deputy Governor of Barbados to Lords of Trade and Plantations, 9/14/1685, CO 1/58, #56, 56I, Colonial State Papers, Public Records Office, British National Archives, Kew, London.

authorities drew between convict servants who were raced as white and "hired" servants who possessed rights as Christians, highlighted how closely tethered race, commodification, and rebellion were to the architects of England's emerging empire of traffic. The greatest threat to elite rule on Barbados in 1685 was not a revolt of enslaved peoples against the whites but of the trafficked against common English masters. These anxieties generated numerical distinctions that helped colonial and metropolitan authorities measure the threat of a rebellion of the raced. The 1680 census compiled by Barbadian sugar planters listed two categories of indentured labor, "hired servants" and "white servants," the latter being transported convicts whom the local militia was hired to police, along with the growing number of the island's African slaves.[26]

The work that counting people by skin color accomplished would soon change, as whiteness was reimagined as a set of customary rights and legal privileges for Christians of European heritage. Yet that process took time and was resisted by trafficked "whites" across much of the colonial period, who continued to form strategic alliances with enslaved Africans, running away from common masters and on occasion plotting rebellions against common enemies.[27] When whiteness became better established as both an ideology and a set of prescriptive rights, the relationship between trafficking and race nonetheless remained tightly interwoven. Even as freedom became racialized as an inherent expression of white identity, trafficking remained vital to its meaning. To make the value of whiteness visible, defenders of white rights made victimhood the emotive cornerstone of white racial identity. In that highly elastic accounting of historical suffering, numbers played a vital if imprecise role, a way of insisting that white suffering or *white slavery* was a crime whose costs far exceeded any crimes associated with the enslavement of African peoples across the Americas. Counting slaves, white as well as Black, comprised one of the most effective vehicles for naturalizing an ideology of white supremacy, one

[26] Governor Sir Jonathan Atkins to Mr. Blathway, CO 1/44, April 1, 1680, #47, Colonial State Papers, Public Records Office, British National Archives, Kew, London.

[27] One of the most dramatic of such events was the servant slave conspiracy of 1741 in New York City in which four Irish immigrants, three of them servants, and twenty-six African slaves were executed as part of an alleged plot to burn colonial New York to the ground and overthrow common masters. See Peck, "Mobilizing Race: Atlantic Slave-Servant Conspiracies;" chapter 4 of *Race Traffic*; and Jill Lepore, *New York Burning: Liberty, Slavery, and Conspiracy in Eighteenth-Century Manhattan* (New York: Viking, 2005).

that policed not only enslaved people but also any trafficked white who might find common cause with them.[28]

2.2.2 Rethinking the Uses of Abolitionist History

This brief reprise of the historical relationship between numeracy, race, and human trafficking suggests several vantages from which modern abolitionists might rethink their work. First, counting slaves has historically benefitted governmental authorities, whether or not they defend or protect the rights of their subjects. The United States State Department exemplified that bureaucratic windfall, gaining the power to assess and grade the anti-trafficking efforts of every nation on the planet while exempting itself from evaluation until 2009. Given the fact that slavery is officially illegal and a highly controversial problem, most counts of "modern slaves" have been intensely political, as the prominence of human trafficking conversations in diplomatic communications recently made visible.[29] Yet rather than acknowledge the vexed relationship between counting slaves and the national anxieties that slave-counting has generated, many contemporary abolitionists have been largely silent about the role of western democracies in fomenting human trafficking, preferring instead to define the problem as one of third-world backwardness, cultural corruption, or statelessness. David Batstone, for example, blamed human trafficking primarily on war and the statelessness that it creates, quoting as his authority Senator Samuel Brownback of Kansas, who wrote that there are "fifty million refugees and displaced persons" today. "This ready reservoir by the stateless presents opportunity rife with exploitation by human traffickers."[30] While there is little doubt that refugees have been exploited by traffickers, neither Brownback nor Batstone paused to consider the relationship between immigration policies within western democracies and the trafficking of refugees, or the broader immigration restrictions that propel many migrant men and

---

[28] The language of white slavery emerged as a toxic tool in the arsenal of white supremacists surprisingly late, only in the late 1840s and 1850s when southern nationalist George Fitzhugh made white slavery and white victimhood the cornerstone of his polemic against free labor arguments in the Republican Party. See chapter 12 "Antislavery and White Supremacy, 1850–1860," of *Race Traffic*.

[29] For an analysis and explication of the rich documentary record that the WikiLeaks' exposé of diplomatic correspondence generated for researchers on human trafficking, see Judith Kelley, *Scorecard Diplomacy: Grading States to Influence their Reputation and Behavior* (New York: Cambridge University Press, 2017).

[30] Batstone, *Not For Sale*, 11.

women to pay traffickers in the first place. The omission of immigration policy from the diagnostic arsenal of modern abolitionism is striking, given how powerful counting people has been in defining immigrants as topics of public debate. Neither Siddharth Kara nor his mentor Kevin Bales asked a single question about immigration, citizenship status, or migration policy in their hundreds of interviews with trafficked people.[31] Exempted from their inquiries are the political actors who enforce increasingly militarized immigration policies across the borders of the developing and the developed world.[32]

The second insight that a history of counting slaves highlights is the intrinsic connection between notions of racialized victimhood, the emotive heart of white supremacy, and contemporary practices of human trafficking. If one considers the political status of undocumented peoples today, many of them trafficked by middlemen to get into western democracies, the centrality of race to the contemporary human trafficking crisis is obvious. One wonders how a fuller appreciation of race might shift the way abolitionists and governments count modern slaves. Would the United States fare as well in the annual Trafficking in Persons (TIP) Report if the hundreds of thousands of undocumented men and women who are currently detained in private prisons across the nation, many of them held without legal counsel or due process rights, were counted as modern slaves? Certainly, many of them are unfree to move, to contact their families, or if they work while in detention, to earn wages. If one recognizes how twined race and human trafficking have been over the past four centuries, we can see clearly that Kevin Bales was premature in suggesting that "in the new slavery race means little."[33] Bales is certainly correct to insist that Black skin color is not a precondition for contemporary bondage. But when he concludes that "the criteria of enslavement do not concern color, tribe, or religion," he neglects the powerful role of racism and nationalism in shaping the global political economy from which human trafficking currently derives as well as perceptions of modern slavery itself, including who gets counted as one.

Two examples underscore the importance of racism and nationalism in shaping how both policy-makers and citizens in western democracies

---

[31] Bales, "A Note on Research Methods," 203–207; Kara, *Sex Trafficking*, 222.

[32] The best work on the relationship between migration policies and human trafficking has been done by Anne Gallagher. See her *The International Law of Human Trafficking* (Cambridge: Cambridge University Press, 2010), 218–275.

[33] Bales, *Disposable People*, 32.

perceive the stakes of "modern slavery." In the immediate aftermath of the 9/11 terrorist attacks on the United States, an obscure white nationalist group known as the Omdurman repurposed the newly emergent concept of modern slavery as "white slavery" to justify a sustained war against both Muslim nations and the people of color who allegedly threaten the freedom of white people, especially white women.[34] Their narrative, which effectively linked Islamophobia to the long history of white supremacist propaganda focusing on the protection of sexually endangered white women, would soon become a blockbuster movie in Hollywood, with little stigma or fringe status. The movie *Taken* (2008), in which Muslim men capture, traffic, and try to enslave a father's virginal white daughter until he stops them with righteous patriarchal violence, not only revived white slavery narratives but dramatically expanded the global visibility of modern slavery and white supremacy in 2007. Even if most of the people in the twenty-seven million estimate were people of color, a global public responded to the spectacle of an endangered white virgin, a trope that launched Hollywood's rise to prominence a century earlier with *The Birth of a Nation* (1915).[35] Then, as now, images of trafficked white virgins command attention, linking ideas seemingly in tension – white supremacy and antislavery – into a seamless whole.

Perhaps because of the unhappy twining of white supremacy and sex trafficking in the past and the present, authors of the annual TIP Report have labored hard to suppress race from discussion or analysis. No mention has been made of "white slavery" in the annual TIP Reports that the US Department of State has published annually since 2002. The photographs of trafficking victims in the TIP Reports have also de-emphasized white victimhood, with whites comprising just ten percent of all the victims portrayed and more than half originating in Asia and another quarter from Africa.[36] But a closer look at the racial makeup of each type of victim within the TIP Reports between 2004 and 2014, a decade spanning the presidencies of both George W. Bush and Barack

---

[34] The images produced by the Omdurman, a sequence of six, entitled "White Slavery in Saudi Arabia." I discuss them in greater depth in Gunther Peck, "The Shadow of White Slavery: Race, Innocence, and History in Contemporary Anti-Human Trafficking Campaigns," in *The Power of the Past: History and Statecraft*, eds. Hal Brands and Jeremi Suri (Washington, DC: Brookings, 2015), 213–214.

[35] Pierre Morel, dir., *Taken* (Los Angeles, 20th Century Fox, 2008). For a fuller discussion, see Peck, "The Shadow of White Slavery," 215.

[36] Peck, "The Shadow of White Slavery," 216–217.

Obama, suggests persistent biases about who gets counted and portrayed as a victim of sex or labor trafficking. Fully three-quarters of the white victims portrayed in the TIP Reports experienced sex trafficking, while just an eighth of the white victims were trafficked for labor. By contrast, nearly three quarters of the Black victims within TIP were trafficked for labor while just one fifth trafficked for sex.[37] But the authors of TIP offered no evidence to support those suppositions, largely because there is little evidence to support them. Indeed, despite evidence to the contrary, the annual TIP reports present a centuries-old narrative between 2004 and 2014: white female bodies are trafficked for sex, while Black bodies are trafficked for labor. Black women trafficked and coerced into sex work remain largely invisible.

If the shadow of white slavery is alive and well in TIP images, it also seems to be apparent in the implementation of the Trafficking Visa or the T Visa. Administered by the Department of Justice, the T Visa is available to any victim of human trafficking who would experience "unusual or severe harm" if they were returned by US border authorities to their home country. Ostensibly a humanitarian visa for trafficked migrants fearing deportation, the T Visa possesses the dubious distinction of being the only undersubscribed visa in the entire US immigration system, a result of the demanding requirement that recipients prosecute their traffickers. Remarkably, however, there is little detailed government data about who has received the T Visa, who has been denied it, or the background of either group, a surprising omission given the importance of numbers in the global fight against modern slavery.[38] The best evidence is impressionistic and anecdotal. According to immigrant advocacy groups, the five hundred or so T Visa recipients each year do share some common features. They are much more likely to comprise women and children and are also far more likely to have been trafficked for sex rather than for labor. Taken as a group, T Visa recipients confirm the notion that a hierarchy of victimhood exists

---

[37] Ibid., 218.

[38] There is little academic literature on the implementation of the T visa. For an overview of the T Visa program, see Alison Siskin and Lions Wyler, "Trafficking in Persons: US Policy and Issues for Congress," *Congressional Research Service*, December 23, 2010. For a brief discussion of the T visa, see Peck, "The Shadow of White Slavery," 226–227. For an explication and analysis of the efforts of European states to protect rather than deport trafficking victims, see Gallagher, *The International Law of Trafficking*, 100–103.

among the trafficked: sex trafficking is the most severe crime, the one that persuades US authorities to act.[39]

Analysis of the T Visa's weaknesses and its failure to reach even a small fraction of the thousands who are allegedly trafficked into the United States each year raises troubling questions about the exact function of trafficking estimates and the anti-trafficking policies they inform. The supposition by contemporary abolitionists is that counting modern slaves will inform the work of policy-makers, shaping how and where they implement their ideas. But the Department of Justice's resistance to even a basic accounting of the T Visa's lengthening track record suggests an alternative reading of how border bureaucrats have used numbers, now and in the past. Numbers are especially useful in fomenting calls for legislative action and bureaucratic expansion; they are less helpful when used to hold authorities to account, to challenge their interests as stake-holders in the problems they police. Given the selective counting of trafficked people, we might ask whether current anti-trafficking policies are in fact designed to succeed? Or, like the Spiriting Law of 1670, do today's anti-trafficking policies work best when they fail, when they establish a powerful moral purpose and an elusive enemy that justifies bureaucratic funding and growth over time?[40] Contemporary abolition-ists need not abandon their commitment to rigorous research to acknow-ledge the ironic impact of modern slave counts. The question is not how modern abolitionists might improve numerical estimates of human traf-ficking, but how they might reimagine their work as both advocates for governmental action in the developed world and as critics of it.

For assistance in that task, I turn to the historical abolitionists who organized coalitions capable of sustaining political change and holding political authorities accountable at the same time. I begin with one of the most prodigious and creative researchers in the history of abolition, Englishman Thomas Clarkson, whose sweeping investigation into the political economy of the slave trade, *The Substance of the Evidence*, in

---

[39] For critiques of the T visa's requirements, see Jocelyn M. Pollack and Valerie Hollier, "T Visas: Prosecutorial Tool or Humanitarian Response," *Women and Criminal Issues*, 20, no. 1–2 (2010), 127–146.

[40] During the late nineteenth century, immigrant padrones served as a vehicle for expanding the US Bureau of Immigration's authority and funding, an immigrant entrepreneur, like today's coyotes, who benefitted from the very policies that sought to curtail their capacity to traffic immigrants. See Peck, *Reinventing Free Labor*, 106–111. Peter Andreas advances similar arguments in *Smuggler Nation: How Illicit Trade Made America* (Oxford: Oxford University Press, 2013).

1789 played a crucial role in setting Great Britain on a path toward the abolition of the slave trade just two decades later. Clarkson used several kinds of numbers in his investigation, including calculations about the mortality rates of both slaves and sailors on board slave ships and the amount of space that slaves possessed in the holds of ships when transported across the Atlantic. These calculations were part of a broader theme articulated throughout *The Substance of the Evidence* of the larger cost of the slave trade to British national interests. Not only was the slave trade horrifically immoral, Clarkson contended, but its costs also were crushing the very heart and soul of Britain's imperial navy, which experienced the slave trade as the "grave of our marine," as one sailor put it.[41] National and humanitarian interests came together as a seamless whole in Clarkson's report, a call to action that crossed and reconfigured ideological boundaries within Great Britain in 1789.

The political impact of Clarkson's evidence reflected how he conducted his research and with whom he collaborated. Clarkson wove consistency and comparability into the varied testimonies that comprised the bulk of *The Substance of the Evidence*, seeking always to be "disinterested and unbiased" in his methods and insisting that he "propose the same queries to all." Equally important, Clarkson anchored the truthfulness of his evidence not in aggregate numbers, but in the testimonies of those English subjects with the closest access to the slave trade: mariners and slaves, whose firsthand knowledge of slave ships was vast and irrefutable. The result was not simply an abolitionist argument from the mouths of mariners and slaves but something far more authoritative and devastating: "a regular and systematic history of the slave trade," as Clarkson put it, one that made the trade's systemic violence visible through the sheer repetition of first-hand evidence.[42] Clarkson's consistent questions about treachery in the slave trade, about coercion in the recruitment of sailors, about the inhumanity of slave ship captains toward slaves and sailors alike, provided coherence to the depositions and a narrative backbone from which themes and variations emerged almost naturally. The fusion of national and humanitarian imperatives was no accident, but a deliberate effort to link abolitionists' strategic and idealistic objectives.

For contemporary abolitionists, there is much to learn from the substance of Thomas Clarkson's evidence. He established many of the

---

[41] Thomas Clarkson, *The Substance of the Evidence of Sundry Persons on the Slave Trade* (London, 1789), 17.
[42] Ibid., iv.

epistemological values associated with precise and accurate numbers – objectivity, clarity, and truthfulness – without slave counts, instead deploying repetition and consistency across his diverse testimonies. He made the immorality of the slave trade visible by featuring crimes that were systemic rather than individual in nature, the unethical work of an entire class of historical actors. One of the most provocative aspects of Clarkson's evidence was that it provided a collective portrait of what little difference ship captains' individual character made once they entered the trade. The good men who reluctantly became captains of slave ships in Clarkson's evidence were each transformed by the tyrannical power they wielded over slaves and sailors alike. The root cause of slave captains' taste for cruelty was not individual moral weakness, but the nature of tyranny on slave ships, the systemic and abusive power generated by this "nefarious traffic." One mariner summarized the progression as follows. "The Captains of Guinea-men are tolerable on their first sailing," but then "their cruelty begins to shew itself on their arrival upon the coast ... After they have been there a little time, it has no bounds."[43] Only rarely did Clarkson deploy a simple number to summarize how the slave trade corrupted England's maritime leadership. Out of twenty slave ships that Clarkson surveyed, just three possessed captains who were "men of common humanity."[44] Individual morality and humanity were no match for the systemic evils that the African slave trade unleashed. Only its immediate abolition could emancipate slaves, sailors, and ship captains alike from the immorality and national shame that it constituted.

By linking a powerful political critique of slavery to national redemption, Clarkson fused idealistic and pragmatic objectives into a single powerful narrative. As one of the world's first social scientists, Clarkson was also a ferocious critic of entrenched governmental interests, fearless in his desire to use his research to unmask the hypocrisy that economic and political power created. For modern abolitionists who are reluctant to engage their critics or are focused on defending their access to resources which governmental authorities curate and provide, Clarkson would be skeptical and impatient, mindful as he was of the duplicitous and crafty ways that government actors appropriate and subvert antislavery rhetoric. Clarkson was hardly alone among abolitionists in seeking to fuse idealism and pragmatism when engaging government actors. When the African American abolitionist Maria Stewart first spoke to a mixed gender

[43] Ibid., 16.
[44] Thomas Clarkson, *An Essay on the Impolicy of the African Slave Trade* (London, 1788), 48.

and mixed-race audience about abolition in 1831 in Boston, she did not cede the nation to the violent critics of abolition and of Black people, even though most free Black citizens in the North had already been disfranchised. Instead, she demanded her place within a racially just and redeemed nation, arguing that the US constitution was an antislavery text more than two decades before Frederick Douglass's fifth of July speech. Stewart ended her speech with the emphatic code "AND WE CLAIM OUR RIGHTS."[45] Frederick Douglass likewise labored tirelessly to secure political rights and power for Black citizens despite what seemed perpetual setbacks. During the 1860 election season, even as the Republican Party that he supported came to national power, Douglass courageously critiqued the soul-crushing ways white political allies betrayed their best values by defeating a Black suffrage proposal in New York State.[46] For Douglass, as for many abolitionists, engagement with political authorities offered few tangible results or victories before 1865.

Disagreements among abolitionists about how to use research, history, and personal narratives to engage and change political institutions were as ferocious as they were unresolved over the course of eight decades of sustained activism on both sides of the Atlantic. But those conflicts also expanded their dynamism, influence, and ultimate impact within both British and American political culture. If today's abolitionists would benefit from a better appreciation of how counting slaves has historically bolstered nationalist and white supremacist causes, contemporary critics of modern abolitionism might learn from how historical abolitionists successfully combined humanitarian and activist imperatives in their organizing. Some of the sharpest contemporary critics of the new abolitionism reductively view it as a simple reincarnation of American and/or western imperialism, a political "discourse" that rationalizes interventions against the rights and needs of women across the first and third worlds.[47] Humanitarianism has been corrupted by imperial, national, and

---

[45] Maria Stewart , "Religion and the Pure Principles of Morality, the Sure Foundation on Which We Must Build," The Liberator, October 8, 1831, reprinted in Marilyn Richardson, ed., *Maria W. Stewart: America's First Black Woman Writer* (Bloomington: Indiana University Press, 1987), 40.

[46] David W. Blight, *Frederick Douglass: Prophet of Freedom* (New York: Simon & Schuster, 2018), 325–326.

[47] See for example Jo Doezema, *Sex Slaves and Discourse Masters: The Construction of Trafficking* (London: Zed Books, 2010); Gretchen Soderlund, "Running from the Rescuers: New US Crusades against Sex Trafficking and the Rhetoric of Abolition," *National Women's Studies Association Journal* 17, no. 3: 64–87. Some of the historical

patriarchal designs in this line of reasoning, or was never free of them in the first place. But that line of critique neglects the work and example of radical humanitarians like Maria Stewart, who spoke truth to power in the 1830s while organizing political coalitions that could challenge the immoral policies harming slaves and free Black and female citizens across the nation. Stewart's attributed her capacity to challenge authority to a universal "religious spirit" which emboldened "women of all ages," to make them "by turns martyrs, apostles, warriors, and divines and scholars." Stewart used that radical universalism to call out inequalities within Boston's antislavery community as well. "Few white persons of either sex," she boldly observed "are willing to spend their lives and bury their talents in performing servile labor."[48] Servitude was not slavery, but neither was it truly free. Undergirding Stewart's radicalism was an unsparing critique of the American nation and a powerful, abiding sense of patriotism. "America is indeed a seller of slaves and the souls of men," Stewart lamented, before thundering to Black and white abolitionists "I am a true born American."[49]

What Stewart and Clarkson would make of contemporary abolitionists and their critics is a matter of speculation and educated guesswork. Would they be moved by the creative ways abolitionist researchers have used the 13th amendment to fight human trafficking within and outside American borders?[50] Would they be outraged by the incarceration of millions of people of color and undocumented peoples at home a century and a half after the passage of the 13th amendment? Would they agree with feminist critiques of the misuses of the 13th amendment to criminalize prostitution globally? Perhaps Clarkson and Stewart would be inspired and outraged by the perplexing uses and abuses of antislavery ideology. This much we do know. For both figures, a radical critique of government immorality and patriotism went hand in hand. They were not so much choices as

---

abolitionists were no strangers to imperialism, of course, a point made persuasively and provocatively by Joel Quirk in his essay, "Uncomfortable Silences: Contemporary Slavery and the 'Lessons' of History," in *From Human Trafficking to Human Rights: Reframing Contemporary Slavery*, eds. Alison Brysk and Austin Choi-Fitzpatrick (Philadelphia: University of Pennsylvania Press, 2012), 25–43.

[48] Maria Stewart, "Religion and the Pure Principles of Morality," 46, 71.   [49] Ibid., 40.

[50] Kevin Bales and Austin Choi-Fitzpatrick make the creative argument that because the Thirteenth Amendment forbids any US citizen from owning a slave, anywhere, the most unruly of all the United States' constitutional amendments does in fact serve as a global weapon for fighting coercion and enslavement. See their co-authored "The Anti-slavery Movement: Making Rights Reality," in Bryst and Choi-Fitzpatrick, *From Human Trafficking to Human Rights*, 210–211.

necessary components of the political worlds they inhabited and sought to change. To juxtapose humanitarian commitments from national ones was strategically foolish as well as dangerous, handing the nation to the very interests who demonized them, empowering the actors who benefitted from slavery in the name of white nationalism. If we aspire to make history in fighting the scourge known as modern slavery, we do in fact need to learn from the past, from the debates about history that abolitionists generated, and from the spectacular disagreements among them that shed light on our dilemmas in the present. The question for contemporary abolitionists is not whether trafficked peoples should be counted, but what they should do with those accountings. How might numbers help those who have been trafficked to organize? How might numbers be used to inspire progressive change in law and simultaneously challenge government authorities when they abuse people? How can research into human trafficking reduce the crisis of visibility that foments virulent forms of white supremacy and skepticism about modern slavery? For answers, I urge readers to revisit the history of radical antislavery with fresh and curious eyes, and also to read the terrific writers in this volume, whose passions and disagreements about fighting modern slavery suggest hope if not outright solutions to this pressing moral and political crisis.

3

Working Analogies

Slavery Now and Then

Anna Mae Duane and Erica R. Meiners

3.1 INTRODUCTION

In 2019, a year in which shocking headlines have become routine,
one particular announcement was met with relief, but not with surprise.
"Twelve Detained Babies," CBS News announced, "Have Been Released
from ICE Custody."[1] The tangled logic behind such a headline, the
reasoning that makes the surreal yoking of the words "detained" and
"baby" a phrase that has material and legal legibility, is itself intertwined
in another impossible pairing: Modern Slavery. Both those who applaud
and decry the incarceration of migrant youth draw on the lexicon of
modern slavery to make their case. Pro-border wall factions argue that
detention is necessary to save innocent children who are in danger, specifically from voracious child sex traffickers, the cruelest villains in the
global saga of "modern day slavery." In this telling, the tension between
vulnerability, protection, and punishment collapse in one another, as
babies – the epitome of innocence – are incarcerated to protect them
from a slavery that somehow would take away the freedom for which
their vulnerability has already made them disqualified.[2] On the other end
of the political spectrum, those who are horrified by the prospect of
subjecting a child to incarceration also see slavery at the heart of the

---

[1] Kate Smith, "12 detained babies have been released from ICE custody in Dilley, Texas"
CBS News, March 4, 2019.
[2] For example, House Republican Matt Gaetz argued that even with noted abuses in deten-
tion centers, sex traffickers in the free world pose a greater danger. See Julia Conley,
"'Shocking' Report Reveals Thousands of Migrant Children Have Been Sexually Abused
While in US Custody," *Common Dreams*, February 26, 2019.

harms being inflicted. Immigration and human rights activists have repeatedly made the case that the family separations at the border echo the cruelties inflicted by nineteenth-century American enslavers, who would tear children from parents in order to increase profits and productivity.[3]

We draw on this extreme example of "detained babies" to tease out how the historical analogy between chattel slavery and contemporary forms of state violence are themselves undergirded by a series of inter-twined legal and emotional regimes embedded in our understanding of childhood, and by extension, the borders of the human itself. Analogies to slavery circulate in contexts already saturated with contradictory mean-ings: care can be rendered equivalent to ownership, and innocence is both a prerequisite for freedom and a disqualification for it. This chapter's response to the governing question of "what works?" does not focus on current monitoring or data-gathering practices aimed at solving problems inherent in the myriad abuses categorized under "modern slavery." Instead our focus turns to the stories that define what the problems are and what history has to tell us about solutions. In particular, we seek to unravel the thick metaphorical coverings of childhood that envelop the emotional and legal depictions of slavery and abolition.

As coauthors, one a scholar of the literature of chattel slavery and the other a scholar of carceral studies, we come to this work with our own investments in the emotional resonances of the word "slavery." Our purpose here is not to litigate who, if anyone, is entitled to use the word "slavery" in the twenty-first century, but rather to lean into the creative possibilities – and responsibilities – inherent to the work of historical analogy. More precisely, we trace the different sorts of work an analogy can do by attending to two parallel invocations of slavery in the twenty-first century. The first model is the lexicon of modern day slavery that titles this volume – a movement that seeks to name and address human traffick-ing, coercive labor, and a host of other dehumanizing abuses. The second invocation of slavery is used primarily in the United States to draw atten-tion to the violence of the prison industrial complex (PIC). These scholars and activists purposely invoke the memory of slavery and the language of abolition to offer analysis and critique of mass incarceration. By exploring these two often-contradictory approaches to the invocation of slavery in twenty-first century scholarship, we trace how a belief in historical

---

[3] DaNeen L Brown, "'Barbaric': America's Cruel History of Separating Children from their Parents," *Washington Post*, May 31, 2018.

progress and an emotional investment in the power of innocence – both concepts embedded in our understanding of childhood – have helped to forge vexed and contradictory definitions of slavery and freedom.[4]

3.2 THE WORK OF HISTORICAL ANALOGY

How is it that one word – slavery – can be deployed to further completely opposite ends? Even as it evokes divisive racial and colonial histories, the term "slavery" somehow has the capacity to accommodate an incredibly diverse, and often paradoxical set of political arguments and legal practices. The fight against "modern slavery" – often used interchangeably with "human trafficking" – has, among its foot soldiers, individuals as varied as George W. Bush, Steve McQueen, Eve Ensler, Dame Judi Dench, Robert Mugabe and Ivanka Trump to name just a few.[5] In this international conversation, the well-known history of chattel slavery's horrors lends moral weight to the remarkably popular work of anti-slavery activism and scholarship. References to an antislavery past are cited often across a variety of media. This new abolitionism relies heavily on identifying abusive practices, rescuing those who are being abused, and prosecuting those who are guilty.[6] This call for prosecution is especially strident in response to sex work and sex trafficking, particularly when children are considered among the victims. As with other forms of law enforcement, the attribution of childhood innocence and adult guilt are shaped by assumptions attached to race, class, and sexual orientation.[7]

---

[4] While most scholars who identify as Prison Industrial Complex (PIC) abolitionists would likely not use the term "modern day slavery" to describe the US carceral state, people who organize against the PIC with an abolitionist lens do use this language and invoke this analogy.

[5] Joel Quirk and Anne Bunting, eds., *Contemporary Slavery: Popular Rhetoric and Political Practice* (Vancouver: UBC Press, 2017), 8.

[6] Elizabeth Bernstein, "Militarized Humanitarianism Meets Carceral Feminism: The Politics of Sex, Rights, and Freedom in Contemporary Antitrafficking Campaigns," *Signs: Journal of Women in Culture and Society* 36, no. 1 (2010): 45–71; Jennifer Musto, *Control and Protect: Collaboration, Carceral Protection, and Domestic Sex Trafficking in the United States* (Berkeley: University of California Press, 2016); Stephen Dillon, "Possessed by Death: The Neoliberal-Carceral State, Black Feminism, and the Afterlife of Slavery," *Radical History Review* 2012, no. 112 (2012), 113–125.

[7] Erica Meiners, *For the Children? Protecting Innocence in a Carceral State* (Minneapolis: University of Minnesota Press, 2016); Laura Soderberg, "Writing the Criminal Child: Antebellum Prison Records, Parenting Manuals, and the Rise of the Incorrigible Child," *J19* 6, no. 2 (2018), 307–334.

The carceral solutions posed by those fighting one particular instantiation of modern slavery is, for many scholars in the United States, the very process by which chattel slavery's logics continue to destroy the lives of people of color. Prosecution and incarceration, rather than a means of fighting modern slavery, is, in these scholars' eyes, a means of extending slavery's reach into the twenty-first century. As critics including Dennis Childs, Ruth Wilson Gilmore, Michelle Alexander, and others have argued, the work of mass incarceration itself echoes and extends the practices of historical slavery.[8] Now, as then, they argue, the institutions behind mass incarceration yield profits for the powerful, particularly the state, at the expense of people of color.[9] In sum, the chasm between these two definitions of slavery is so wide that it can accommodate the portrayal of a migrant toddler as deserving *both* protection and incarceration.

3.3 THE RHETORICAL WORK OF CHILDHOOD IN UNDERSTANDING SLAVERY AND FREEDOM

Children haunt the legal and imaginative rhetoric defining and combatting modern day slavery, as they facilitate a sentimental model of care that negates the rights of those who require caretaking. In other words, children occupy the role of victims who need rescue, and who, because of that need, are particularly disqualified for freedom. This duality finds its origin in the Enlightenment philosophy that undergirds much of current legal thought. John Locke's profoundly influential vision of Enlightenment freedom has, at its heart, an opposition between adult and child, a binary separated by capacity for reason. Consent became the prerequisite for political citizenship in the same moment when children were defined as people who cannot consent. In other words, when John Locke

---

[8] Dennis Childs, *Slaves of the State: Black Incarceration from the Chain Gang to the Penitentiary* (Minneapolis: University of Minnesota Press, 2015); Ruth Wilson Gilmore, *Golden Gulag: Prisons, Surplus, Crisis, and Opposition in Globalizing California* (Berkeley: Univ of California Press, 2007); Michelle Alexander, *The New Jim Crow: Mass Incarceration in the Age of Colorblindness* (New York: New Press, 2012).

[9] Ruth Wilson Gilmore provides a reminder to center the state and not simply private industry in our critiques of the PIC, and to avoid the "tendency to aim substantial rhetorical and organizational resources at the tiny role of private prison firms in the prison-industrial complex, while minimizing the fact that 92 percent of the vast money-sloshing public system is central to how capitalism's racial inequality works." Ruth Wilson Gilmore, "The Worrying State of the Anti-Prison Movement," *Social Justice: A Journal of Crime, Conflict & World Order*, February 23, 2015, accessed May 18, 2020, www.socialjusticejournal.org/the-worrying-state-of-the-anti-prison-movement/.

wrote that children are "not born in [a] full state of equality, though they are born to it," he simultaneously changed the terms of government, and created a means of excluding the young from it.[10] The social contract assumes that all participants come to it as fully consenting independent subjects, and thus disqualifies those who do not meet the criteria.[11] Thus the child was the only subject from whom freedom could be ethically kept.[12] Indeed denying rights to other populations – women and enslaved people to take two examples – were often justified by comparing them to children.[13] The child symbolizes the state of subjection that we are all born to, and destined to grow out of, and in that space between vulnerability and consent, freedom is a boon that only qualified adults can bestow.

Nineteenth-century antislavery literature (which inspires much of modern slavery's rhetoric) was entranced with the idea of the child as someone whose powerlessness required extraordinary actions from those with power. Indeed, even slavery apologists made the case that vulnerability both obliterated a person's consent and guaranteed that they would receive privileged treatment from those who had no legal obligation to recognize their rights. In 1857, proslavery writer George Fitzhugh argued that "the dependent exercise, because of their dependence, as much control over their superiors in most things as those superiors exercise over them." It was "an invariable law of nature," Fitzhugh insisted, "that weakness and dependence are elements of strength, and generally sufficiently limit that universal despotism, observable throughout human and animal nature."[14] The "natural" response to dependence, as imagined here, renders individual rights beside the point. As Saidiya

[10] John Locke, *Second Treatise of Civil Government*, sixth edition (London: A. Millar et al., 1764), VI. Par. 55.

[11] Martha Nussbaum, *Frontiers of Justice: Disability, Nationality, Species Membership* (Cambridge: Harvard University Press, 2006).

[12] Locke's philosophical cordoning off of children has been supported in later years by scientific, moral, and criminal statutes all of which deny children access to rights that adults enjoy; John Wall, "Can Democracy Represent Children? Toward a Politics of Difference," *Childhood* 19, no. 1, (2012): 86–100; Annette Ruth Appell, "Representing Children Representing What: Critical Reflections on Lawyering for Children," *Columbia Human Rights Law Review* 39, no. 3 (2007): 573–636.

[13] Holly Brewer, *By Birth or Consent: Children, Law, and the Anglo-American Revolution in Authority* (Chapel Hill: University of North Carolina Press, 2012); Anna Mae Duane, *Suffering Childhood in Early America: Violence, Race, and the Making of the Child Victim* (Athens: University of Georgia Press, 2010), 1; Corinne T. Field, *The Struggle for Equal Adulthood: Gender, Race, Age, and the Fight for Citizenship in Antebellum America* (Chapel Hill: University of North Carolina Press, 2014).

[14] George Fitzhugh, *Cannibals All! Or Slaves without Masters 1857* (Cambridge: Belknap, 1971), 204–205.

Hartman explains, in this model "the dominated exert influence over the dominant by virtue of their weakness and therefore more formal protections are unnecessary."[15] By rendering the protective instinct a natural response to childish vulnerability, the creation of legal protections becomes not only unnecessary but unseemly. The affect that innocence invokes, surely, is a more potent safeguard than impersonal laws.

This same logic – that helpless innocence inevitably summons a moral response from the powerful – was also deployed in antislavery literature. Woodcuts, pamphlets, and novels all centered endangered children and the feelings they evoked in right-minded people as a means of persuading those with power that slavery was a moral wrong. These tableaus require an appealing innocence on the victim's part and, in its more modern incarnations, punishment for those who abuse that innocence. Take for example, Harriet Beecher Stowe's 1852 international best-seller *Uncle Tom's Cabin*, a novel which made its antislavery case by showcasing the suffering of children, and inviting readers to imagine that harm extended to their own offspring. In one of the most famous scenes in this surpassingly famous novel, the fugitive Eliza rescues her child from the grip of a slave-trader. She carries her child through the night, and, like an action hero, jumps across crashing ice floes to cross the Ohio River to safety. In this scene and others like it, Stowe drew on the seemingly universal power of child vulnerability to create an interracial sympathy that would make slavery intolerable for all.

"If it were *your* Harry, mother, or your Willie," she asked the spellbound reader,

"that were going to be torn from you by a brutal trader, tomorrow morning, – if you had seen the man, and heard that the papers were signed and delivered, and you had only from twelve o'clock till morning to make good your escape, – how fast could *you* walk? How many miles could you make in those few brief hours, with the darling at your bosom, – the little sleepy head on your shoulder, – the small, soft arms trustingly holding on to your neck?"[16]

The child in this scene is an object to be acted on; his potential suffering moves his mother, and through her, the reader, to act, newly empowered by her feelings to solve the problem contained in this small suffering body. The effect of this antislavery novel showcasing child-victims was, in the words of Frederick Douglass, "amazing, instantaneous, and universal."[17]

---

[15] Saidiya Hartman, "Seduction and the Ruses of Power," *Callalloo* 19, no. 2 (1988), 547.
[16] Harriet Beecher Stowe, *Uncle Tom's Cabin* (New York: W. W. Norton, 1994), 43.
[17] Frederick Douglass, *The Life and Times of Frederick Douglass* (Hartford: Park Publishing, 1882), 351.

Its emotional work continues to this day. Little Harry has numerous descendants in consciousness-raising materials warning of the dangers of modern slavery, and suffering children occupy center stage in dozens of articles, books, and websites, which in turn ask the viewer to engage the global problem as a parent might care for a child, often asking white, affluent adults to imagine their own children in the same sort of peril that impoverished children of color inhabit.[18] One infomercial made by the charity World Vision seeks to highlight the dangers of modern slavery by featuring the story of two men selling children with no more fanfare than if they were potted plants. "Some things," the ad intones, "should never be for sale."[19] Their website features a series entitled "Five lives I can't imagine for my son." "The stories of boys who are abused can keep me awake long into the night," the writer confesses. "Since I happen to have sons, I can't help but imagine one of my kids in their places." One of the lives the writer can't help but imagine involves a child coffee harvester, whose "tiny figure" is too "small" to manage the work, the website asks readers to take action to adopt the work of "caring for what's precious," and restore this child to the sort of innocence presumably enjoyed by their own children, including the writer's son.[20]

3.4 CHILDHOOD INNOCENCE IN PRISON ABOLITIONIST THOUGHT

The precious innocence of children that animates so much of the modern fundraising lexicon – and the humanitarian actions that draw upon those funds – has a very different resonance for those who draw on slavery to analogize the abuses of mass incarceration. For them, innocence is a weapon wielded against people of color, even as it is an attribute systematically denied to people of color in the United States, and particularly denied to Black children.[21] The deaths of Travon Martin, Tamir

---

[18] See for example images and narratives that are featured on the following websites for anti-slavery organizations: "Me Ta's Story," Not for Sale, accessed May 18, 2020, www.notforsalecampaign.org/me-tas-story/; and the images on the websites for Anti-Slavery International, www.antislavery.org/ and Free the Girls, https://freethegirls.org/, accessed May 18, 2020.

[19] Alexander Lam, "Child Slave Infomercials," Trendhunter.com, June 15, 2013, accessed May 18, 2020, www.trendhunter.com/trends/child-for-sale.

[20] "Five Lives I Can't Imagine For My Son: Coffee Worker," *No Child for Sale*, accessed May 18, 2020, www.worldvision.ca/no-child-for-sale/resources/five-lives-i-can%E2%80%99t-imagine-for-my-son-coffee-worker.

[21] See for example, P. A. Goff, M. C. Jackson, B. A. L. Di Leone, C. M. Culotta, & N. A. DiTomasso, "The Essence of Innocence: Consequences of Dehumanizing Black

Rice, and others provide heartbreakingly material testimony for the fact that childhood innocence is not uniformly available. Denied the care that childhood innocence should invoke, Black children in the United States are often cast as peremptorily adult, and automatically suspect.[22] Even as Black children are denied care in the United States, child protection continues to be used to deny women, particularly poor, disabled, young, and/or nonwhite women, reproductive and parenting rights. The contradictory logic invoked by such a profoundly incoherent and racialized concept of innocence scaffolds policies that harm actual children in the name of protecting an ephemeral vision of sacred childhood.[23]

3.5 THE INNOCENCE OF HISTORY

In response to child-victims trapped in perpetual bondage, rendered especially vulnerable by the very youth that disqualifies them for many basic rights, those fighting modern slavery often construct historical time as a process of growing into an increasingly civilized maturity. In this developmental view of history, those of us living in the present must act to banish outdated practices that, like a stubborn child, refuse to give way. As they stretch the work of long-dead abolitionists forward to twenty-first century problems, modern slavery scholars and activists build upon several assumptions about the progressive march from past to present and future. We can turn to William Lloyd Garrison, or Frederick Douglass, the argument runs, and employ their successful strategies against the problems we now face. Yet there is a strange disconnect even as proponents find inspiration in the similarities between abolitionisms old and new. If the actions of past abolitionists were successful, then why does slavery keep popping up in unexpected places? The relationship between past and present in this model functions much like a reflection in a hall of mirrors. We can see a relationship between two disparate events, as one echoes the other, but

---

Children," *Journal of Personality and Social Psychology* 106, no. 4 (2014), 526–545; Kimberlé Williams Crenshaw, *Black Girls Matter: Pushed Out, Overpoliced and Underprotected* (New York: African American Policy Forum, 2015), accessed May 18, 2020, www.atlanticphilanthropies.org/wp-content/uploads/2015/09/BlackGirlsMatter_Report.pdf.

[22] Meiners, *For the Children?*

[23] Michelle Chen, "The Department of Homeland Security's 'Baby Jails'," *The Nation*, October 25, 2015.

the lines of cause and effect are obscured. In these disjunctions between then and now lay our own historical innocence.

That innocence emerges in our collective shock at the incongruity of slavery in modern times, even as awareness of its reach grows every year. The author of the anti-modern slavery text *A Crime so Monstrous: Face to Face with Modern Slavery* asks us to imagine, in an increasingly spectacular series of hypotheticals, that the South had won the Civil War, that Pearl Harbor had never happened, and that Hitler went unchallenged by the Confederate States of America. Finally, the author asks us to confront the most outrageous counterfactual of all. "Imagine" he asks us, "a world where the ideologies that endorsed slavery still stood."[24] Slavery, it's clear, only belongs in such a perverted alternate reality: not our own. "Despite the fact that many people believe that slavery no longer exists," one website declares, "an estimated five million children are in slavery worldwide, including in the UK."[25] Slavery, in this model, is not supposed to be here – it as an outdated regime that we all thought we had left behind. The children who are ensnared in its grip, like slavery itself, are caught in a time warp, needful of rescue from adults who have advanced beyond such primitive practices.

The conception of slavery as a throwback, as a feudal form of labor practice destined to be shed, like swaddling clothes, by the rise of modern industrial capitalism has been with us since before legal emancipation. In the early 1800s, Southerners in the United States began to defend slavery as their "peculiar institution." The phrase provided a form of comfort to Northerners then and to many modern slavery activists now. It suggests that slavery was a quirk, a peculiar aberration that could be quarantined from the nation's progress into an enlightened future defined by free labor. The work of Karl Marx, Adam Smith, and a host of historians have reinforced this particular set of assumptions about slavery's decidedly pre-modern provenance.[26] We have outgrown such barbarism, the argument runs, our systems have banished it to the shadows. When Mitch McConnell, US Senate Majority Leader, declares that slavery was

---

[24] E. Benjamin Skinner, *A Crime So Monstrous: Face to Face with Modern Day Slavery* (New York: Free Press, 2009), xv.

[25] "Child Slavery," Anti-Slavery International, accessed May 18, 2020, www.antislavery.org/slavery-today/child-slavery/.

[26] Cedric Robinson was among the first to refute the idea that somehow capitalism was a repudiation of feudalism, and the hierarchies embedded therein. Cedric Robinson, *Black Marxism: The Making of the Black Radical Tradition* (Chapel Hill: University of North Carolina Press, 2000).

"something that happened 150 years ago, for whom none of us currently living are responsible,"[27] that innocence becomes weaponized, and white Americans, like newborn babes, cannot possibly be blamed for the systems that have placed them where they are.

Because modern commercial and legal systems were in place for the process that allegedly killed slavery the first time, and because they share in the presumed historical innocence of a post-emancipation world, they are now duly enlisted as part of the solution for the predations of modern slavery. One antislavery organization, the Polaris Project, dedicated considerable resources to creating a report that delineated twenty-five types of slavery, each with a particular business model currently employed by traffickers.[28] But rather than drawing a conclusion that there is much in contemporary capitalism that translates easily to slavery, the report instead argues that businesses must excise the alien presence of slavery lurking in their shadows. The proper response to these abuses, Polaris argues, is "actual, active commitment and effort on the part of businesses that unwittingly, but regularly intersect with traffickers, victims, and survivors." Even as the organization evokes the language of chattel slavery – Polaris, after all, refers to the North Star, a key point of navigation for enslaved African Americans – their report testifies to present day capitalism's innocence of that particular history. The global businesses they target are "unwittingly" intersecting with slavery's practices, as if the work of global capitalism has no relation to the regime of racial capitalism that emerged in tandem with chattel slavery. As slavery is seen as an interloper within benign systems, the solutions to the problem slavery poses is to utilize the tools of the systems themselves – business plans, technology, legal proceedings – to eradicate it. While it is undoubtedly necessary to draw attention to the existence of traffickers and labor abuses within corporate supply chains, research indicates that efforts from within such systems often fall far short of anything approaching the abolition of such practices. An extensive analysis of data on such self-policing efforts

---

[27] Ted Barrett, "McConnell Opposes Paying Reparations," *CNN Politics*, June 19, 2019, www.cnn.com/2019/06/18/politics/mitch-mcconnell-opposes-reparations-slavery/index.html.

[28] "Polaris's research team analyzed the data and developed a classification system that identifies twenty-five types of human trafficking in the United States. Each one has its own business model, trafficker profiles, recruitment strategies, victim profiles, and methods of control that facilitate human trafficking." Polaris, "On-Ramps, Intersections, and Exit Routes" Polaris Project, July 1, 2018, https://polarisproject.org/on-ramps-intersections-and-exit-routes/, 5.

revealed "the lack of effectiveness, transparency, and traceability" in the ethical certification programs that many global corporations have created to address their "unwitting" participation in, and subsequent benefit from, a supply chain that supports a host of coercive labor practices.[29]

While modern slavery activism often views slavery as an aberration, a monstrous Peter Pan who must be forced to grow out of old ways, for those who draw on analogies of slavery to explain and resist the evils of mass incarceration, the past is not something we outgrow. Rather it is the very institutions that allegedly ensure and enhance freedom from past abuses that ensure that those abuses are reproduced. As Stephen Dillon writes, even as our modern institutions produce "the neutral discourses of equality, diversity, freedom, and opportunity, neoliberalism [and the pursuit of capital it champions] necessitates force, punishment, warfare, immobilization through incarceration, and the uneven distribution of social and biological death."[30] In this model, the analogy between past and present slavery is reimagined as a recursive genealogy in which the past is not dead, but rather the site of perpetual reproduction. For these scholars, to pretend as if slavery's predations are aberrations represents a dangerous form of amnesia that disavows the multiple forms of violence our allegedly advanced historical moment requires. In response to some readings of classical Marxism that view chattel slavery as an outmoded form of labor superseded by capital accumulation, theorists like Jodi Melamed, invoking Cedric Robinson's work, argue that all capitalism is always *racial* capitalism: "Capital can only be capital when it is accumulating, and it can only accumulate by producing and moving through relations of severe inequality among human groups."[31]

In this critique, the etymological and chronological preciseness that insists on dividing past from present itself another means of facilitating a dangerous historical innocence. To draw from an especially eloquent formulation of this rebuttal, W. E. B. Du Bois has argued that strategic forgetting at the heart of historical innocence allows racial capitalism to morph from chattel slavery to colonialism and capitalism, disavowing such connections, even as it continues to do the work of extracting value from subjugated brown and Black bodies.

It all became a characteristic drama of capitalist exploitation, where the right hand knew nothing of what the left hand did, yet rhymed its grip with uncanny

[29] Genevieve LeBaron, *The Global Business of Forced Labor: Report of Findings* (SPERI, University of Sheffield, 2018), 48.
[30] Dillon, "Possessed by Death."
[31] Jodi Melamed, "Racial Capitalism," *Critical Ethnic Studies* 1, no. 1 (2015): 76–85, 77.

timeliness; where the investor neither knew, nor inquired, nor greatly cared about the sources of his profits; where the enslaved or dead or half-paid worker never saw nor dreamed of the value of his work [now owned by others]; where neither the society darling nor the great artist saw the blood on the piano keys; where the clubman, boasting of great game hunting, heard above the click of his smooth, lovely, resilient billiard balls no echo of the wild shrieks of pain from kindly, half-human beasts as fifty to seventy-five thousand each year were slaughtered in cold, cruel, lingering horror of living death; sending their teeth to adorn civilization on the bowed heads and chained feet of thirty thousand Black slaves, leaving behind more than a hundred thousand corpses in broken, flaming homes.[32]

As Joy James suggests, anti-PIC abolitionists do not understand history as a linear narrative, in which the primitive and barbarous gets left behind in the progressively enlightened march toward the future. Christina Sharpe, rather than seeing history as prologue, writes about modern (Black) life and death "in the wake" of chattel slavery: "In the wake, the past that is not past reappears, always, to rupture the present."[33] Avery Gordon describes the "haunting" or the "seething presence" of histories that "loiter in the present."[34] Frank Wilderson sketches a continuum that stretches, "despite changes in its 'performance' over time," across "slave ship, Middle Passage, Slave estate, Jim Crow, the ghetto, and the prison-industrial complex."[35] Firmly rooting chattel slavery as co-constitutive with capitalism, these scholars challenge how mainstream historical discourses have redefined "slavery" itself to signify the very antithesis of progress. Life and value, freedom and bondage, "civil society" and its subjects, have all been defined through the conceptions of the human that were forged and resisted in the construction of chattel slavery, colonialism, and the paternalism that enabled them both.

Insisting on chronologies that blur the neat boundaries between past and present, this body of work sees historical rigor as a bait and switch that distracts us from the ways that slavery and its legacies, far from being anomalous in the present, are in fact the bedrock upon which we stand. It

[32] W. E. B. DuBois, *The World and Africa* (New York: Intl Pub Co; 1979), 74. We are indebted to Walter Johnson's work for bringing our attention to DuBois's formulation of this question. Walter Johnson, "To Remake the World: Slavery, Racial Capitalism, and Justice," *Boston Review*, Forum 1, February 20, 2018, https://bostonreview.net/race/walter-johnson-slavery-human-rights-racial-capitalism.

[33] Christina Sharpe, *In the Wake: On Blackness and Being* (Durham: Duke University Press, 2016), 9.

[34] Avery Gordon, *Ghostly Matters: Haunting and the Sociological Imagination* (Minneapolis: University of Minnesota Press, 2008).

[35] Frank Wilderson III, *Red, White, and Black: Cinema and the Structure of U. S. Antagonisms* (Durham: Duke University Press, 2010), 75.

is only when we engage with our own complicity can we begin to accomplish anything like abolition. "If unfinished liberation is the still-to-be-achieved work of abolition," Ruth Wilson Gilmore argues, "then at bottom what is to be abolished isn't the past or its present ghost, but rather the processes of hierarchy, dispossession, and exclusion."[36] Those processes are embedded in the language we use, the analogies they support, and the unequal distribution of human worth facilitated by our commonsense myths of innocence and progress.

3.6 RADICALLY UNDOING THE WORK

Juliette Hua has suggested that analogy limits the possibilities for liberation by offering dichotomies as solutions. In other words, historical analogy yokes together nouns – there are slaves now, and there were slaves then. In these rhetorical equations, we lose track of the verbs. The actions that facilitate exploitation, the assumptions made, and the profits produced simply don't fit within the analogy's structure of thought, which is at heart, an act of comparison, not a delineation of cause and effect. The two-pronged comparison between chattel and modern slavery can reduce options to binaries: we move subjects from the bad category to the good one. We protect the innocent from the guilty, dutifully moving people from the box marked "slave" to the box marked "free." In Hua's words, we reduce a systemic problem to individual status. We focus on "subjects [consumers, criminals traffickers, 'slaves']" when the real work is to wrestle with "the terms through which [these] subjects emerge."[37]

But analogy can be expansive as well as reductive. As Yogita Goyal suggests, "the analogy to slavery can be enlisted to yield broader visions of justice and reparation, but only if we refuse to settle the meaning of either term compared."[38] Instead, we would have to deploy analogy to

[36] Ruth Wilson Gilmore, "Abolition Geographies and the Problem of Innocence," in *Futures of Black Radicalism*, eds. Gaye Theresa Johnson and Alex Lubin (London: Verso Books. Kindle edition, 2017), 4442.

[37] Yogita Goyal, "The Logic of Analogy: Slavery and the Contemporary Refugee," *Humanity: An International Journal of Human Rights, Humanitarianism, and Development*, 8, no. 3 (Winter 2017): 543–546, 544.

[38] Julietta Hua, "Modern Day Slavery: The Analogy Problem in Human Trafficking Reform" in *Panic, Transnational Cultural Studies, and the Affective Contours of Power*, ed. Micol Seigel (New York: Routledge, 2018).

deliberately proliferate, rather than reduce, the avenues through which we understand what chattel slavery was in the past and how we wrestle with its multiple legacies in the present. Rather than looking at the dizzying panoply of modern abuses and discerning whether or not they are equivalent to chattel slavery, we might draw upon the ambiguity that surrounds definitions of modern day slavery as an impetus to further complicate our approach to how enslaved people in the past defined both freedom and bondage, and to draw from those possibilities. Such purposeful ambiguity does not require abandoning the work of historical analysis, or even historical analogy, but does ask us to resist the myths of progress that these endeavors so often support. Giving up on historical innocence does not mean giving up on hope. The radical work of achieving justice, in Ruth Wilson Gilmore's words, "goes back in time-space not in order to abolish history, but rather to find alternatives to the despairing sense that so much change, in retrospect, seems only ever to have been displacement and redistribution of human sacrifice."[39]

On several registers, historians are carrying out this work of complicating progress. Much of the recent scholarship on racial capitalism has been borne out of a recognition that the experience of formerly enslaved people across the world was often vastly different than the clean break between slavery and freedom imagined in emancipation documents. Fully engaging with the messy overlaps of slavery, Jim Crow policies, and mass incarceration requires a capacious reimagining of the present's innocence to demand reparations that would not only atone for past sins, but also offer new chronologies and widened possibilities.[40]

The building blocks of modern democracy – reason, consent, capitalism – cannot be disentangled from chattel slavery, and the language we use needs to address that entanglement. We need to imagine history, and the solutions we create in terms other than a developmental model that views the degradation of enslavement a stage we can outgrow or discard, leaving those in the present innocently aghast. So for us, the response to the

---

[39] Gilmore, "Abolition Geographies and the Problem of Innocence," 4442.

[40] Eric Williams, *Capitalism and Slavery* (Chapel Hill: University of North Carolina Press, 2014); Edward E. Baptist, *The Half has Never Been Told: Slavery and the Making of American Capitalism* (London: Hachette UK, 2016); Jack Lawrence Schermerhorn and Calvin Schermerhorn, *The Business of Slavery and the Rise of American Capitalism, 1815–1860* (New Haven: Yale University Press, 2015). For more on the contemporary movement of reparations for African Americans moving from the political margins toward the center see Sheryl Gay Stolberg, "At Historic Hearing, House Panel Explores Reparations," *New York Times*, June 19, 2019.

guiding question "what works?" is to suggest that we grapple with how our current structures, enabled by assumptions about human development and, historical progression are not working toward transformative justice.

Rather than blaming or discarding the embedded analogy in the term "Modern Slavery," comparing this use of terminology with the way the language of slavery and abolition is deployed by anti-PIC activists can complicate the definitions of both sides of the equation. These revised definitions, we suggest, must address not only the legacies of brutality and dispossession but also the commonsense logic of property and paternalism that find ideological cover in the supposedly neutral figure of a child-not-ready-for-freedom. By shifting our focus from nouns to verbs, we can better wrestle with the realization that the oppressed who need rescue by law and by business are in fact exploited by the profit drive at the heart of business itself and disempowered by the law's privileging of autonomy and maturity. The very vulnerability we purport to protect is in fact engineered by those who profit from it.

Undoing the work that got us here involves both scholarship and practice that disrupts the way ideas of innocence and dependence are embedded in both how we understand and battle modern slavery and the terms by which we define a large portion of the people who suffer from it. Attending to analogy also offers the possibility of reorienting legal and scholarly approaches to children themselves, whose reduction to metaphor has kept them from being engaged as people from whom justice, not to mention freedom, has historically been withheld. If we insist on acknowledging and untangling the multiple investments in a conception of childhood that naturalizes a lesser form of humanity, we will be forced to reorient the terms on which we understand both slavery and liberation. We can then begin to retheorize vulnerability outside of what philosopher Iris Marion Young has termed a "daddy state" in which punishment and protection are mutually constitutive.[41] If we foreground children as actors and even leaders in our labor, business, cultural, feminist analyses of the problems contained under the terminology of Modern Slavery, we are confronted anew with insights that scholars have been pointing out – that individual rights are not sufficient, and that communal solutions created outside of legacies of law and capital are required. Here again, the radical use of the terms both abolition and slavery by anti-PIC scholars provides

---

[41] Iris Marion Young, "The Logic of Masculinist Protection: Reflections on the Current Security State," *Signs: Journal of Women in Culture and Society* 29, no. 1 (2003), 1–25.

a useful roadmap. Over the past fifteen years, a number of organizations have sprung up, from Creative Interventions and the Storytelling and Organizing Project in Oakland to the Safe Outside the System Collective with the Audre Lorde Project in New York. Many of these organizations self-identify as abolitionist, as engaged in practicing transformative justice or community accountability, and/or as groups who are building alternative responses to harm that do not center policing or incarceration. These organizations create and proliferate "in the moment" tools to enable other responses to harm beyond prison – and engage in community transformation by attempting to dismantle systems and practices that produce and naturalize forms of violence.[42] Often led by queer and Black young folks, these organizations are building a transformative vision of abolition that does not depend on buy in from legal or business authorities.

While we have foregrounded this work by anti-PIC scholars in the United States, this sort of innovation is not new or unique to that country. The work of children imagining collective forms of advocating for children's security by themselves has already taken hold in many places across the globe. Peru, for instance, has been a leader in supporting politically active collectives of working children, where young people advocate for just and equitable structures that would allow safety and security while still ensuring their full participation in economic and political life.[43]

For theorists Stefano Harney and Fred Moten the object of abolition is "[n]ot so much the abolition of prisons but the abolition of a society that could have prisons, that could have slavery, that could have the wage, and therefore not abolition as the *elimination* of anything but abolition as the *founding* of a new society [emphasis ours]."[44] We end with this counterintuitive use of language – abolition becomes an act of creation, rather than negation – to suggest that eradicating the use of analogy in modern slavery studies is not necessarily the way to move toward what works, but

---

[42] For example, the response of the Black Youth Project 100 (BYP 100) to the ongoing violence of policing in Chicago that targets young Black folks for premature death, is the demand to shrink the city's investments in policing. When 40 percent of Chicago's operating budget is already spent on policing, they identify their Fund Black Futures campaign as abolitionist as it demands resources for public education, healthcare, and transit, and not for reforming policing. https://byp100.org/

[43] Jessica Taft, "Supporting Working Children as Social, Political, and Economic Agents," *Beyond Trafficking and Slavery*, openDemocracy.com, March 24, 2016, www.open democracy.net/beyondslavery/jessica-taft/supporting-working-children-as-social-polit ical-and-economic-agents.

[44] Stefano Harney and Fred Moten, *The Undercommons: Fugitive Planning & Black Study* (Brooklyn: Autonomedia 2013), 114.

made the idea that slavery exists in the modern world seem alien in the first place. Our response to the question "what works?" asks us to fundamentally reassess the beliefs that undergird how we determine what success is, what freedom looks like, and the tools by which we determine whether those goals are being achieved.

4

Free Soil, Free Produce, Free Communities

Kevin Bales and Alison Gardner

4.1 INTRODUCTION

In the context of fighting modern slavery and human trafficking today, this chapter explores the centrality of community organizing to past anti-slavery movements and examines the continuing role for community-based activism, with a focus on the United States (US) and the United Kingdom (UK). While civil society-based strategies for catalyzing antislavery action are increasingly incorporated into wider international development programs,[1] they are more rarely discussed in relation to developed economies, with emphasis more often falling on the efforts of legislators, policy-makers, and NGOs. In arguing for a broader community-mobilization perspective, we identify the historic role of three convening forces – faith, commerce, and place – in stimulating individuals to action, challenging social norms, sharing the message, and weaving diverse anti-slavery responses together. We reflect on the ways in which these forces generated action in the past, and consider their ongoing relevance to community-based antislavery initiatives in the present day.

As we move back in history it is not difficult to discover people working at the local level and organizing to attain common goals, often to do with human rights, but this is rarely called "community organizing." It would seem that the public preference for telling history through the individual lives of "great" men and women often precludes recounting the efforts,

---

[1] Kavi Ramburn, Maurice Middleberg and Terry FitzPatrick, *Catalyzing a Civil Society Movement against Slavery* (Washington, DC: Free the Slaves, 2018), accessed February 10, 2020, www.freetheslaves.net/wp-content/uploads/2018/10/Catalyzing-a-Civil-Society-Movement-Against-Slavery-Oct-2018-web.pdf.

FIGURE 4.1 *The Black Man's Lament*, or *How to Make Sugar*[2]
Source: Image from British Library online gallery: Amelia Opie, *The Black Man's Lament*, or *How to Make Sugar*, London: Harvey & Darton, 1826. Used with permission.

dedication, and effectiveness of small and large groups at the local level. Thus, abolition in Britain becomes the story of William Wilberforce, the famous aristocrat and parliamentarian who campaigned for the abolition of the Slave Trade and emancipation over nearly four decades. As this contemporary illustration demonstrates, it is the big man graciously accepting the petitions of little people, who may then act to free the supplicating slave.

Although Wilberforce became a mouthpiece for the cause of abolition, he was only able to press the British Parliament toward abolition because of the large number of petitions and testimonials flooding in from all over Britain (see Figure 4.1). From the earliest days, it was clear that the antislavery argument spread via existing community networks, and three core points of convergence arose within communities of faith, commerce, and place.

---

[2] Amelia Opie, *The Black Man's Lament; or, How to Make Sugar* (London: Harvey & Darton, 1826), accessed February 9, 2020, www.bl.uk/onlinegallery/onlineex/carviews/t/022zzz000112712u00002000.html.

4.2 THREE HISTORICAL FOCAL POINTS FOR ABOLITION:
FAITH, COMMERCE, AND PLACE

Community organizing, and the way in which faith, commerce, and place worked together, was a source of energy, ideas, and resources of the antislavery movement. After the first antislavery petitions were delivered to parliament and tabled by parliament in 1783,[3] the antislavery movement was dramatically overtaken by an innovative campaign based in large part on place-centered community organizing. The Society for the Abolition of the Slave Trade was established in May 1787. It brought together members of a Quaker antislavery committee formed four years earlier with Anglican abolitionists such as the young Thomas Clarkson and Granville Sharp, a lawyer who had been involved in legal cases on behalf of enslaved Africans. The importance of the Society for the Abolition of the Slave Trade cannot be overstated. It set out to shift public and political opinion and action toward abolition with a three-fold strategy: firstly, to provide the public with books, pamphlets, and prints, advertising through the main medium of the time the ideas underlying the abolitionist position. Secondly, the Society built up a network of local contacts, "agents," and "country committees" to organize local chapters and activities; and thirdly, they employed Thomas Clarkson as a full-time "travelling agent" who would support local groups, guide them in uniform campaigning when appropriate, and collect any information that would be useful to the antislavery cause. This community organizing strategy is shown in the minute books of the Society from the very first meetings of the leadership, usually known as the London Committee. Within a few years, "There was an abolition committee in every major city or town in touch with a central committee in London."[4]

While the publication of books, pamphlets, and posters was important to fuel local groups, community organizing was the key to unlock the first major campaign of 1787–1788 in which more than 100 petitions arrived at parliament carrying around 60,000 signatures. Supported by that broad-based campaign, a year later in 1789 Wilberforce made his first speech in parliament against the slave trade. Local organizing had clearly set the stage. When the first abolition bill was defeated in 1791, abolitionists mounted another campaign in 1792 and deluged parliament with an additional 519 petitions

---

[3] David Brion Davis, *The Problem of Slavery in the Age of Revolution, 1770–1823* (New York: Oxford University Press, 1999), 215.
[4] Adam Hochschild, *Bury the Chains* (London: Pan Macmillan, 2005), 107.

carrying some 390,000 signatures. If Wilberforce was now a force in parliament, he had been lifted high by an organized groundswell from across the communities of Britain. As John Oldfield notes, while "the industrial north provided the most enthusiastic support for abolition, every English county was represented [in the petition campaign] in 1792, in addition to which Scotland and Wales made significant contributions."[5] This volume of active support could not be ignored and the petitions could no longer be relegated to "lie upon the table." Pressed to vote, parliament was resolved by 270 votes to 85 that the slave trade should be gradually abolished. That indicative resolution, however, was to have little immediate effect, indeed the larger antislavery movement itself found itself stymied in a period of political retrenchment with the outbreak of the French Revolution and the resulting war with France.

The enforced political hiatus imposed by the long war with France did not end the antislavery campaign, but it was significantly slowed and regularly thwarted in its political aims by a government and parliament focused on armed conflict. While local groups continued to meet, public expressions for abolition slowed almost to a stop in the hostile wartime atmosphere. From 1794 to 1797 the movement went through a low point, the organizing (London) committee only met six times, and eleven bills were lost in parliament from 1792 onwards. Thomas Clarkson, the key organizer and researcher, suffered a breakdown, and retired with his family to the Lake District.

Frustrated but not cowed, the activists at national and local level continued to organize and diversify their campaigning tactics. In the face of suppression, the campaign evolved and generated more innovative techniques for social change, harnessing the commercial potential of fashion and mass-media communications. Possibly the best-remembered are the graphic images propagated in large numbers and widely disseminated. One was Josiah Wedgwood's slave medallion with the motto "Am I Not a Man and a Brother?" Thomas Clarkson wrote that the medallion was put to many uses: "ladies wore them in bracelets, and others had them fitted up in an ornamental manner as pins for their hair. At length the taste for wearing them became general, and thus fashion, which usually confines itself to worthless things, was seen for once in the honourable office of promoting the cause of justice, humanity and freedom."[6] A second

---

[5] John Oldfield, "British Anti-Slavery" *BBC History*, 2011, accessed September 5, 2018, www.bbc.co.uk/history/british/empire_seapower/antislavery_01.shtml.

[6] Thomas Clarkson, *The History of the Rise, Progress and Accomplishment of the Abolition of the African Slave Trade by the British Parliament* (London, 1839), 417.

image used with great effect was the drawing or diagram of the slave ship Brookes, first appearing in a broadsheet published in December 1788 by the Plymouth Chapter of the Society for Effecting the Abolition of the Slave Trade. The image was published in several formats and editions, in newspapers, pamphlets, books, and posters. For a contemporary viewer it would have had a powerful effect, as it was common knowledge that travel by sailing ship was cold, wet, dangerous, and unhealthy in the best of circumstances. An eighteenth-century viewer would quickly discern that packed slaves would be chained down, lying in their own vomit and excrement and that of their neighbors, that there would be little light or circulation of air, and that this would last for weeks or months. It was a shocking realization and once the viewer had momentarily placed him or herself into the image, it would have brought home the intense suffering involved. Both of these images were extended further through their use on merchandise, cufflinks, cameos, framed and colored pictures and prints, seals, medallions, and Wedgwood china.

One of the most powerful means of community engagement and organizing was the invention by the abolitionist movement of what we now call "ethical consumption." While political campaigning was very difficult during the war years, campaigning around economic and consumption behavior expanded rapidly. A pamphlet by William Fox denouncing the purchase and use of slave-made sugar was published in 1791 and in four months sold 70,000 copies.[7] It is estimated that 300,000 people joined the "anti-saccharite" boycott of slave-produced sugar. The boycott was primarily a community organizing campaign. Women controlled the purchasing and use of sugar in the household, and local groups of women were key to the success of the boycott. In Birmingham, for example, abolitionist women worked in groups to visit some four-fifths of the homes in the city pressing the idea of abstaining from slave-made sugar among the city's wives and mothers. By the 1820s there were some seventy abolitionist women's groups operating in local communities around the UK.[8]

There was also a positive action related to the negative action of boycott. In the second large-scale campaign against slave-made goods, a parallel "free produce" movement grew as well. Free Produce stores stocked clothing, dry goods, shoes, soaps, ice cream, candy, vegetables and other agricultural produce, fruit, rice, and any other "free"

---

[7] Davis, *The Problem of Slavery*, 381.
[8] Clare Midgley, *Women against Slavery: The British Campaigns, 1780–1870* (New York: Routledge, 1995), 45.

commodity that could be sold in opposition to those tainted by slavery.[9]
Free Produce was never more than a small part of the overall market,
probably smaller than the Fairtrade goods available today, but it meant
that families and communities were able to address slavery and other
human rights challenges through immediate actions in their homes and
cities. It is this active participation in the work of abolition at the local
level, however small in effect, which helped to sustain antislavery movements of the past.

To change the course of a country deeply engaged in the international
slave trade also required changing the thinking of a large number of
people within that country. We may mark success in the passage of
a law, but such political acts in a democracy (even a democracy as flawed
as that of eighteenth- and nineteenth-century Britain) are the result and
outcome of larger changes in the minds and public opinion of a sufficient
proportion of a country's population. It was in the home, amongst friends
and peers, in the community, where change first occurred. For that reason,
it is important to look deeper than the easily visible signs, the marches,
petitions, and rallies of community organizing and activism and grasp the
less visible but driving forces of changing thought, of evolving moral
precepts, and of a widening global view of responsibility that formed the
bedrock upon which abolition was built.

4.3 WHY COMMUNITIES ARE KEY

In practice human rights don't occur when they are written down; they
occur when a community or a society agrees that such rights exist. The
first step leading to the emergence of a human right is the redefinition of
a particular human activity from functional and acceptable to being
morally untenable – a violation of personhood. An important step, possibly the key step, in the social and legal evolution of the human perception of enslavement was its redefinition as an evil act. This popular
redefinition did not happen all at once but over decades, or one could
argue, centuries. The abolitionist movement was, above all else, a moral
movement, designed to convince the populace that slavery was an iniqui-
tous activity. The assumption was that if slavery came to be generally
perceived as morally wrong, then that perception could be translated into
legislation. But if slavery, widely seen as a (perhaps regrettable) necessary

---

[9] Julie L. Holcomb, *Moral Commerce: Quakers and the Transatlantic Boycott of the Slave
Labor Economy* (New York: Cornell University Press, 2016), see especially chapter 5.

economic activity was to be redefined as a morally reprehensible act, how was that change to be carried out in the minds of those who were not enslaved? Especially as they were separated by thousands of miles and great cultural gulfs from those who were enslaved?

For an antislavery movement to succeed, the convincement that slavery was wrong and must be abolished had to occur in the minds of many thousands of individuals, not solely in the minds of a few privileged politicians. Nor was the impetus for reflection and redefinition likely to occur in some great mass event led by an advantaged few. Instead, thousands of people had to come to a personal recognition and decision, possibly influenced by the people around them, and possibly through what they had been told, seen, read, or witnessed. For Thomas Clarkson deep research into the slave trade for his prizewinning essay piled up in his mind an avalanche of empathy. He explained what happened when his own redefinition occurred, when slavery "wholly engrossed my thoughts. I became at times very seriously affected ... I frequently tried to persuade myself in these intervals that the contents of my Essay could not be true. The more however I reflected on them ... the more I gave them credit. ... a thought came into my mind, that if the contents of the Essay were true, it was time some person should see these calamities to their end." For Clarkson redefinition quickly translated to a personal commitment to action, that he was the person who "should see these calamities to their end."[10]

In today's vernacular, the popular mental redefinition of slavery was an idea that went viral within Great Britain and then the United States. The critical role of communities in this process becomes clear if we stop analyzing social change through the actions of elites, and recognize social change is actually the physical manifestation of a spreading idea. Through that lens we see that it is the family, the church, the club, the sports-team, the workmates, the friends, the people who inhabit one's immediate social world, and only occasionally outside influences, that carry the "infection" of viral ideas.

Like all infectious ideas, the condemnation of slavery had had minor earlier outbreaks. Meltzer notes that around 2,100 years ago two Jewish communities, the Essenes and the Therapeutae, not only rejected slavery as evil, but he also points out that "to condemn slavery as powerfully as these two sects did was extraordinary for that time. No one else in antiquity seems to have advanced that far. Not until certain radical Protestant sects appeared many centuries later did the world hear slavery

---

[10] Clarkson, *History*, 83.

denounced so sweepingly."[11] If the radical Protestant sect of Quakers were especially receptive to this infectious idea in the 1780s it was likely because earlier Quakers such as John Woolman and Benjamin Lay[12] had spoken and written and demonstrated against slavery – though they were regularly ignored or suppressed. Their communities were not yet ripe for infection.[13] Likewise, for the first antislavery movement, the authentic voice of Olaudah Equiano, a self-redeemed slave living in Britain who published a popular autobiography, *The Interesting Narrative of the Life of Olaudah Equiano or Gustavus Vassa, the African* (1789), was another route to privileging the experience of the victim of slavery, translating it into a vehicle for empathy. But while the absorption of this new perspective was an important step, the elaboration of that idea into action formed the next crucial stage.

4.4 MORAL RESPONSIBILITY AT A DISTANCE

Clarkson moved rapidly from realization and redefinition to the assumption of personal responsibility and action, but for most people that is at best a gradual process. Likewise, the extension of empathy beyond what might be called its natural borders often falls at the first (literal) gate. Sympathy, in the eighteenth century, rarely extended beyond one's own neighbors, and even then could be radically diminished by notions of class or religious profession. A less explored attribute of the first antislavery movement was its extension of concern, an indicator of redefinition, across continents and cultures. Take for example the 1688 document sent by Quakers in Germantown Pennsylvania to the Monthly (local area) Meeting of Quakers. It reads in part:

Now tho they are black, we can not conceive there is more liberty to have them slaves, as it is to have other white ones. There is a saying that we shall doe to all men licke [like] as we will be done ourselves; macking [making] no difference of what generation, descent or Colour they are. and those who steal or robb men, and those who buy or purchase them, are they not alicke? Here [in Pennsylvania] is liberty of conscience wch is right and reasonable; here ought to be likewise liberty of the body, except of evildoers, wch is an other case. But to bring men hither, or to

---

[11] Milton Meltzer, *Slavery: A World History* (New York: DeCapo, 1971), 44.

[12] John Woolman, *The Journal and Major Essays of John Woolman*, ed. P. P. Moulton (Richmond: Friends United Press, 2007); Marcus Rediker, *The Fearless Benjamin Lay: The Quaker Dwarf Who became the First Revolutionary Abolitionist* (New York: Verso, 2017).

[13] An interesting area for study would be to explore or determine the conditions which make a group, community, or population most receptive to a particular viral idea.

robb and sell them against their will, we stand against. In Europe there are many oppressed for Conscience sacke [sake]; and here there are those oppressed wch are of a Black Colour.[14]

Though convoluted (the authors were not writing in their first language) the text is clear enough. It calls upon the Golden Rule (Matt. 7:12, "Do unto others . . ."), which was also reflected in a fundamental Quaker belief that there is a spark of the divine in every human being, thus making all persons equal in God's spirit, and that one should try to recognize and "answer that of God in everyone." This is a statement of universality and common humanity, and growing from that statement is an assumption that there can be no border, no limit of race or station, to empathy. While the document may presage the Universal Declaration of Human Rights (1948), so does the reception of this early document by other Quakers predict the political reaction to abolition. Having received this epistle, the local area Monthly Meeting of Quakers kicked the radical document upstairs to the Quarterly (regional) Meeting, who did the same, passing it up to the annual Yearly (national) Meeting. At the Yearly Meeting it was finally "placed upon the table" for no further action. Viral ideas often grow slowly and then reach a stage of exponential growth.[15] For the ideas of equality and abolition, the highly infectious stage would not arrive until 100 years later with Clarkson and the London Committee.

When the viral idea of abolition reached the epidemic stage after 1787, it generated a larger and more varied translation of idea into action. Both the boycott campaigns and the Free Produce movement are key examples of this. Both were aimed at specific political outcomes only as secondary goals; their primary focuses were on personal choice and community action. Both were answers to the internal question that comes from recognition that an existing and accepted activity like slavery must be seen in a new light – that it is morally wrong. That is the question of the extent of moral responsibility. If one knows that an action is wrong, if one feels empathy with those who suffer from that action, and if one wants to live in a way that diminishes that wrong, how far does one's personal responsibility to act against evil extend?

Viral ideas often generate conundrums when they alter existing world-views. One conundrum was this: Does my responsibility to work against

---

[14] Brycchan Carey, *From Peace to Freedom: Quaker Rhetoric and the Birth of American Antislavery, 1657–1761* (New Haven: Yale University Press, 2012), see especially chapter 2.
[15] For an explanation of this process, see Malcolm Gladwell, *The Tipping Point* (London: Abacus, 2000).

slavery transcend my responsibility to provide for my family, support my coworkers, and participate in community? It is fair to say abolitionists have grappled with these questions for hundreds of years, and human rights activists continue to do so today. For most activists, then and now, the answers to these questions are found partially in one's conscience, and partially within one's community. This is especially so if there is a community of the like-minded, people who are also grappling with their consciences.

Consider again the Free Produce movement. The unknown author of a Free Produce article entitled "How Do You Know" set out the parameter of responsibility in this way: "let us remember that . . . however far we may be from the scene of their sufferings in the physical world, in the moral world we are standing beside them."[16] This statement encapsulates the second stage of infection of the viral idea of abolition, the step that moves not just from convincement to action, but removes all limits to action. Today we both celebrate and sometimes feel oppressed by this sequela of moral infection. We celebrate the extension of responsibility and name NGOs with global reach Médecins Sans Frontières and Beyond Borders, while, at the same time, trying to rein back the acceptance of universal responsibility so that all other personal responsibilities are not overwhelmed. This dilemma is an inheritance from the first antislavery movement, from a general and community-based awakening to universalist ideas of what is right and what are rights. This transformation came about through moral redefinition that then led to political change. Our assertion, our argument, is that moral redefinition occurs in individuals and is led by groups – leading by example, suggesting and sharing, working together to express moral choices through considered action. Our next question is how does this viral idea and its consequent dilemmas play out today within what some regard as the anti-slavery movement of today?[17]

4.5 WHAT ROLE DO COMMUNITIES PLAY IN ANTISLAVERY ACTION TODAY?

If we view communities as an agent for nurturing and transferring new social norms, it is important to also acknowledge that fragmentation often

---

[16] Holcomb, *Moral Commerce*, see especially chapter 5.
[17] Kevin Bales & Zoe Trodd, eds., *The Antislavery Usable Past: History's Lesson for How We End Slavery Today* (Nottingham: The Rights Lab, 2018), 6.

characterizes our experience of community in modern culture. In the past, *community* was often used to refer to the body of the people as a whole, but more recently a plural form (communities) has emerged to demark distinct groups within the context of wider society. In the Oxford English Dictionary, community is used to describe people connected by place, culture, religious society, ideology, or interests and pursuits, as well as online social networks, meaning that community no longer requires physical proximity. All these different forms represent publics united by a common factor, though we also need to beware viewing communities simplistically as homogenous or apolitical, as they have multiple internal fault lines and overt or covert power dynamics. This is not wholly a modern phenomenon: indeed a great deal of historical writing has analyzed the fault lines and power dynamics of the early anti-slavery movement.[18]

In keeping with this complex picture, communities form part of the solution to slavery and trafficking, but are also deeply implicated in the underpinning problems. The 2018 Trafficking in Persons (TIP) report took the role of communities as its central theme, emphasizing that "National governments cannot do these things alone. Their commitments to this issue are more effectively realized in partnership with the communities that face it, including local authorities, NGOs and advocates, and individual community members who are often the eyes, ears, and hearts of the places they call home."[19] However, identifying and acting upon community-based drivers for slavery is not an unproblematic process. Slavery and trafficking are frequently enacted through community links and we know that social norms and cultural institutions such as the caste system can be used to justify exploitation[20]. Would-be antislavery activists must simultaneously steer clear of ill-founded ethnocentric judgments on diverse social practices, while also avoiding a shift from a universalist view of human rights into normative moral relativism that fails to recognize and name exploitation.

Community mobilization and action remain a crucial part of the solution. Importantly, we need to look beyond the role of NGOs to wider

---

[18] See for example Henry Mayer, *All on Fire: William Lloyd Garrison and the Abolition of American Slavery* (New York: St Martins, 1998).

[19] US Department of State, *Trafficking in Persons Report* (Washington, DC: US Department of State Website 2018), 2, accessed February 10, 2020, www.state.gov/reports/2018-trafficking-in-persons-report/.

[20] Austin Choi-Fitzpatrick, *What Slaveholders Think* (New York: Columbia University Press, 2018).

social actors. While NGOs have in the past – and today – used community-based action to challenge entrenched slavery, it is important to underline that engagement with NGOs should not be taken as proxy for the involvement of wider civil society. Indeed, the historical example demonstrates that if the potential of community-based action is to be released, anti-slavery principles and the fundamental elements of a slavery-free society need to move beyond the sphere of activism and become embedded within the conscious and unconscious decision-making of wider publics.

But are the convening forces of the past – faith, business, and place – still as potent in our information-rich, connected, and globalized world? We will argue that they are. Faith has been a key historic driver for action, and we will argue that despite persistent discourses on the waning influence of religion in developed economies (particularly the Christian church), faith-based organizations continue to offer a moral challenge, convening role, networks, and resources which are otherwise often profoundly lacking in a fragmented and impoverished post-austerity governance landscape. Meanwhile looking toward the role of commerce, we consider how businesses might be encouraged to engage at a civic and community level in initiatives that impact locally and globally beyond the supply chain and reflect on the value of ethical consumerism and branding in constructing virtual communities.

Communities of place have also been important in anchoring the past antislavery movement, and we will examine the significant role towns and cities can play in antislavery work, as well as their potential to unify fragmented governance responses, create survivor-centered responses, and lever-in additional resources through collaboration with civil society. Our aim is to uncover the latent potential in moving the focus of anti-slavery activity today beyond a narrow focus on top-down legislation, government policy, criminal enforcement, and the role of NGOs.

4.6 THE ROLE OF FAITH NETWORKS

We often hear that participation in formalized religion is decreasing, for instance in the UK in 1983, one in three people did not affiliate with a religion, whereas in 2010 the figure was one in two.[21] Despite this, faith-

---

[21] Alison Park, Elizabeth Clery, John Curtice, Miranda Philips, and David Utting, eds., *British Social Attitudes 28, National Centre for Social Research* (London: Sage, 2012), 180, accessed February 10, 2020, www.bsa.natcen.ac.uk/media/38966/bsa28-full-report.pdf.

based organizations continue to play a fundamental role in responding to contemporary slavery, and faith participation in the antislavery movement appears to be increasing. Transnational networks include the Global Freedom Network, which has been bringing faith leaders together from across the world to sign a global declaration against modern slavery since 2014.[22] There is also strong faith representation in Alliance 8.7, which brings church and influencers together in a network which spans international borders. Jeffrey Barrows has identified numerous faith-actors present in the US anti-trafficking movement, working at societal, community, and organizational and interpersonal levels.[23] A recent report found that 48 percent of organizations that primarily or exclusively focused on modern slavery in the UK were faith-based (the majority Christian).[24] Many anti-trafficking organizations such as the Medaille Trust, Hope for Justice, International Justice Mission, and City Hearts have faith at their roots, while faith-based service providers are critical in underpinning the UK's support for victims and survivors, with the Salvation Army currently holding the main contract for the UK National Referral Mechanism. Both the Catholic Church and Church of England have launched projects with the aim of using church networks to mobilize congregations toward antislavery activity. So how do we explain this continuing level of commitment from faith bodies, and what is its significance for engaging communities in the modern antislavery movement?

For faith actors in the modern movement, antislavery principles continue to resonate as strongly with theology as they did for the late eighteenth-century Quakers. Barrows demonstrates how sacred texts underpin a common call to empathy and responsibility within Jewish, Christian, Islamic, and Baha'i traditions.[25] The 2014 joint declaration against modern slavery signed by religious leaders participating in the

---

[22] Global Freedom Network, "A United Faith against Modern Slavery," (Nedlands, Australia: Minderoo Foundation, 2016), accessed February 10, 2020, https://cdn.global freedomnetwork.org/content/uploads/2017/02/06155946/GFN-A-United-Faith.pdf.

[23] Jeffrey Barrows, "The Role of Faith-Based Organisations in the US Anti-Trafficking Movement," in *Human Trafficking is a Public Health Issue*, eds. Chisolm-Straker, Makini, and Hanni Stoklosa (Cham, Switzerland: Springer International, 2017), 277–291.

[24] Hannah Lewis, Gwyneth Lonergan, Rebecca Murray, Emma Tomalin, and Louise Waite, *Faith Responses to Modern Slavery* (Sheffield: Economic and Social Research Council, 2020), accessed February 10, 2020, www.sheffield.ac.uk/socstudies/news/report-launch-faith-responses-modern-slavery.

[25] Barrows, "The Role of Faith-Based Organisations."

Global Freedom Network declared: "In the eyes of God each human being is a free person whether girl, boy, woman or man, and is destined to exist for the good of all in equality and fraternity. Modern Slavery . . . is a crime against humanity."[26] Faith organizations are already frequently involved in serving the most vulnerable and marginalized in society, not just spiritually but through provision for basic needs such as food, education, healthcare, and housing. They are key pro-social community actors able to provide myriad resources ranging from physical meeting space to local leadership for community initiatives.[27] This means there is a considerable overlap between work they are already engaged with and anti-trafficking activism. They are also embedded in localities, with an enduring presence that renders them able to build relationships of trust and sustain action over the long term.[28]

The Christian church has taken a particularly high-profile role in the modern antislavery movement. Some criticism – mainly levelled at the Christian evangelical movement in the US – has suggested that the engagement of religious groups has led to an excessive focus on sex-trafficking, as well as a misguided short-term focus on "rescue."[29] Critics may also point to questions over the moral legitimacy of Christian denominations to provide leadership on this issue, given its history of profiting from chattel slavery, and the continuing shadow of sexual abuse scandals, which call into question its ability to serve vulnerable people.

However, in the US and the UK the current paucity of mainstream funding for antislavery service provision means that there are wide gaps which could not be filled without engagement from the church and other faith groups.[30] In the US there is a tradition of services being provided through philanthropy, but in the UK, recent public spending cuts of more than 30 percent at a local level have seen a move away from dependence on a secular state provision to embrace the resources which faith

---

[26] Global Freedom Network, "A United Faith against Modern Slavery," 25.

[27] Ingrid Storm, "Civic Engagement in Britain: The Role of Religion and Inclusive Values," *European Sociological Review*, 31, no. 1 (2015): 14–29.

[28] John Frame, Mia Tuckey, Lili White, and Emma Tomalin, "Faith and Freedom: The Role of Local Faith Actors in Anti-modern Slavery and Human Trafficking," The Joint Learning Initiative on Faith and Local Communities (2019), accessed February 10, 2020, https://aht-ms.jliflc.com/resources/ams-ht-scoping-study/.

[29] See for instance Barrows, "The Role of Faith-Based Organisations," and Ruth Graham, "How Sex Trafficking Became a Christian Cause Célèbre," *Slate*, March 5, 2015, accessed February 10, 2020, www.slate.com/articles/double_x/faithbased/2015/03/christians_and_sex_trafficking_how_evangelicals_made_it_a_cause_celebre.html.

[30] Lewis et al., "Faith Responses to Modern Slavery."

communities can provide, such as youth work, provision for basic needs, and social care. In this climate, faith-based actors have been welcomed as partners in implementing local antislavery strategies, with more than 60 percent of respondents to a Church of England survey indicating that their local diocese was involved in multiagency antislavery action.[31] Research with the Anglican Church's Clewer Initiative identified four main roles that the church could play in antislavery partnerships including as a catalyst and campaigner to exercise "prophetic voice" and challenge cultural indifference to injustice; a convener to mobilize communities and draw partnerships together; a carer and commissioner – taking responsibility both in the immediate neighborhood and at a distance, through investments and funding; and as a critical friend providing continuity to social justice campaigns, beyond the limited cycle of politics (see Figure 4.2).

The Clewer Initiative has also adopted a broad perspective on modern slavery, emphasizing different manifestations and pointing to the responsibility of communities in both generating and addressing problems.[32] Their model takes an asset-based approach, building on local strengths and resources to engage congregations. The result is a diverse program of activity exploring a wide range of interventions, from the relatively low commitment of asking members to use a "safe car-wash" phone app, to embedding training on modern slavery in safeguarding programs and engaging with at-risk clients in foodbanks and homeless night shelters. However, there are challenges for their work, particularly in challenging anti-immigrant biases that occur within as well as beyond congregations; securing the time and human resources needed to co-ordinate activity; and reaching beyond the Anglican network in a "viral" sense to draw upon the resources of other church denominations, and communities of different faiths and none. This is particularly important given that churchgoers identified as Anglican have halved in recent years[33]

There are also dilemmas inherent in the interface between faith, activism, and politics. While principles such as fair trade are widely shared, definitions of sexual exploitation are more divisive, and can split religious communities. Antislavery activists within the church comment on the

---

[31] Alison Gardner and Ben Brewster, "The Clewer Initiative: An Appreciative Inquiry," University of Nottingham Rights Lab 2020, forthcoming.
[32] Pat Ashworth, "People Trafficking: A Build-up of Traffic," *Church Times*, August 3, 2018, accessed February 10, 2020, www.churchtimes.co.uk/articles/2018/3-august/features/features/people-trafficking-a-build-up-of-traffic.
[33] Park et al., *British Social Attitudes* 28, 180.

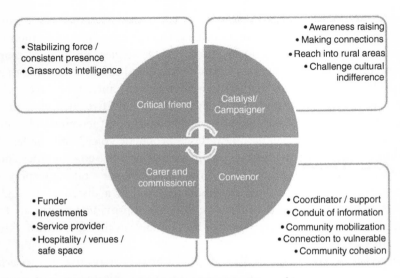

FIGURE 4.2 Roles for the church in antislavery partnerships
Source: Gardner and Brewster (2020).

need for the church to use its "prophetic voice" to challenge issues of injustice, but engagement with justice issues such as immigration and labor regulation inevitably means that any prophetic voice will carry a political message, which can be an uncomfortable challenge for both faith leaders and politicians. Nonetheless, while more work is needed to understand the reach and significance of the role of faith organizations in the global antislavery movement, it is clear that in the UK and the US they retain a key role in community mobilization and continue to be vocal – and practical – in emphasizing the need for moral responsibility both in relation to their locality and at a distance.

4.7 BUSINESS AS A CORPORATE CITIZEN AND THE ROLE FOR ETHICAL CONSUMERISM

Just as nineteenth-century businesses played a crucial role in the antislavery agenda, the prosperity of places is still intimately connected to the success of local businesses and local (as well as global) business practices can be influential in shaping civic and community action. The UK factory "villages" of Bourneville, New Earswick, and Port Sunlight provide lasting legacies to the way in which Victorian employers including Cadbury, Rowntree, and Leverhulme engaged proactively to improve the physical, economic, and social landscape inhabited by their employees. However, modern equivalents to the "model villages" are difficult to find, and as LeBaron shows in this volume, a globalized marketplace coupled with the increasing length and complexity of supply chains means that even those businesses marketing goods with ethical and fair-trade branding are often failing to effectively address the welfare of precarious workers.

The local economy has also long provided the basis of city finance and governance in the US, and this situation is increasingly mirrored in the UK, with the localization of business rates and a focus on city-region economies.[34] As local levels of pay, company registrations and the existence of formal employment opportunities form key determinants for economic prosperity, policy-makers such as local governments and industrial strategists have a clear interest in encouraging businesses to engage with the antislavery agenda. There are furthermore multiple roles that businesses play in community-based action, beyond examining their own supply chains. This includes a civic leadership role in influencing local decision-makers, sharing intelligence with enforcement agencies, training staff and implementing good labor practices, raising awareness with clients, and providing support for survivors. Yet two successive surveys of multiagency antislavery partnership work across the UK show that many local partnerships were struggling to engage with business partners, with the majority of partnerships dependent upon statutory, voluntary and faith-sector partners for funding and administration.[35]

More widely, while the 2015 UK Modern Slavery Act was innovative in including a requirement for businesses to publish a modern slavery supply chain transparency statement if they had a turnover of more than £36 million, the Act has often resulted in a narrow focus on legal compliance, with a particular emphasis on the importance of transnational business supply chains. Nearly half of all top businesses currently ignore the regulations completely and the majority of UK businesses are in any case small and medium-sized employers (SMEs), meaning that many do

---

[34] Vivien Lowndes and Alison Gardner, "Local Governance under the Conservatives: Super-austerity, Devolution and the 'Smarter State'," *Local Government Studies* 42, no. 3 (2016): 357–375.

[35] Alison Gardner et al., "Collaborating for Freedom," (Nottingham: University of Nottingham Rights Lab, 2017), accessed February 10, 2020, www.antislaverycommissioner.co.uk/media/1186/collaborating-for-freedom_anti-slavery-partnerships-in-the-uk.pdf. A 2020 update to this report is forthcoming.

not meet the turnover threshold.[36] Research by the Chartered Institute of Procurement and Supply in 2016 suggested that SMEs were less engaged with the antislavery agenda and that out of 263 businesses with turnovers under £36 million, nearly two-thirds (61 percent) of small business were unaware of the UK's Modern Slavery Act, and its impact on them, 67 percent of SMEs did not take any steps to tackle the issue, and 75 percent did not know what to do if modern slavery was found in their supply chains.[37]

Some businesses have been proactive in embracing antislavery campaigns, often inspired by advocacy from staff members. The international banking giant HSBC has shown systemic commitment to the antislavery agenda, both through senior leadership support for national anti-trafficking initiatives and through local training for frontline branch staff, which has resulted in modern slavery prosecutions. HSBC also chairs the UK's Joint Intelligence and Money-Laundering Taskforce, a financial industry network that provides intelligence toward investigations of transnational trafficking operations, and has developed banking provision aimed specifically at survivors. Meanwhile in the UK, the Co-operative Group, which focuses mainly on supermarket and service-industries (with an annual turnover £9.5 billion), has provided industry leadership both in its hometown of Manchester and further afield. The group's strong historic roots in social entrepreneurism and ethical trading encourage a vigorous approach to monitoring supply chains (albeit, that these measures have limitations, as LeBaron demonstrates). The Co-op has worked with leading survivor support charities to pioneer an employment scheme for survivors of modern slavery – Bright Future – which is now being rolled out to other businesses across the UK.

Government is also an important client for many businesses, and although central and local UK government were originally exempted from supply chain transparency statement requirements, policy-makers are progressively layering anti-exploitation provisions onto governance, commissioning, and procurement practice. Many UK local authorities are choosing to publish voluntary transparency in supply chain statements,

---

[36] Business and Human Rights Resource Centre, First Year of FTSE 100 Reports Under the UK Modern Slavery Act: Towards Elimination?, Antislaverycommissioner.co.uk (2018), accessed February 10, 2020, www.antislaverycommissioner.co.uk/media/1189/first-year-of-ftse-100-reports-under-the-uk-modern-slavery-act_towards-elimination.pdf.

[37] Chartered Institute of Procurement and Supply, UK SMES Overwhelmingly Unaware of the Modern Slavery Act's Impact on Them, CIPS News, Mar 29, 2016, accessed February 10, 2020, www.cips.org/en-gb/who-we-are/news/uk-smes-overwhelmingly-unaware-of-the-modern-slavery-acts-impact-on-them-cips-research-finds/.

with 126 statements noted by the Local Government Association in 2020.[38] This development is further reinforced by the 2013 Social Value Act, which requires commissioners of public sector services to consider the wider social, economic, and environmental benefits of their purchasing decisions. Modern Slavery Procurement guidance issued by the UK Cabinet Office in September 2019, which applies to all central government departments, executive agencies, and non-departmental public bodies also advocated a set of activities to embed antislavery measures throughout the procurement cycle and reiterated the UK central government's commitment to publishing a voluntary transparency statement.[39]

Yet despite these examples, more could be done to encourage businesses to engage with antislavery governance, leadership, and ethical business practice at a local level, particularly amongst small and medium-sized employers. Small businesses in particular retain a mutually beneficial connection to their communities, which could provide a motivating factor to engage with locally-based antislavery initiatives if targeted campaigns were developed.[40] National industrial strategy and local governments could also more proactively mitigate risks of exploitation when planning the types of industry they wish to attract to an area, keeping a balance between higher and lower-risk industries, and offering support to small and medium-sized employers in meeting costs, such as constructing transparency statements and providing staff training. In addition, despite recent investment in key regulators such as the Gangmasters and Labour Abuse Authority, further resources are needed to enforce existing local regulators such as environmental health and trading standards. Without this legislative and incentive-based framework, it seems likely that

[38] Local Government Association, Modern Slavery in Supply Chains, Local Government Association, local.gov.uk (2020), accessed February 10, 2020, www.local.gov.uk/topics/community-safety/modern-slavery/supply-chains.

[39] H.M. Government, Procurement Policy Note 05/19: Tackling Modern Slavery in Government Supply Chains, Gov.uk, September 18, 2019, accessed February 10, 2020, www.gov.uk/government/publications/procurement-policy-note-0519-tackling-modern-slavery-in-government-supply-chains.

[40] Lähdesmäki and Suutari's study on 25 Finnish SMEs demonstrated how the relationship between SMEs and the local community leads to a "circle of reciprocity" where both parties mutually benefit from the interaction. See Merja Lähdesmäki & Timo Suutari, "Keeping at Arm's Length or Searching for Social Proximity? Corporate Social Responsibility as a Reciprocal Process between Small Businesses and the Local Community," *Journal of Business Ethics*, 108, no. 4 (2012): 481–493. Recent research by Alison Gardner and Akilah Jardine (forthcoming) has also found that SMEs become more engaged in discussions about modern slavery when relevance is demonstrated to their community and networks.

engagement in local and community-based antislavery initiatives will remain limited to a narrow selection of corporations with the resources as well as the commitment to make an impact.

However, when we move away from the traditional connection between business and spatial communities to consider the influence of virtual communities, the power of individual consumers and corporate brands to apply pressure for new patterns of ethical consumption is only just starting to be explored. For example, sophisticated social media techniques are beginning to be deployed by NGOs, such as using well-known YouTube influencers to produce viral videos examining exploitation in the footwear industry.[41] This is a new type of convening, using technology and branding to bring together diverse communities of followers, who appreciate the value of corporate reputations as well as the impact of consumer choice. Such strategies are still new to the antislavery movement, but present fresh opportunities to engage and sustain broad-based community engagement in campaigns. Yet at the same time, they problematize the act of consumption: if exploitation-free goods frequently cannot be ensured as LeBaron suggests, are consumers still willing to suffer themselves through forgoing sought-after brands or goods in order to see their ethical dilemma resolved?

4.8 COMMUNITIES OF PLACE

One urgent challenge for the contemporary antislavery movement revolves around the need to cohere the fragmented actions being undertaken by a range of different actors. Bales and Soodalter strongly advocate multiagency working, and in a passage entitled "How to make your city a slave-free city" outline a number of stepping stones to address slavery using a place-based approach to mobilization, which centers on developing engagement with antislavery action across a specific geographical community, town, or city.[42] Their recommendations for action include developing civic and community ownership for the concept, public awareness raising, training for frontline staff in public services, action on slavery-free supply chains, and monitoring progress on an ongoing basis.

---

[41] See Jacques Slade UNBOXING: The REAL Price of SNEAKERS, YouTube, May 15, 2018, accessed February 10, 2020, www.youtube.com/watch?v=5CBTMHyutQU.

[42] Kevin Bales and Ron Soodalter, *The Slave Next Door* (Berkeley: University of California Press, 2009), 192–194.

These principles have been used in the UK County of Nottinghamshire to inform multiagency action and assist with communication, with enforcement added as an additional priority that needed to be approached in partnership. The main coordination group, Nottinghamshire Modern Slavery Partnership, has adopted the concept of a "slavery-free Nottinghamshire" to help communicate its antislavery work. The partnership includes representatives from local government, police, labor enforcement, NGOs, faith organizations, and local businesses. It links with community-based action through a Nottingham voluntary sector forum, and a "Slavery Free Notts" faith network. Actions to date have included launching an antislavery pledge for local institutions and businesses, multiagency enforcement exercises, encouraging public sector partners to publish modern slavery transparency statements, developing a pilot program to improve long-term survivor support, and commissioning a rolling training program for staff and voluntary sector partners who are working in direct contact with the public. A multi-agency "problem-profile" is under development to better articulate known and emergent forms of exploitation, and a "slavery and exploitation risk assessment conference" has been established by the City Council, in conjunction with police, to review cases of vulnerable adults who are potentially at risk of exploitation. The work has attracted local and national media coverage as well as inspiring similar initiatives in other parts of the Midlands including Birmingham and Sandwell.

The US has also encouraged the development of community and place-based responses to slavery, with 42 anti-trafficking taskforces of federal, state, and local providers funded by the US Office for Victims of Crime (OVC) and the US Bureau of Justice Administration (BJA) since 2004. For example, in Orange County, a Human Trafficking Taskforce, initiated in 2004, brings together six law enforcement agencies, 60 partner agencies and more than 200 volunteers in a structured and survivor-centered program to address modern slavery. Supported by state grant funding, the Community Service program and local Salvation Army, and with a core staff of seven full-time equivalents, the partnership raises awareness of modern slavery, provides training for law enforcement, and wraparound care for survivors including therapy and legal support, guided by the survivor's progress (sometimes extending over more than two years). More than one hundred community volunteers are engaged through meetings that take place twice a month, with expert speakers ensuring that partners are kept up to date on emerging issues.

There are several advantages inherent within a place-based approach to addressing modern slavery. First, the strapline of "slavery-free community" is an aspiration that is easy to grasp and promote, although it needs to be emphasized that "slavery-free" is more of a journey than a destination. The aim is not to create a naive belief that all forms of exploitation will be eradicated, but to create an environment that can be resilient against slavery taking root. Second, a slavery-free community places an emphasis on widespread community responsibility, moving beyond an enforcement-focused approach, and allowing challenge to consumer behaviors and actions. It also helps to tie together separate campaigns around awareness, training, supply chains, intelligence, and victim support through a place-based focus that can tap into local civic pride and local strengths. It contains elements and potential actions that every type of organization can relate to and participate in, whether public, private, voluntary, or community-based.

However, despite the logic of a place-based approach, further research is needed to understand precisely what actions can best be addressed at community level. We need to examine in more detail the complexities of the theory of change underpinning the ideal of a slavery-free community, including its relationship to the wider historical, structural, and legislative context. Questions which require further consideration include who is best placed to provide civic and community leadership, what are the optimal approaches for awareness campaigns, how can we create effective local strategies for survivor support, and what are the best mechanisms for systematically gathering and sharing evidence. This is particularly challenging in the UK context, where local partnership responses have developed organically over different geographies and with minimal guidance or core funding to promote consistency.[43] Such factors may also be very culturally and locality specific, suggesting a need for national and international cross-comparison work.

4.8 CONCLUSION

Communities remain part of the problem and an essential part of the solution for responding to contemporary slavery. Faith, commerce, and place still play an important role in generating momentum, particularly as conveners for the diverse groups and individuals that create campaign energy and resources. Leaders in these networks can help to challenge

---

[43] Gardner et al., "Collaborating for Freedom."

existing norms, whether through campaigning action, or radical internal reform in supply chains. They are also a good starting point for sharing the (often still poorly understood) message that slavery still exists, and that communities have an essential role to play in breaking the cycle of exploitation.

However, there are a number of key differences between community responses to historic slavery and those required for contemporary slavery. Although at a simplistic level the crime appears similar, the motives of "perpetrators" and the drivers behind the different types of offence included under the umbrella term of "modern slavery" are more complex to uncover and address. Chattel slavery was a norm that was once commonplace and then rendered unacceptable. Now that practice is widely outlawed, the norms that sustain the existence of contemporary slavery are significantly more subtle and multifaceted. Issues requiring "moral redefinition" in relation to manifestations of modern slavery include the effects of patriarchy (particularly the normalization of violence against women); unrestrained markets; a lack of empathy for others' suffering that Pope Francis terms "the globalization of indifference";[44] and an individualistic and materialistic culture prevalent in the global north that privileges luxury for some communities over the quality of life of others. Such problems are deep-seated in our power structures, beyond the influence of any one industry,[45] and the solutions politically contested, which implies discomfort for institutions such as faith bodies, businesses, and national and local governments in seeking solutions. This, in itself, need not be a barrier to abolition: the British economy was once substantially invested in the transatlantic slave trade, but that was overturned.

Perhaps the most significant challenge at this point is the effectiveness of community and civil society groups in clarifying and naming the moral dilemmas that affect their own communities and creating a consensus on the best path for decisive action. History tells us that suggestions for radical cultural and social change will often be put off for future consideration by either literally or metaphorically being "placed upon the table" but that persistence and diversification of campaign tactics can contribute to change over the longer term. In addition, the multifaceted nature of

---

[44] "Pope Francis Warns against 'Globalisation of Indifference' in Lenten Message," *Catholic Herald*, January 27, 2015, accessed February 10, 2020, https://catholicherald.co.uk/pope-francis-warns-against-globalisation-of-indifference-in-lenten-message/.

[45] Karen E. Bravo, "The Role of the Transatlantic Slave Trade in Contemporary Anti-Human Trafficking Discourse," *Seattle Journal for Social Justice* 9, no. 2 (2011): 555–597.

modern slavery is also its weakness, and this is where the potential of community-based action lies. Drivers for modern slavery – once identified – can be unpicked piece by piece, issue by issue – just as other ancient tools of repression such as child sexual exploitation and female genital mutilation are being undone. The tools for mass communication and the sharing of viral ideas are also more powerful than ever before. Communities can be constructed and mobilized within hours, both locally and across continents and time-zones. As face-to-face communications improve, the distance over which our moral responsibility must be extended has grown less significant. We also know more now about techniques for achieving social and individual change than we have ever done before. Our capacity to "nudge" and influence is increasingly sophisticated.[46] In this context, the potential for sustainable changes in behavior and practice is magnified, and ending slavery – community by community – appears a more achievable prospect.

---

[46] For a review of the interaction of behavioral economics and public policy see Peter John, *How Far to Nudge? Assessing Behavioural Public Policy* (Cheltenham: Edward Elgar, 2018).

5

Ambivalent Abolitionist Legacies

The League of Nations' Investigations into Sex Trafficking, 1927–1934

Jessica R. Pliley

5.1 INTRODUCTION

Modern abolitionists look to the past to find inspiration. They seek heroes to emulate, tactics to embrace, and strategies to follow. They also make arguments that antislavery and anti-trafficking campaigns of the past need to be pulled into the present to fight a new, more insidious form of human trafficking and modern slavery. Most of the "saving," "rescuing," awareness raising, and fundraising of contemporary activists focus on fighting sex trafficking.[1] When activists pull on the past in their fight against contemporary sex trafficking, they frequently turn to the history of antislavery abolitionism that offers seemingly uncomplicated heroes – like Frederick Douglass, William Wilberforce, and Harriet Tubman – and a victorious narrative. For example, Operation Underground Railroad, a current group that operates out of Utah, claims the legacy of Harriet Tubman, requests donations of a "Lincoln" ($5), and utilizes paramilitary tactics to liberate children (always portrayed as children of color).[2] Similarly, the Polaris Project, which runs the US National Human Trafficking Hotline, is named after the North Star that guided enslaved people to freedom and, according to its own publications, was also

[1] See ILO et al., *Global Estimates of Modern Slavery: Forced Labour and Forced Marriage* (Geneva: ILO, 2017), 16; Kamala Kepadoo, "The Modern-Day White (Wo)Man's Burden: Trends in Anti-Trafficking and Anti-Slavery Campaigns," *Journal of Human Trafficking* no. 1 (2015): 8–20, 10.

[2] Garrett Nagaishi, "'From Utah to the Darkest Corners of the World': The Militarism of Raid and Rescue," in *Popular and Political Representations: Beyond Trafficking and Slavery Short Course*, Volume 1, eds. Joel Quirk and Julia O'Connell Davidson (BTS, 2015), 50–52.

inspired by the Underground Railroad.[3] Odes to British abolitionist William Wilberforce are also common, to such a degree that the 2000 Trafficking Victims Protection Act became the Wilberforce Trafficking Victims Protection Reauthorization Act in 2008; in 2006, the University of Hull launched the Wilberforce Institute to study modern slavery. The historical movement to abolish slavery inspires.

Campaigns to abolish sex slavery and prostitution emerged from anti-slavery abolitionism in the nineteenth century to challenge the legitimacy and legality of sexual marketplaces throughout the world. These campaigns peaked in the period between World War I and World War II, when delegates to the League of Nations – the precursor to the United Nations – debated sex trafficking, produced international sex trafficking conventions, and investigated the extent of global sex trafficking. Rarely do these activists turn to the history of anti-prostitution and anti-trafficking abolitionism,[4] yet this history of abolition is distinct from the fight against chattel slavery. It also had its share of successes, emerging as the dominant paradigm within international civil society in the interwar period. Yet, the abolitionists – reformers dedicated to abolishing state-regulated prostitution – offer contradictory lessons about the collateral damage of anti-trafficking campaigns and policy.[5]

Rather than romanticized histories about abolitionists, the key lessons contemporary activists should heed from historic abolitionism – viewed through a sex trafficking lens – are that such struggles have long been intertwined with anti-sex, anti-feminist, and anti-prostitute agendas; have

---

[3] Polaris, "Combatting Human Trafficking and Modern-Day Slavery: Ten Years of Impact, 2002–2012," 3, accessed May 18, 2020, https://polarisproject.org/wp-content/uploads/2019/12/Polaris-Ten-Years-of-Impact.pdf.

[4] There are some exceptions. Global Centurion, an NGO devoted to ending the demand for commercial sex, includes an essay about Josephine Butler on its website, Laura J. Lederer, "Josephine Butler: A Century Long Battle to End International Sex Trafficking," Global Centurion, accessed May 18, 2020, www.globalcenturion.org/about/publications/josephine-butler-a-century-long-battle-to-end-international-sex-trafficking/. The Salvation Army includes a celebration of its historic ties to Butler. "The Army's History in Fighting Sexual Trafficking," Salvation Army International, accessed May 18, 2020, www.salvationarmy.org/ihq/maiden-tribute-story. Truckers Against Trafficking has an award named the "Josephine Butler Abolitionist Award for Policy Development," *Truckers Against Trafficking Newsletter* 4, no. 1 (January 2013), 3, accessed May 18, 2020, https://truckersagainsttrafficking.org/wp-content/uploads/2018/02/TAT1stQuarter2013Newsletter.pdf.

[5] Global Alliance Against the Traffic in Women (GAATW), ed. *Collateral Damage: The Impact of Anti-Trafficking Measures on Human Rights around the World* (Bangkok, Thailand: Global Alliance Against the Traffic in Women, 2007).

frequently resulted in the exertion of coercive state power in the form of increasingly rigid border control infrastructures and carceral regimes; and are characterized by fraught and discriminatory racial politics. Examining the anti-trafficking movement during the interwar period reveals that the politics of anti-prostitution abolitionism were fraught with disagreements about how to understand commercial sex. The interwar anti-trafficking campaign was divided between feminist abolitionists and paternalist abolitionists, with the paternalists emerging as the more powerful branch due to their close ties to government officials and leaders in the era's major nongovernmental organizations. At the same time, corporate interests funded international research. These investigations reflected the geopolitical concerns of the Americans who conducted the report, including the white supremacist worldview of these investigators. And the final recommendations urged stricter border control and the criminalization of prostitution. Contemporary antislavery activists note, the past can teach us much; and this chapter suggests that it can also warn us of the (un)intended outcomes of our approaches.

5.2 DISCOVERING THE PROBLEM: WHITE SLAVES AND THE ORIGINS OF INTERNATIONAL CAMPAIGNS AGAINST TRAFFICKING

The remarkable visibility of commercial sex provoked anti-prostitution reform movements among evangelical Christians and women's rights activists in the latter half of the nineteenth century. In the United Kingdom, Josephine Butler launched a campaign to overturn the Contagious Diseases Acts (CD Acts) passed by parliament in 1864, 1866, and 1869. These laws empowered police to detain women suspected of selling sex in designated British cities. Butler and her allies protested the ways that these laws enshrined a double standard of sexuality that men needed sexual access to women, but required women to be chaste. Butler rejected what she saw as the state-sanctioned commercialization of poor women's sexuality maintained via state control over women's freedom of mobility. The campaign against the CD Acts culminated in parliament's repeal of the CD Acts in 1886.[6] Concern about sex slavery in brothels animated former antislavery abolitionists in the United

---

[6] Judith R. Walkowitz, *Prostitution and Victorian Society: Women, Class, and the State* (Cambridge: Cambridge University Press, 1980).

States, who saw brothel slavery and the "slavery of sex" as the next campaign to wage in their lives devoted to social justice. They called themselves the "new abolitionists."[7] Significantly, Butler and her feminist allies protested the criminalization of women who sold sex, understanding that police and the power of the state posed some of the most significant dangers to women who sold sex and their neighbors. Meanwhile, they condemned third-party profiteering from women's sexual labor, whether from a madam, pimp, doctor, policeman, or the state in cases of regulated prostitution. By the late nineteenth century social purity reform animated Christian activists and women's rights organizations seeking to eradicate the scourge of what was called white slavery.[8]

The term *white slavery* emerged during the 1880s campaigns against prostitution and trafficking in the United Kingdom and the United States to draw attention to the traffic in young white women who had been fraudulently offered jobs in domestic service in foreign counties yet been placed into brothels far from the protections of home. The rhetoric of white slavery consistently painted the threat to these women as a foreign "other" and the victims as innocent, young white girls. The term has particular valence because it paradoxically linked whiteness with enslavement; two statuses thought to be diametrically opposed. As historian Gunther Peck notes, "white slaves were enslaved not because of their skin color, but in spite of it."[9] More to the point, the term *white slavery* implied that women selling sex in brothels had no volition, because they had been trapped by poverty, desperation, fraud, force, or coercion. In this way, the term had the possible effect of converting all women who sold sex into sex slaves. The term was characterized by its extraordinary slipperiness, though it consistently contained a racial connotation.[10] American activist Clifford Roe observed in 1911, that "The phrase,

---

[7] Jessica R. Pliley, *Policing Sexuality: The Mann Act and the Making of the FBI* (Cambridge: Harvard University Press, 2014), 19–20. For "new abolitionists" see Josephine Butler, "New Abolitionist Work throughout the World," London: British, Continental and General Federation for the Abolition of State Regulation of Prostitution, 1885.

[8] Pliley, *Policing Sexuality*, 23–26; David J. Pivar, *Purity Crusade: Sexual Morality and Social Control, 1869–1900* (Westport, CT: Greenwood Press, 1973), 135–157.

[9] Gunther Peck, "Feminizing White Slavery in the United States: Marcus Braun and the Transnational Traffic in Women's Bodies, 1890–1910," in *Workers Across the Americas: The Transnational Turn in Labor History*, ed. Leon Fink, (New York: Oxford University Press, 2011), 224.

[10] Jessica R. Pliley, "Protecting the Young and the Innocent: Age and Consent in the Enforcement of the White Slave Traffic Act," in *Child Slavery before and after Emancipation: An Argument for Child-Centered Slavery Studies*, ed. Anna Mae Duane, (New York: Cambridge University Press, 2017), 158–161.

white slave traffic, is a misnomer, for there is a traffic in yellow and Black women and girls, as well as in white girls. However, the term has become so widely and extensively used that it seems futile to ever change it."[11] Coinciding as it did with the height of scientific racism, the white slavery rhetoric formed an important bulwark of white supremacy in the early twentieth century, and race and nativity often drew the boundary between a victim of white slavery and a deviant, often racialized, prostitute.[12]

In the United States by the 1910s, prominent private individuals, cities, states, and the federal government conducted studies into prostitution, white slavery, and vice to more accurately gauge the number of sex slaves. Muckraking journalist George Kibbe Turner published an exposé that declared New York City to be "a Leading Center of the White Slave Trade of the World."[13] In response, the city of New York convened a grand jury led by John D. Rockefeller, Jr., one of the wealthiest men in America, to investigate prostitution in the Big Apple. Though the grand jury was instructed to meet for only 30 days, Rockefeller kept it in session for over six months, and he spent $250,000 of his own money to fund the investigation (over $6.3 million in today's money). The grand jury's findings confirmed that "a traffic in bodies of women does exist," but that it was carried out informally.[14] In the United States, these findings would be echoed in the over forty municipal investigations into vice and prostitution launched between 1910 and 1916, as well as the federal government's investigation into white slavery that was published to great publicity in 1909 as part of the Congressional Immigration Commission.[15] Taken together, these US investigations produced three lasting developments – legal reform, new investigative techniques, and the proliferation and consolidation of anti-vice voluntary organizations.

---

[11] Clifford Roe, *The Horrors of the White Slave Trade: The Mighty Crusade to Protect the Purity of Our Homes* (Chicago: Clifford B. Roe and B. S. Steadwell, 1911), 97.

[12] The term white slavery has a particularly racial connotation in English, French (*la traite des blanches*), and Spanish (*la trata de blancas*). It lacks this racialized connotation in German (*der Mädchenhandel*) and Russian (*torgovliia zhenshchinami*), and Polish (*biała niewola*). Though, in regions where German, Russian, and Polish were commonly spoken, trafficking had an especially anti-Semitic connotation.

[13] Brian Donovan, *White Slave Crusades: Race, Gender, and Anti-vice Activism, 1887–1917* (Chicago: University of Chicago Press, 2006), 90.

[14] Quoted in Gretchen Soderlund, *Sex Trafficking, Scandal, and the Transformation of Journalism, 1885–1917* (Chicago: University of Chicago Press, 2013), 156.

[15] Ruth Rosen, *The Lost Sisterhood: Prostitution in America, 1900–1918* (Baltimore: Johns Hopkins Press, 1983), 14; Pliley, *Policing Sexuality*, 51–54; Katherine Benton-Cohn, *Inventing the Immigration Problem: The Dillingham Commission and Its Legacy* (Cambridge, MA: Harvard University Press, 2018), 155–157.

The US investigations into prostitution, trafficking, and vice immediately prompted significant legal reform in local, state, and federal laws related to prostitution. Each city that conducted a vice investigation closed its red-light district within months of its investigation.[16] By 1915, forty-five of the forty-eight states in the US had passed an anti-white slavery law to prohibit pandering and third-party profiteering from commercial sex.[17] At the federal level, Congress passed the 1910 White Slave Traffic Act that prohibited taking a woman or girl over state, territorial, or reservation borders for the purposes of prostitution, debauchery, or "any other immoral purpose," and Congress fortified US immigration law with the 1910 and 1917 immigration acts that made the selling of sex by foreign-born women and the profiteering from sexual labor a deportable offense.[18]

The investigations encouraged many voluntary organizations concerned with prostitution and trafficking to eschew the sentimental tone that had characterized anti-prostitution tracts of the late nineteenth century, and instead, to adopt a more rational, social scientific tone. Most significantly, the Rockefeller grand jury investigation prompted Rockefeller to establish the Bureau of Social Hygiene, a privately-funded organization that would fund and conduct research on prostitution-related matters and develop policy recommendations. As scholar Gretchen Soderlund notes, in this effort "Rockefeller discovered a new role for the private philanthropist: to inform social policy and shape public opinion on important social issues."[19] The Bureau of Social Hygiene would wield an outsized influence as it funded the American Social Hygiene Association, formed in 1913. The American Social Hygiene Association (ASHA) was devoted to "promoting public health and morality" by supporting sex education, advocating for a single standard of morality of men and women, lowering sexually transmitted infection rates, and eradicating prostitution.[20] ASHA developed a form of

---

[16] Joseph Mayer, *The Regulation of Commercialized Vice: An Analysis of the Transition from Segregation to Repression in the United States* (New York: Klebold Press, 1922), 11.

[17] Mayer, *The Regulation of Commercialized Vice*, 31.

[18] Martha Gardiner, *The Qualities of a Citizen: Women, Immigration, and Citizenship, 1870–1965* (Princeton: Princeton University Press, 2005); Eithne Luibhéid, *Entry Denied: Controlling Sexuality at the Border* (Minneapolis-St. Paul: University of Minnesota Press, 2002); Grace Peña Delgado, "Border Control and Sexual Policing: White Slavery and Prostitution along the US-Mexico Borderlands, 1903–1910," *Western Historical Quarterly* 43, no. 2 (2012), 157–178.

[19] Soderlund, *Sex Trafficking*, 160.

[20] Ruth Clifford Engs, *The Progressive Era's Health Reform Movement: A Historical Dictionary* (Westport, CT: Praeger, 2003), 22.

paternalist abolitionism – paternalist because ASHA favored laws that targeted "bad" women while also treating women as children, abolitionist because it called for the eradication of state-regulated prostitution – that contrasted to the feminist abolitionism of Josephine Butler and her ideological heirs.[21]

Even though local concerns drove local campaigns, trafficking was conceived of as a social problem that had international dimensions. Consequently, anti-vice organizations sought to host international conventions to explore what could be done transnationally and internationally to halt the traffic in women and girls. The year 1877 saw the first international anti-white slavery meeting held in Geneva. That meeting was followed by meetings in London in 1899, Paris in 1902, Madrid in 1910, and London in 1913. These meetings provided a space for delegates to find common ground, articulate similar challenges, and establish international norms codified in the first international anti-trafficking agreement: the 1904 International Agreement for the Suppression of the White Slave Traffic.[22] At its most basic, the 1904 agreement established the principle that its signatories should be sharing information about traffickers. The 1910 International Congress for the Suppression of the White Slave Traffic built on the foundations of the 1904 agreement and required signatories to criminalize the prostitution of women by force or fraud and to

---

[21] This distinction between feminist abolitionist and paternalist abolitionist positions would be replicated in the international arena by the competition between the International Abolitionist Federation (IAF) and the International Bureau for the Suppression of the White Slave Traffic (IB). The IAF was the international branch of Josephine Butler's British organization and had its headquarters in Geneva. It called for the abolition of state-regulated prostitution and for the combatting of trafficking. The IB that grew out of the Christian purity organization the National Vigilance Association was founded in 1886. The National Vigilance Association operated as a social service organization that sought to ensure the enforcement of British anti-vice laws, and consequently, it was closely aligned with the British state. See Stephanie Limoncelli, *The Politics of Trafficking: The First International Movement to Combat the Sexual Exploitation of Women* (Stanford: Stanford University Press, 2010), 42–60.

[22] The convention also established travelers' aid relief in railway stations and ports, set up protocols for the repatriation of foreign prostitutes, and regulated employment agencies that operated in more than one country. Over twenty countries, including the leading imperial powers, eventually signed the world's first international anti-trafficking treaty. The original signatories of the 1904 agreement included Belgium, Denmark, France, Germany, Italy, the Netherlands, Portugal, Russia, Spain, Sweden and Norway, Switzerland, and the United Kingdom. Later adherents included Australia, Austria, Brazil, Bulgaria, Canada, China, Cuba, Czechoslovakia, Finland, Hungary, India, Japan, Luxembourg, Monaco, New Zealand, Poland, Siam, Uruguay, and the United States.

prohibit the prostitution of minors defined as female migrants below the age of twenty.[23]

One challenge of creating international agreements that codified international humanitarian norms was the divisive issue of state-regulated prostitution and its relationship to sex trafficking. Some cities and countries managed prostitution by treating prostitution as a form of disreputable work by registering women who sold sex, requiring regular examinations by physicians, and restricting the selling of sex to licensed sites located in specific neighborhoods. Conceived as both a public health measure and a policy that promoted social order, regulation was most associated with the French who were among the first to implement it in 1803. Other counties adopted the policy, including, but not limited to, Argentina (1875–1934), Austria-Hungary, Belgium (1844–1947), Czechoslovakia (1918–1922), Germany (1830–1871, 1891–1927, 1933), Greece (1922–1955), Italy (1860–1958), Japan (1871–1946), Mexico (1872–1942/1943), the Netherlands (1852–1913), Poland, Portugal, Russia (1843–1917), Spain, Sweden (1859–1919), Switzerland (1896–1925), and the Ottoman Empire/Turkey (1880–present).[24] Regulation became a routine feature of colonial regimes, embraced even by countries that denounced registration within their metropoles, like the United States and the United Kingdom.[25] The 1904 and 1910 agreements did not directly address the relationship of the state-regulated brothels and

---

[23] Limoncelli, *The Politics of Trafficking*, 9. The original signatories of the 1910 agreement included Austria, Belgium, Denmark, France, Germany, Italy, the Netherlands, Portugal, Russia, Spain, Sweden, Switzerland, and the United Kingdom. Later adherents included Bulgaria, Canada, China, Cuba, Czechoslovakia, Finland, Japan, Monaco, New Zealand, Norway, Poland, Siam, South Africa, and Uruguay.

[24] Stephanie A. Limoncelli, "International Voluntary Associations, Local Social Movements and State Paths to the Abolition of Regulated Prostitution in Europe, 1875–1950," *International Sociology* 21, no. 1 (January 2006): 31–59, citation on 35; and Stephanie A. Limoncelli, "The Politics of Humanitarianism: States, Reformers, and the International Movement to Combat the Traffic in Women, 1875–1960," PhD diss. (University of California at Los Angeles, 2006), 59; Mark David Wyers, "Selling Sex in Istanbul," in *Selling Sex in the City: A Global History of Prostitution, 1600s–2000s*, eds. Magaly Rodríguez García, Lex Heerma Van Voss, and Elise Van Nederveen Meerkerk, (Leiden: Brill, 2017), 278–305, 285, 294.

[25] Jessica R. Pliley, "The FBI's White Slave Division: The Creation of a National Regulatory Regime to Police Prostitutes in the United States, 1910–1918," in *Global Anti-Vice Activism: Fighting Drink, Drugs, & "Immorality," 1880–1950*, eds. Jessica R. Pliley, Robert Kramm, and Harald Fischer-Tiné, (Cambridge: Cambridge University Press, 2016), 233–235. It is important to point out that in cities and countries that embraced prostitution through regulation, the vast majority of transactional sex occurred clandestinely, outside of the gaze of the state.

sex trafficking, but among abolitionists – feminist and paternalist – in Great Britain and the United States there was a growing belief that state-licensed brothels stimulated the international demand for sex trafficking.[26] The debate between regulationists and abolitionists would shape international anti-trafficking politics in the interwar period.

5.3 CODIFYING INTERNATIONAL NORMS: THE LEAGUE OF NATIONS AND THE TRAFFIC IN WOMEN, 1919–1939

After World War I, the League of Nations became the site for the international discussions of white slavery, though in 1919 the term "white slavery" was discarded in favor of the more accurate and less racially inflected term of "traffic in women." The League hosted an international conference on the trafficking of women and children held in Geneva in the summer of 1919. The most important outcome of this conference, attended by representatives from thirty-three countries, was the establishment of the Advisory Committee on the Traffic in Women and Children (TWC) that would meet annually to coordinate the ongoing international fight against sex trafficking. The TWC met for the first time in 1922, and was composed of delegates from nine countries and representatives – called assessors – from five nongovernmental organizations. Charged with advising the League Assembly and Council of strategies to fight the traffic in women and children, the TWC functioned as a clearinghouse for the legal codes of each member state that addressed sex trafficking, reported incidences of trafficking throughout the world, and noted any activities undertaken by international anti-sex trafficking voluntary organizations. For a while, Butler's feminist abolitionist position was represented on the TWC, though they would quickly be overshadowed by paternalist abolitionists from the United States.[27]

---

[26] Limoncelli, *The Politics of Trafficking*, 38.

[27] The scope of the TWC extended beyond just an interest in prostitution. Over its existence, the committee studied the employment of women abroad, the use of women as police officers, the traffic in alcohol and obscene publications and their perceived contributory role in prostitution, the treatment of female prisoners, entertainment work for women, age of consent laws, and the general migration of women. Jessica R. Pliley, "Claims to Protection: The Rise and Fall of Feminist Abolitionism in the League of Nations' Committee on the Traffic in Women and Children, 1919–1937," *Journal of Women's History* 22, no. 4 (Winter 2010): 90–113; Metzger, "Toward an International Human Rights Regime," 60–61; Leila J. Rupp, *Worlds of Women: The Making of an International Women's Movement* (Princeton: Princeton University Press, 1997),

Though the United States never joined the League of Nations, US interests directed much to the TWC's activities in pursuit of what scholar Eva Payne has called "America's sexual exceptionalism."[28] At the 1923 meeting the US delegate to the TWC Grace Abbott "revolutionized League methods"[29] when she suggested that instead of talking about the traffic in women and children in vague terms, what the League needed was "to obtain official and accurate information regarding the existence and nature of the traffic in women and children."[30] The TWC enthusiastically embraced Abbott's idea, especially when the Rockefeller's Bureau of Social Hygiene agreed to underwrite the study to the tune of $75,000 ($1.1 million today).[31] Rachel Crowdy, the head of the League's Social Section, wrote Abbot that her proposal had been embraced by the League's Council because, "I think really that there was a general feeling that in the past the voluntary organizations had perhaps exaggerated the extent of the traffic and that the Governments had minimized it, and that it would therefore be of the greatest possible value for the actual extent of the traffic to be accurately gauged at last."[32] The study would be conducted by the expert vice investigators of ASHA.

215–217; Karen Offen, *European Feminisms, 1700–1950: A Political History* (Stanford: Stanford University Press, 2000), 355–356. It is notable that the committee did not analyze prostitution from a labor perspective, although issues of women's employment and low wages were threaded throughout the committee's work. Within the structure of the League, and indeed the gendered imaginations of the elite participants of the TWC, issues of work belonged in the ILO, issues of women's vulnerabilities to the TWC in the Fifth Committee (Social Questions), and issues of women's rights and nationality to the League's First Committee (Constitutional and Legal Questions).

[28] Eva Payne, "Purifying the World: Americans and International Sexual Reform, 1865–1933," (PhD diss., Harvard University Press, 2017).

[29] Florence Brewer Boeckel, "Women in International Affairs," *Annals of the American Academy of Political and Social Science*, 143; Women in the Modern World (May 1929): 230–248, citation on 234. Abbott, head of the U.S.'s Children's Bureau, was invited to sit on the TWC in 1922 and she served irregularly through 1934. Although the United States never joined the League, it did frequently send non-official representatives to the League's technical committees, including the TWC. Robyn Muncy, *Creating a Female Dominion in American Reform, 1890–1935* (New York: Oxford University Press, 1991), 89–92.

[30] League of Nations, *Advisory Committee on the Traffic in Women and Children: Minutes of the Second Session* (Geneva: LNP, 1923), 27.

[31] Metzger, "Toward an International Human Rights Regime," 66. The Rockefeller Foundation was an important source of funding for the League of Nations Library and humanitarian efforts. Warren K. Kuehl and Lynne K. Dunn, *Keeping the Covenant: American Internationalists and the League of Nations, 1920–1939* (Kent, OH: Kent State University Press, 1997), 132.

[32] Rachel Crowdy to Grace Abbott, October 9, 1923, League of Nations, Advisory Committee on Traffic in Women and Children. "Dossier concerning the representation of the United States of America." Document No. 12/21502/13720, Dossier No. 13720,

In the United States, ASHA had developed a reputation as being the go-to organization for investigating issues related to prostitution, developing policies on prostitution and lobbying for those policies. Initially, ASHA focused on investigating the contours of vice economies and lobbying city and state governments to pass new anti-prostitution laws. On the state level, many states adopted ASHA's model definition of prostitution that eradicated the commercial element of the crime: "prostitution should be defined to include the giving or receiving of the body, for hire, or the giving or receiving of the body for indiscriminate sexual intercourse *without hire*."[33] This definition laid the foundation for legally treating the brothel-based prostitute and the more elusive promiscuous woman as one in the same.

During World War I, ASHA capitalized on the wartime conditions to promote federal laws that targeted prostitutes while perfecting its investigative techniques for locating clandestine prostitution; both of these developments would come to bare on the League's trafficking study. ASHA partnered with the US federal government to develop US prostitution policy that would support the military's goals of keeping men "fit to fight."[34] The American Plan, as it was called, had two aspects. First, the Conscription Act of 1917 established "pure zones" that prohibited indiscriminate sex between unmarried peoples within 5 miles (and later 10 miles) of all military installations in the United States and led to the closing of 116 red light districts.[35] Second, the Chamberlain–Kahn Act of 1918 implemented an ambitious public health agenda by encouraging states to pass public health laws that required the detention of women suspected of a sexually transmitted infection, forced gynecological exams, and incarceration of those found to be infected, all justified in the name of

League of Nations Registry Files, 1919–27, Record Group 8, Box 649, League of Nations Archives, Geneva, Switzerland.

[33] See David J. Pivar, *Purity and Hygiene: Women, Prostitution, and the "American Plan"* (Westport, CT: Greenwood Press, 2002), 130; Kristin Luker, "Sex, Social Hygiene, and the State: The Double-Edged Sword of Social Reform," *Theory and Society* 27, no. 5 (October 1998): 601–634, 614, emphasis added. Twenty states adopted ASHA's model law entirely, 32 states based built their laws off of ASHA's model law.

[34] Nancy K. Bristow, *Making Men Moral: Social Engineering During the Great War* (New York: New York University Press, 1996), 21; Allan M. Brandt, *No Magic Bullet: A Social History of Venereal Disease in the United States since 1880* (New York: Oxford University Press, 1985).

[35] Pliley, *Policing Sexuality*, 122–129.

public health with no due process protections.[36] Over 30,000 women would be incarcerated in federally funded facilities during the war, and untold numbers would be detained under state laws. Also during the war, ASHA attorney Bascom Johnson perfected ASHA's undercover investigative techniques for the US Army by training field agents to scour cities and towns for prostitution.[37] These field agents interviewed police officers, health officers, and social workers; they examined local laws and ordinances; they investigated detention facilities, jails, and reformatories, and they nosed around reported brothels and dingy hotels.[38] When US forces disembarked in France, they tried to bring aspects of the American Plan with them. From ASHA's perspective, as Payne writes, "more than any other country France represented old world sexual decay through regulated prostitution."[39] US officials launched a campaign of surveillance, detention, and harassment based on the model developed by ASHA in the United States, even though they lacked the jurisdiction to alter French laws.[40]

With the conclusion of the war, ASHA searched for a new project. In some ways it was a victim of its own success; by 1919 it had successfully changed the prostitution laws throughout the United States and had driven prostitution underground. ASHA soon focused on encouraging the US Immigration Bureau "to coordinate the activities of the Federal and state official agencies dealing with immoral aliens, so that their deportation might be facilitated."[41] Within the first ten years of ASHA's existence, the organization had closed down the remaining red-light districts in the United States, criminalized prostitution and promiscuous sex, developed and implemented a draconian quarantine law that targeted promiscuous women, encouraged the deportation of "immoral women," and attempted to export these policies to the heart of the regulationism – France. The invitation to conduct the League of Nations' study on trafficking offered ASHA the opportunity to export its sexual exceptionalism to the world.

When Grace Abbott attended the League of Nations TWC meeting in 1923 she brought with her the offer to pay for an international study from Rockefeller and the Bureau of Social Hygiene. The money came with the

---

[36] Scott Wasserman Stern, "The Long American Plan: The U.S. Government's Campaign against Venereal Disease and its Carriers," *Harvard Journal of Law & Gender* 38 (2015): 373–436.

[37] Payne, "Purifying the World," 185.   [38] Stern, The Trials of Nina McCall, 127.

[39] Payne, "Purifying the World," 166.   [40] Payne, "Purifying the World," 212–213.

[41] Stern, The Trials of Nina McCall, 182.

implicit guarantee that ASHA would conduct the on-the-ground portion of the investigation, not the Body of Experts composed of members of the TWC. ASHA attorney Bascom Johnson saw the League of Nations as an ideal site to export US prostitution policy – criminalizing prostitution coupled with a deportation regime – to the rest of the world. He wrote "we welcome any move by the various governments designed and calculated to restrict the importation of alien prostitutes into any country."[42] Johnson told Abbott that ASHA would appreciate it if she would, "Urge a pronouncement in favor of abolishing the open brothel, on the ground that the brothel furnishes the greatest single incentive for international and national traffic, as it is a sure market for the disposal of women and girls."[43] Abbott wisely kept her own council when she raised the idea of the League study, choosing not to inflame delegates from regulationist countries which might have voiced their opposition to an investigation led by abolitionists. Nevertheless, Johnson's advice lays bare ASHA's commitment to an abolitionist, immigration-restrictionist analysis of prostitution and trafficking.

ASHA relied on the methods it had developed in the United States during WWI to conduct the League study. First, the Body of Experts sent a questionnaire to official governmental institutions inquiring about local conditions and local laws. Second, ASHA investigators met with officials working in law enforcement and social work. Third, ASHA investigators slipped into the seedy world of prostitution in each of the 112 cities they visited. In each place the investigators, in Bascom Johnson's words, "associated with souteneurs [pimps] and prostitutes, frequented their clubs and cafes, visited the houses of prostitution, and became well acquainted with the madames, assistant madames, and inmates [women who sold sex]."[44] After thoroughly exploring the world of vice with their undercover techniques, the investigators correlated the official statements with the data collected from the interviews of 6,500 people connected to the sex trade.

---

[42] Bascom Johnson to Grace Abbott, February 21, 1923, Folder: Grace Abbott Correspondence, Box S180, League of Nations Archives, Geneva, Switzerland.

[43] Bascom Johnson to Valeria Parker, Memo: Matters for Consideration While in Europe, March 1, 1923, Folder: Grace Abbott Correspondence, Box S180, League of Nations Archives, Geneva, Switzerland.

[44] Bascom Johnson, "Part II of the Report of the Special Body of Experts on Traffic in Women and Children—Draft," pages 6–7, SW45 165:10, Staff Mss, Bascom Johnson Mss, 1929–35. Publications. Staff Manuscripts. Bascom Johnson Manuscripts. (Box 165, Folder 10), American Social Health Association Records, 1905–1990 (SW 45); University of Minnesota Libraries, Social Welfare History Archives, Minneapolis, MN.

After two years of investigating conditions in Europe, Eastern Europe, North Africa, the Caribbean, South American, and North America, ASHA and the League published the report in two parts. Part I detailed a comprehensive synthesis of the findings, describing the contours of the traffic, explaining sources of the trafficking, examining the role of third-party profiteers, and offering recommendations to halt the traffic. Part II included individual reports on the conditions, legal context, and ongoing efforts to eradicate the traffic in each of the 28 countries visited, listed in alphabetic order. Part I sold out of its first run of 5,000 within weeks of publication.[45]

Part I of the League's groundbreaking 1927 study mercilessly implicated state regulation of prostitution as the primary cause of trafficking throughout the world. The authors called on the elimination of licensed brothels and stricter immigration controls. In 1928, H. Wilson Harris published a shorter, popular (and sentimental) version of the League's study entitled *Human Merchandise*.[46] Harris went further than the League report in implicating regulation, stating that "once a direct connection between the international traffic and the licensed house in an individual country is acknowledged, it becomes impossible to warn the League off the subject of licensed houses on the grounds that that is a purely domestic question."[47] Harris correctly identified that the issue of abolition was gaining momentum in the TWC, and indeed after the damning assessment of the 1927 special report, the TWC sought to specifically address regulated prostitution. Rachel Crowdy claimed that it was a "miracle that a report which condemns the system of licensed houses and registration, should have been accepted ... by any Committee on which the nationals of countries having licensed systems were represented!"[48]

The report declared that prostitution could not be considered as legitimate work, and consequently women migrating to work in brothels, even legal

---

[45] The nine known investigators include: Bascom Johnson, Paul Kinsie, Samuel Auerbach, George Worthington, Walter Clarke, F. H. Whithin, Walter Brunet, Christina Galitzi, and Chloe Owing. There were a few unidentified investigators. See Jean-Michel Chaumont, Magaly Rodríguez García, and Paul Servais, eds., *Trafficking in Women, 1924–1926: The Paul Kinsie Reports for the League of Nations*, Vol. 1, Historical Series No. 2 (Geneva: United Nations, 2017), 12–14. H. Wilson Harris, *Human Merchandise: A Study in the International Traffic in Women* (London: Ernest Binn, 1928); the book cost six shillings. Daniel Gorman, *The Emergence of International Society in the 1920s* (Cambridge: Cambridge University Press, 2012), 80, 84–85.

[46] Harris, *Human Merchandise*, x.   [47] Ibid.

[48] Rachel Crowdy to Alison Neilans, March 22, 1927, 3AMS/B/11/03, AMSH Papers, Box 70, Women's Library, London School of Economics, London, UK.

state-regulated brothels, were not regarded as legitimate economic migrants. The investigators embraced the abolitionist perspective when it erased the agency of women who sold sexual services by declaring, though each woman had migrated to sell sex in new marketplaces and "technically she might not have been brought to this condition by force or fraud, but actually she is deceived at every step."[49] This assertion contradicted the testimony of the vast majority of women that investigator Paul Kinsie interviewed, who claimed to travel of their own volition and admitted to selling sex in Europe prior to their travels.[50] The authors of the report dismissed the accounts of women that they migrated, in the words of one French woman, "To make money."[51] For the authors of the 1927 report, exploitation from third parties such as pimps and brothel managers converted foreign women who sold sex into sex slaves regardless of their volition.

ASHA's findings reflected a particularly Anglo-American global geography of vice that was infused with racial assumptions about nonwhite peoples, and biases against non-Protestant peoples. Argentina was imagined as a racially profligate place where Jewish criminality ran amuck, facilitated by Argentine officials embracing of state-regulated prostitution.[52] Rio de Janeiro occupied a similar place in American imaginations. In South America, especially in Brazil, American investigators encountered women that confused their racial understanding of the world. When looking at Rio de Janeiro, American investigators mapped "race onto nationality" by thinking of all Brazilians as Black, and therefore converting all white women they encountered into foreign, trafficked women.[53] Similarly in Mexico, ASHA investigator George Worthington considered all Mexican women to be Indian and therefore searched the country for "real white slavery" by looking for white women (presumed to be non-Mexican).[54] In the Mediterranean Middle East and North Africa, as Liat Kozma has documented, ASHA conceived of trafficking as a crime that only applied to European women, ignoring the migration

[49] League of Nations, *Report of the Special Body of Experts*, Part I, 18–19.

[50] For examples see Chaumont, Rodríguez García, and Servais, eds., *Trafficking in Women*, 26, 41, 48, 58, 60, 65, and 68.

[51] Chaumont, Rodríguez García, and Servais, eds., *Trafficking in Women*, 68.

[52] Mir Yarfitz, "Polacos, White Slaves, and Stille Chuppahs: Organized Prostitution and the Jews of Buenos Aires, 1890–1939" (PhD diss., University of California Los Angeles, 2012), 77.

[53] Payne, "Purifying the World," 255; Cristiana Schettini, "Between Rio's Red-Light District and the League of Nations: Immigrants and Sex Work in 1920s Rio de Janeiro," *IRSH* 62 (2017): 105–132.

[54] Payne, "Purifying the World," 254.

(some of it forced) of non-European women in the region.[55] Finally, two of the ASHA investigators spoke Yiddish. This fact led to an over-representation of Jewish pimps and brothel managers in the final report. In the United States and Europe, trafficking had long been considered a particularly Jewish crime, and reports of Jewish traffickers had become a staple of anti-Semitism of the early twentieth century.[56] The American global imaginary of vice and trafficking that was reflected in the findings of the League's 1927 study prompted objections from many corners of the world that did not agree with American assessments.

5.4 DEBATING METHODS AND MOTIVES: RESPONSES TO THE 1927 STUDY

The League's study soon generated opposition and critiques, especially from those countries that sought to defend the ways they managed commercial sex. The structure of the report provoked much complaint, especially Part Two that offered detailed country reports that read like an atlas of vice. The Body of Experts noted that "we wish to make it clear that when countries are referred to by name it is not intended to single out any particular country or to suggest any criticism whatever of its authorities;" despite such statements, individual countries did feel singled out.[57]

The League Committee's Uruguayan delegate Dr. Paulina Luisi voiced concern over Eurocentric bias within the 1927 report. South America was the first geographic area visited by the investigators; additionally, it was in South America where they spent the most time.[58] The report claimed that Buenos Aires was a main destination for traffickers, although it allowed that traffickers maintained an active presence in Montevideo and Rio de Janeiro as well. It also declared that approximately 75 percent of the women in Argentine brothels were foreign-born, implying that they were all victims of organized trafficking

---

[55] Liat Kozma, *Global Women, Colonial Ports: Prostitution in the Interwar Middle East* (Albany: SUNY Press, 2016), 50–51.

[56] Edward J. Bristow, *Prostitution and Prejudice: The Jewish fight against White Slavery, 1870–1939* (New York: Schocken Books, 1982).

[57] League of Nations, Report of the Special Bodies of Experts on the Extent of the International Traffic in Women and Children, Report by Sir Austen Chamberlain, March 8, 1927 C.126.1927.IV, League of Nations Registry Files, 1919–27, Record Group 8, Box 671, League of Nations Archives, Geneva, Switzerland.

[58] Donna J. Guy, *White Slavery and Mothers Alive and Dead: The Troubled Meeting of Sex, Gender, Public Health and Progress in Latin America* (Lincoln: University of Nebraska Press, 2000), 27.

syndicates.[59] Yet, it failed to consider that the majority of the residents in Buenos Aires were foreign born and that most women who sold sex in the city did so in a clandestine manner so as to avoid the high fees associated with registration.[60] Luisi was right to be suspicious of the League investigators' biases against South America. In one of the first planning meetings of the study the committee decided to start the investigation in South America because that is where "most of the specific instances of traffic which has been reported."[61] The Special Body of Experts assumed trafficking to be a South American problem, so from the get-go they set off to confirm their beliefs.

Most objections centered on the methods utilized in the study, but were actually the consequence of diplomatic face-saving. The Italian Ministry of the Interior rejected the conclusions that an active internal traffic in women thrived in Italy, that Italy was an attractive destination for prostitutes from neighboring counties, and that the government did little to protect female entertainers working abroad,[62] writing, "The subject of the investigation was naturally a most difficult one, for it is no easy matter to become intimately acquainted with the haunts of prostitution where lying and deceit are rife. But the difficulties become even greater, when the persons responsible for the investigation are foreigners and do not thoroughly understand the country in which they are operating." He dismissed all the evidence given to the undercover investigators by individual pimps as the product of bragging, saying, "they try to make their audience believe that they are possessed of great skill and cunning, and sometimes even make out that they are the authors of actions which exist only in their own imagination."[63] Similar objections were voiced by the French, Polish, Argentine,

---

[59] Ibid. Anti-white slavery activists had argued that Argentina was a supposed destination since the 1860s. See Donna J. Guy, *Sex and Danger in Buenos Aires: Prostitution, Family, and Nation in Argentina* (Lincoln: University of Nebraska Press, 1991).

[60] Jose C. Moya, *Cousins and Strangers: Spanish Immigrants in Buenos Aires, 1850–1930* (Berkley: University of California Press, 1998), 161; Guy, *Sex and Danger in Buenos Aires*, 16.

[61] League of Nations, Enquiry into the Traffic in Women and Children, "Traffic in Women and Children. Special Bodies of Experts. Report on the Work of the First Session. Approved by the Committee on April 24, 1924," page 6, CTFE/Experts/6, League of Nations Registry Files, 1919 – 1927, Record Group 8, Box 671, League of Nations Archives, Geneva, Switzerland.

[62] League of Nations, *Report of the Special Body of Experts, Part II* (Geneva: League of Nations Publications, 1927), 106.

[63] League of Nations, Traffic in Women and Children. "Part II of Report of Committee of Experts on the Traffic in Women and Children: Observations of Government of Italy."

Brazilian, and Hungarian governments seeking to defend their national reputations from the criticism embedded in the report.

These critiques shaped future League studies. Rockefeller's Bureau of Social Hygiene agreed to pay $125,000 ($2.1 million today) to fund a second study into trafficking that would examine sex trafficking in East Asia, South East Asia, and the Middle East. This study was again conducted by the ASHA's Bascom Johnson, who hoped to replicate the same undercover methods that had been used in the first study, though the Commission of Enquiry was now led by French TWC delegate Eugène Regnault.[64] In one of the first planning meetings for the Far East study, Johnson noted that the Traveling Commission sought "to define International Traffic very strictly and to shut off undercover investigations altogether. I had to explain that I have a man in New York of such unimpeachable character and superhuman abilities that it was incredible to me that any government would refuse his assistance."[65] Regardless of how "superhuman" the ASHA investigator might be, the stinging recriminations of the first study meant that the TWC had grown wary of undercover investigations due to the way that these methods provoked controversy. Grace Abbott reported that members of the TWC opposed the use of American investigators, with many governments insisting on the traveling commission only using "reports submitted by the governments following investigations in their respective countries," and only interviewing established non-profit and governmental officials in each of the thirty-four cities visited.[66] There would be no undercover visiting of brothels nor interviews with women who sold sex or men who facilitated the sex trade. Protection of national reputations required rejecting undercover investigations. Thus, when the League's study was published in 1933, the media largely ignored it because it offered few salacious stories of the sex trafficking of white women.[67] Rather the 529-page study and its shorter

---

Document No. 12/63098x/58719, League of Nations Registry Files, 1919–27, Record Group 8, Box 704, League of Nations Archives, Geneva, Switzerland.

[64] Paul Knepper, "The Investigation into the Traffic in Women by the League of Nations: Sociological Jurisprudence as an International Social Project." *Law and History Review* 34, no. 1 (2016): 45–73.

[65] Bascom Johnson to William F. Snow, September 4, 1930, Box L17:7 International Activities, Bascom Johnson and the Orient, 1930–1933, American Social Health Association, RG SW045, Social Welfare History Archives, University of Minnesota, Minneapolis, MN.

[66] "Reports Reduction in White Slavery," *New York Times* September 24, 1930, 24.

[67] Knepper, "Measuring the Threat of Global Crime," 798–799.

1934 42-page version presented an in-depth analysis of women's labor and migration in the region.

5.5 SIGNIFICANCE: LESSONS TO BE DRAWN FROM THE LEAGUE'S ANTI-TRAFFICKING EFFORTS

What is striking about the history of the interwar debates about trafficking, migratory prostitution, and the regulation of prostitution, as well as the international investigations into trafficking, is the degree to which they foreshadow the modern slavery and trafficking movement of today. Every year since 2000 the United States' Department of State has issued its Trafficking in Persons (TIP) report that seeks to document the extent of trafficking and modern slavery throughout the globe. And every year its publication spurs an annual ritual of outrage as journalists produce sensational headlines warning of the scourge of trafficking. Yet almost 100 years ago, in 1927, the League of Nations published the first study on the extent of international sex trafficking, generating effusive headlines like "Secret Shame Told to World," "Girls Lured Revealed," "League Finds White Slavery," and "War Against White Slavery."[68] The report offered a stunning indictment of legalized and regulated prostitution, arguing that the "system of licensed houses" in countries that regulated prostitution "stimulated" demand for the international traffic in women.[69] It asserted a particularly American paternalist abolitionist view of prostitution and trafficking that had a white supremacist thread woven throughout.

The 1927 study promoted an abolitionist perspective that also reflected an American geography of vice that upheld white supremacist understandings of morality and sexuality. By focusing on the individual cases of trafficking by Jewish migration brokers and pimps, the authors of the 1927 report ignored the structural conditions that led women who sold sex to migrate. Repeatedly, French women told the investigators that they had turned to prostitution to survive during World War I and that the poor economic conditions in Europe prompted them to seek better opportunities in the Americas. Instead of highlighting the sex-segregated labor market that kept women's wages low, the sexual double standard making

---

[68] "Secret Shame Told to World," *Los Angeles Times* December 10, 1927, 18; "Girls Lured Revealed," *Los Angeles Times* December 6, 1927, 1; "League Finds White Slavery," *The Austin American* March 13, 1927, 2; "War Against White Slavery," *The Western Daily Press* (Yeovil, England), June 20, 1927, 12.

[69] League of Nations, *Report of the Special Body of Experts*, Part I, 43.

young women vulnerable to seduction and exploitation, or the economic devastation in postwar Eastern and Western Europe, the authors of the report painted a picture of bad men exploiting naïve young women. Building white supremacy into the very foundation of the investigation led the Report to argue that only the more "civilized" policies of immigration restriction embraced by the United Kingdom and the United States could protect girls. The 1927 Report articulated a version of white saviorism that characterizes contemporary anti-trafficking efforts.[70] Immigration restriction emerged as the lasting legacy of the study. Cuba and Hungry reformed their prostitution laws after ASHA investigators visited in 1925, and Uruguay, Poland, Japan, and Argentina all followed suit after the study had been published. The League study promoted a global diffusion of standardized immigration laws devoted to deporting women who sold sex.[71]

The League study encouraged countries to adopt policies of repatriation for foreign women who sold sex because the League investigators pursued a paternalist abolitionist campaign to reject prostitution as a form of labor. In the 1920s, those opposed to regulated prostitution split over the question of state power and women's rights. Feminists abolitionists objected to policies that treated prostitutes as a class, arguing that efforts to limit the right of migration of women who sold sex would be applied to all women migrating alone. Paternalist abolitionists, in contrast, embraced state power, particularly the emerging carceral and border control regimes to punish and control women's behavior. They did so by routinely dismissing the voices of women they were trying to "protect" who argued that they were economic migrants, not sex slaves. This perspective was ascendant in the 1933 International Convention for the Suppression of the Traffic in Women of Full Age, which forbad the employment of all foreign women in legal brothels.[72] Similarly, today, the US State Department does not recognize sex as work even though many of the countries covered by the TIP Reports have legal, regulated prostitution, and the

---

[70] Kempadoo, "The Modern-Day White (Wo)Man's Burden"; Laura María Agustín, *Sex at the Margins: Migration, Labour Markets and the Rescue Industry* (London: Zed Books, 2007).

[71] Adam McKeown, *Melancholy Order: Asian Migration and the Globalization of Borders* (New York: Columbia University Press, 2011), 320.

[72] 1933 International Convention for the Suppression of the Traffic in Women of Full Age, accessed May 18, 2020, https://treaties.un.org/Pages/ViewDetails.aspx?src=TREATY& mtdsg_no=VII-5&chapter=7&clang=_en.

voices of sex workers' rights organizations are often dismissed by abolitionist organizations.[73]

Other similarities abound. In the interwar period, the anti-trafficking world was overshadowed by the outsized influence of capitalists like John D. Rockefeller, Jr., who used his wealth to help ASHA set the international anti-trafficking agenda; now, philanthrocapitalists like Andrew Forrest sets the anti-trafficking agenda through Walk Free's Global Slavery Index (GSI), which has teamed up with the International Labour Organization to produce the global estimates on the number of enslaved people in the world.[74] In the late 1920s, the TWC's undercover methods came under attack for their biased methodology.[75] The controversies over researching incidences of trafficking and slavery continue unabated today. The GSI/ILO claimed in 2018 that 40.3 million individuals are in modern slavery, yet the 2018 US TIP Report listed only 100,409 identified victims for 2017.[76] Discrepancies like this have long troubled scholars of trafficking and fueled critiques of the methodologies of the GSI and TIP Report.[77]

The American-centric perspective ASHA brought to the League study generated controversy and accusations of eurocentrism or American chauvinism in much of the same way that today the US's TIP Report is seen as evidence of the US acting as global sheriff.[78] The 1927 League study also offers an early demonstration of the ways that international rankings get enmeshed in geopolitics and international reputations, which

---

[73] Jo Doezema, *Sex Slaves and Discourse Masters: The Construction of Trafficking* (London: Zed Books, 2010), 130–132.

[74] Janie Chuang, "Giving as Governance? Philanthrocapitalism and Modern-Day Slavery Abolitionism," *UCLA Law Review* 62 (2015).

[75] For an exhaustive inquiry into the study's methods, see Jean-Michel Chaumont, *Le mythe de la traite des blanches* (Paris: La Découverte, 2016).

[76] Global Slavery Index, "2018 Finding: Highlights," accessed May 18, 2020, www .globalslaveryindex.org/2018/findings/highlights/; US State Department, *Trafficking in Persons Report 2018* (Washington, DC: Government Printing Office, 2018), 43.

[77] Gillian Wylie, "Doing the Impossible? Collecting Data on the Extent of Trafficking," in *Trafficking and Women's Rights*, eds. Christien L. van den Anker and Joroen Doomernik (New York: Palgrave MacMillan, 2006), 70–88; Ronald Weitzer, "Miscounting Human Trafficking and Slavery," in *Popular and Political Representations: Beyond Trafficking and Slavery Short Course*, Volume 1, ed. Joel Quirk and Julia O'Connell Davidson (BTS, 2015), 108–111; Anne Gallagher, "The Global Slavery Index is Based on Flawed Data, Why Does No One Say So?," *The Guardian*, November 28, 2014; Sally Engle Merry, *The Seductions of Quantification: Measuring Human Rights, Gender Violence, and Sex Trafficking* (Chicago: University of Chicago Press, 2016).

[78] Janie A. Chuang, "The United States as Global Sheriff: Using Unilateral Sanctions to Combat Human Trafficking," *Michigan Journal of International Law* 27, no. 2 (2006), 437–494.

the US Department of State must frequently contend with its TIP Reports.[79] Lastly, one of the primary outcomes of the League's study was the strengthening of a global border control and deportation regime. Similarly, anti-trafficking rhetoric and policy in the United States, the United Kingdom, and elsewhere have been critical in contributing to support for walls, fences, and fortress Europe.[80]

Given the fact that anti-migrant policies have led to clear harm to vulnerable populations, it is no wonder that when contemporary activists turn to the past, they seize on antislavery abolitionism of the nineteenth century, rather than the anti-trafficking abolitionism of the early twentieth century. Anti-trafficking abolitionism leaves a much more ambivalent legacy. The feminist abolitionists who sought to protect poor women from exploitation from men, the police, and the state lost their influence. The paternalist abolitionists who relied on the billionaire class succeeded in swaying policy and empowering police power and deportation regimes. Women's freedom to migrate became imperiled and carceral systems proliferated.

As much as the past can give contemporary abolitionists heroes to emulate and stories that inspire, it can also offer warnings. The fight against sex trafficking, with its origins in the 1880s, turned on questions about what is legitimate work for women, the rights of women to migrate outside of family oversight, and the role of the nation in protecting its female citizens. This form of abolitionism serves as a warning to contemporary activists to pay attention to the collateral damage caused by stricter border controls. It reminds activists of the way that white supremacy was woven into the warp and weft of earlier anti-trafficking efforts and suggests that anti-trafficking efforts must consider the racial impacts of any carceral policy proposals to ensure that white supremacy is not threaded through them. Finally, it urges activists to prioritize listening to the voices of those they are trying to "protect."

---

[79] Siobhán McGrath and Fabiola Mieres, "Mapping the Politics of National Rankings in the Movement Against 'Modern Slavery'," in *Popular and Political Representations: Beyond Trafficking and Slavery Short Course*, Volume 1, ed. Joel Quirk and Julia O'Connell Davidson (London: openDemocracy, 2015), 102–107.

[80] Wendy Chapkis, "Trafficking, Migration and the Law: Protecting Innocents, Punishing Immigrants," *Gender & Society* 17, no. 6 (December 2003): 923–937; Julia O'Connell Davidson, "New Slaveries, Old Binaries: Human Trafficking and the Borders of Freedom," *Global Networks* 10, no. 2 (2010): 244–261; Elena Shih, "Not in My 'Backyard Abolitionism': Vigilante Rescue against American Sex Trafficking," *Sociological Perspectives* 59, no. 1 (2016): 66–90.

6

Mexico's New Slavery

A Critique of Neo-abolitionism to Combat Human Trafficking (la trata de personas)

Grace Peña Delgado

6.1 INTRODUCTION

Neo-abolitionists decry 40 million people living as slaves in the world today. The figure, they claim, exceeds the number of chattels seized from Africa during the transatlantic slave trade. Freeing today's slaves demands no less than the shared efforts of private citizens and corporate philanthropists to fight the international traffic in persons. To rouse public support for their cause, neo-abolitionists reach backwards in time to invoke analogies to old slaveries, to the ignominy of chattel slavery, and the horror of white slavery. Without equivocation, the wrongs of slaveries past map reflexively onto new forms of exploitation including prostitution. Assertions of similarities between contemporary human trafficking and transatlantic slavery by John Miller, the former Director of the US State Department's Office to Monitor and Combat Trafficking in Persons under George W. Bush, are commonplace. "Trafficking in persons is a euphemism; what we are really talking about is the slave trade," exhorts Miller. "Today we talk about forced laborers or sometimes the phrase sex worker – a work that research shows 80 to 90 percent of people want to escape from. It is important to call it by its real name: slavery."[1] Abolitionists call for the rescue and redemption of trafficking victims. And those most vulnerable to contemporary slavery – poor women,

---

[1] John R. Miller, "The Call for a 21st-Century Abolitionist Movement," *Intercultural Human Rights Law Review*, vol. 1, 41–42 (2006): 37–42. For a later iteration of Miller's speech with modifications to this quote, see John R. Miller, "Human Trafficking? Call It What It Is: Slavery," *Wilson Quarterly*, Summer 2008, accessed May 21, 2019, https://wilsonquarterly.com/quarterly/summer-2008-saving-the-world/.

immigrants, and children – require strong border safeguards and forceful laws against traffickers.[2]

Neo-abolitionists' international movement to fight contemporary slavery produces results. In 2000, the United Nations passed the Protocol to Prevent, Suppress and Punish Trafficking in Persons, Especially Women and Children, one of three supplementary protocols of the United Nations Convention against Transnational Organized Crime. The anti-trafficking law, referred to as the Palermo Protocol or the Trafficking Protocol, encouraged neo-abolitionists to re-channel prior nationally centered efforts into transnationally coordinated campaigns to mount an international crusade against modern day slavery. With few exceptions worldwide, neo-abolitionists mobilized otherwise rival organizations and political parties into influential, coalition-based, global activism against contemporary slavery, whose conditions, they stress, lie in commercial sexual exchange, debt bondage, and child sex tourism. Modern day abolitionists call on scholars and business leaders to single out and remove slavery from corporate supply chains. They harness energies of university students to rescue and redeem sexual slaves from the clutches of madams or pimps. Neo-abolitionists encourage corporate philanthropists to use investments and profits "to fight slavery, not feed slavery."[3] Modern day slavery, a phenomenon that is neither defined nor recognized in international law, has never faced such a formidable foe.

In Mexico, neo-abolitionism is the principal framework to combat human trafficking (*trata de personas*) as modern day slavery.[4] Mexican neo-abolitionists like their counterparts in the United States, Great Britain, and Argentina, summon images and historical references to the transatlantic slave trade even as an understanding of slavery bears little resemblance to its definition in international law as the control of persons as property. Nor do today's abolitionists puzzle over the manner in which

---

[2] UN General Assembly, United Nations Convention against Transnational Organized Crime resolution / adopted by the General Assembly, January 8, 2001, A/RES/55/25, accessed August 25, 2019, www.refworld.org/docid/3b00f55b0.html.

[3] CorpTrav, "Corporate Social Responsibility: The Code and Human Trafficking," accessed May 17, 2019, www.corptrav.com/about-us/corporate-social-responsibility/global-initiative-to-fight-human-trafficking/.

[4] For similar conclusions see *Hispanics in Philanthropy*, "Una mirada desde la organizaciones de la Sociedad civil a la Trata de Personas en Mexico," 14, 28; Marta Lamas, "Feminismo y prostitución: la persistencia de una amarga disputa," *Debate Feminista* 51 (2016); and Jiménez Luz Del Carmen Portilla, "Apuntes sobre la emergencia del régimen antitrata contemporáneo en México," *Kula: Antropólogos del Atlántico Sur. Revista de antropología y ciencias sociales* Num. 17 (Diciembre 2017): 38–55.

states extended the right of ownership of people to those who were politically free and racially white. Neo-abolitionists disregard the international definition of slavery to draw a faulty analogy between chattel slavery and contemporary human trafficking. On the contrary, a sweeping understanding of "trafficking as modern day slavery" is customary discourse among neo-abolitionists, including those in Mexico. "But human trafficking is now called modern-day slavery for good reason," contends Rosi Orozco, Mexico's most influential abolitionist and co-founder of the Pentecostal Church, Casa Sobre la Roca (House on the Rock) and president of the nongovernmental organization, United Commission Against Trafficking (*Comisión Unidos Vs. Trata*). "It is slavery, quite simply. It involves people who are chronically abused and have no ability to stop it."[5] As a member of the Mexican Chamber of Deputies under the PAN (Partido Acción Nacional or National Action Party) from 2009 to 2012 and president of the Special Commission to Combat Trafficking in Persons, Orozco helped to abrogate Mexico's original national anti-trafficking law (2007) for one that aligned with neo-abolitionism.

In 2012, Mexico's congress passed a neo-abolitionist anti-trafficking law, "The General Law to Prevent, Sanction and Eradicate Crimes of Trafficking in Persons and Protect and Assist Victims of those Crimes" (Ley General Para Prevenir, Sancionar y Erradicar los Delitos en Materia de Trata de Personas y Para la Protección y Asistencia a las Victimas de estos Delitos).[6] Instead of limiting the number of crimes of contemporary slavery by defining exploitation unique to its qualities in Mexico, the law intended a capacious understanding of human trafficking. The General Law promulgated twenty-six crimes. Nine involved sexual matters.[7] Servitude, slavery, the exploitation of the prostitution of others or any other forms of sexual exploitation, labor exploitation, forced begging, and organ trafficking are among the crimes classified as modern day

---

[5] Rebecca Blair, "Mexico Human Rights Activist, Rosi Orozco," *Freedom*, 46, no. 2 (2014), accessed September 15, 2019, www.freedommag.org/issue/201409-under-influence/pro file/rosi-orozco.html.

[6] Cámara de Diputados del H. Congreso de la Unión (2012). Ley General Para Prevenir, Sancionar y Erradicar los Delitos en Materia de Trata de Personas y Para la Protección y Asistencia a las Victimas de estos Delitos, Nueva Ley Diario Oficial 14–06- 2012, Government of Mexico, accessed May 18, 2020, www.gob.mx/cms/uploads/attachment/ file/310904/LEY_GPSEDM_TRATA_19–01-2018.pdf.

[7] Comisión Nacional de los Derechos Humanos (CNDH), Diagnóstico sobre la Situación de la Trata de Personas en México 2019, 12. From hereon referred to as CNDH 2019 Diagnóstico.

slavery.[8] To increase the number of felonies, the General Law eliminated "means" from the definition of human trafficking, thus positioning it against the international definition of human trafficking. While the Palermo Protocol comprehends trafficking as a series of three inter-dependent processes – action, means, and purpose – Mexico's law considers "means" an aggravating, non-essential matter determining a crime of human trafficking. Coercion, force, or abuse of power is unnecessary for a crime of human trafficking.[9] The irrelevance of consent in Mexico's General Law comprehended Articles 13 and 20, "the exploitation of the prostitution of others or other forms of sexual exploitation" as prostitution and prostitution as contemporary slavery.

The elastic usefulness of Mexico's anti-trafficking law has proven to be a political game-changer. Authorization of the measure occurred after a brief debate among customarily discordant political parties. Enforcement of the act took effect soon after its passage. States strengthened their existing trafficking laws or established new regulations to conform to the national law. And these changes fostered new patterns. As the discourse of sex trafficking as modern day slavery took hold, cases prosecuted for sexual exploitation, including prostitution, were on the rise. Neo-abolitionists touted high arrest counts as victories and drew attention to efforts that helped trafficking victims "reach full social reintegration toward a new life."[10] With the benefit of the General Law, although dubious according to labor rights and feminist critics, neo-abolitionism gained traction within anti-feminicide (*feminicidio*) circles as a potential legal instrument to fight gender violence and sexual exploitation. The drift of anti-feminicide politics toward neo-abolitionism,

---

[8] Ley General Para Prevenir, Sancionar y Erradicar los Delitos en Materia de Trata de Personas, Article 10, 7. Exploitation of a person is understood to include: I. Slavery, according with article 11; II. Servitude (Article 12); III. The prostitution of others or any other form of sexual exploitation (Articles 13 and 20); IV. Labor Exploitation (Article 21); Forced Labor (Article 22); forced begging (Article 24); the use of children to commit illicit activities (Article 25); illegal adoption (Article 27); forced marriage (Article 29); organ, tissue, and cell trafficking (Article 30); illicit biomedical experimentation on human being (Article 3).

[9] Scholars are beginning to address Mexico's broad definition of exploitation in its human trafficking law. The seminal essay on the topic is Guadalupe Correa-Cabrera and Arthur Sanders Montandón's "Reforming Mexico's Anti-Trafficking in Persons Legislation," *Mexican Law Review* 11, no. 1 (2018): 3–30, 6.

[10] Rita Maria Mellado-Prince Contreras, Legal Representative of the United Commission vs. Trata to Alejandro Angeles, n.d., editor of Forbes Mexico Digital Communication Media, accessed May 18, 2020, https://cdn.forbes.com.mx/2019/06/Respuesta-FORBES-en-li%CC%81nea.pdf.

although incomplete, departed from customary feminist advocacy of labor and sex worker rights for greater individual freedoms, including the right to migrate across national borders despite prospective risks. As Mexico's anti-trafficking law made analogous any circumstance or practice of force, violence, and exploitation to the withholding of human freedom, it provoked a familiar debate – although an unusual one for Mexico – over prostitution as sexual violence reminiscent of the Anglo-European Sex Wars of the mid-1970s through the 1980s. By 2012, feminists allied with neo-abolitionists in an atypical union to oppose sexual exploitation (read prostitution) as gender violence. This stance put neo-abolitionists and feminists at odds with the time-honored system of licensed prostitution and longstanding support for labor and sex workers' rights.

In this chapter, I examine why neo-abolitionism took hold in Mexican politics at the turn of the twenty-first century, even as anti-prostitution movements intermittently surfaced in civil society from the early twentieth century. While there might be other reasons to account for this, my explanation rests in the alignment of neo-abolitionism with the culturally conservative ideals of the then ruling party, the PAN, to effectuate a federal trafficking law that criminalized prostitution as modern day slavery. It was during the presidency of Felipe Calderón Hinojosa (2006–2012) that political space turned decisively against feminist advocacy and toward the expansion of rule-of-law measures to construe human trafficking as a lucrative enterprise of transnational organized crime. New abolitionists leveraged their political clout to legislate Calderón's view that human trafficking was modern day slavery into federal law. Coupling human trafficking to organized crime brokered a new alliance between Calderón and President George W. Bush based on mutual national security interests. In such a reconfiguration, combating transnational organized crime linked Mexican and US rule-of-law efforts and harsher border controls to anti-trafficking efforts. In fulfillment of the neo-abolitionist discourse of "human trafficking as prostitution and prostitution as modern day slavery," the Mexican state superimposed national security measures to quell drug war violence onto sex workers and immigrants.

***

It took neo-abolitionism several decades to ascend to a place of authority in Mexican national politics. Abolitionist movements demanding an end to transatlantic slavery, and thereafter to suppress the white-slave traffic, did not take hold in Mexico as energetically as they had in British North America or Europe. This is significant. In 1829, Mexico banned chattel slavery and strengthened its abolitionist stance by allowing fugitive slaves from the American South entry into Mexico without reprisal. In the same vein, calls by self-defined "new abolitionists" to end white slavery did not circulate in Mexico as widely as they had in nations with large numbers of southern and eastern European immigrants, purportedly the agents of white-slave traffic. Other forces prevented a national movement from taking hold. Before 1931, Mexico was not a member of the League of Nations and therefore did not pursue abolitionism of prostitution as a part of an international effort to quash white-slave traffic. Nor did a national anti-white slavery campaign originate within Mexico to press for laws against the supposed traffic. From the mid-nineteenth century, tacit and explicit support for controlled prostitution kept neo-abolitionism and its followers in abeyance until the early twenty-first century.

Prostitution regulation began during the French occupation of Mexico (1861–1867) with the Reglamento para el Ejercicio de la Prostitución (Regulations for the Practice of Prostitution). The Reglamento's chief aim was to set up a regime of public prostitution by controlling the spread of venereal disease among *mujeres públicas* (public women or female prostitutes) through increased government intervention, surveillance, and medicalization. Under this regulatory scheme, *mujeres públicas* bore the full burden of disease prophylaxis by submitting to compulsory registration with social hygiene authorities and regular medical inspections for venereal disease. If social hygienists discovered a contagion, mandatory hospitalization of the sex worker followed until they effectuated invisible manifestations of the disease.[11]

Regulated prostitution reinforced existing social divisions of class and gender by holding to a sexual double standard. The belief upheld the idea that male sexual infidelity was a venial sin, while female sexual desire outside of marriage was an aberrant and unforgivable transgression. In the Americas and Europe, the French system provided a culturally acceptable but morally contemptuous alternative to infidelity and homosexuality to preserve

[11] Fernanda Nunez-Becerra, *Prostitución y su repression en la ciudad de México siglo XIX* (Barcelona: Gedisa Editorial, SA, 2002), 17–19; Katherine Elaine Bliss, *Compromised Positions: Public Health and Gender Politics in Revolutionary Mexico City* (University Park: Pennsylvania State University Press, 2001), 27–28.

Mexican middle- and upper-class family honor and female chastity. Regulation likewise functioned as a colonial technology in French-occupied Mexico by providing military troops with steady access to inspected prostitutes. When Great Britain passed the Contagious Diseases (CD) Acts (1864, 1866, and 1869), they relied on portions of the French system of prostitution control. But unlike in Mexico, state-sanctioned prostitution ended following an abolitionist crusade to repeal the CD Acts in 1886.[12] There was no such campaign in Mexico. In fact, a double standard of morality – or as the neo-abolitionist Josephine Butler observed for Great Britain, "prostitution for women ... and vice minus disease for men" – prevailed in Mexico into the late-twentieth century. A nascent labor and sex workers' rights movement recognized and countered the double standard of morality by rejecting prostitution as a "social evil" and advancing laws against police provocation and *clandestina* (streetwalker)-violence.[13]

Mexico's regime of controlled prostitution stood virtually untouched by the global movement against white slavery which promoted national abolition of commercial sex. The outcry to end the traffic in white slaves (the phenomenon did not account for women of color) fueled a series of conferences on "*La traite des Blanches*" that European states and kingdoms attended with near exclusiveness. No Latin America nation, except for Brazil, took part in these meetings or the follow-up conference in Paris in 1904. At this convention, representatives first defined "traffic" as a process of "procuring of women or girls for immoral purposes abroad" and cast it as a lamentable outcome of global migration.[14] An ethos of

---

[12] The CD Acts, initially an experimental and temporary piece of legislation aimed at preventing the spread of venereal diseases among British soldiers, became permanent legislation to regulate prostitution in many parts of the United Kingdom by 1869. For a full discussion of the campaign to repeal the CD Acts see Judith Walkowitz, *Prostitution and Victorian Society: Women, Class and the State* (Cambridge: Cambridge University Press, 1980); and Paul McHugh, *Prostitution and Victorian Social Reform* (London: Croom Helm, 1980).

[13] Abolitionism had its least impact in northern border towns where *zonas de tolerancia* were commonplace. Abolitionism had its greatest impact in Mexico City, the nation's largest urban center after 1940. In that year, municipal officials began to close the city's 118 brothels, arrested dissenting madams, and in the end, displaced over 1,500 women from their one-room cribs where the exchange of money for sex had been a legitimate transaction of the sex market. The quote is modified from Josephine Butler's original to the Federation Conference at Neuchatel, *The Shield*, October 21, 1882, 195. The full quote is "Their system is to obtain prostitution plus slavery for women, and vice minus disease for men!"

[14] International Agreement for the Suppression of the White Slave Traffic, May 18, 1904, 35 Stat. 1979, art. 1, 83.

strong policing animated the 1904 Agreement and encouraged states to set up a central reporting authority to receive and share information on foreign pimps and prostitutes with interested parties. To protect immigrant women and girls against procurers, officials called for greater vigilance at border entry points, railway stations, and on ships.[15] The 1910 International Congress for the Suppression of the White Slave Traffic took up these same measures, but added the elements of force, violence, and intimidation to the definition of the traffic in white slaves.[16] Twenty-two European countries and Brazil signed the 1910 accord while Chile, Colombia, Cuba, and Uruguay were among several nations that later agreed to the Convention.[17] Mexico was not among the nations to sign or agree to the 1910 Convention. Until 1931, Great Britain and the United States refused to recognize its revolutionary government and therefore blocked its membership in the League of Nations.[18] In 1956 – and as a member of the United Nations – Mexico adopted the 1904 International Agreement for the Suppression of the White Slave Traffic and 1910 International Congress for the Suppression of the White Slave Traffic.[19]

Despite Mexico's adherence to international agreements, the commerce in sex thrived in *zonas de tolerancia* (zones of tolerance) even after President Lazaro Cardenas abolished the Reglamento in 1940. "In the end," argues the historian Katherine Bliss, "abolition did not really redeem ... prostitutes or their clients [and] programs that promised to align gender relations neither resolved the problem of female prostitution."[20] Regulated sexual commerce at the state and local levels

---

[15] League of Nations, Protection of Women and Children, White Slave Traffic, Record Group 25, Box, 1403, file no. 1925–82, 35, Library and Archives of Canada, Ottawa, Canada.

[16] International Convention for the Suppression of the White Slave Traffic, art. 2, May 4, 1910, 211 Consol. T.S. 45, 1912, Great Britain, Treaty Series. No. 20.

[17] Ibid., chapter 7.

[18] Manley O. Hudson, "Mexico's Admission to Membership in the League of Nations," *The American Journal of International Law* 26, no. 1 (January 1932): 114–117.

[19] Convención para la Represión de la Trata de Personas y de la Explotación de la Prostitución Ajena, adoptada en la Organización de las Naciones Unidas, Diario Oficial de Federación (DOF) 19 de junio de 1956. Also see Flérida Guzmán Gallangos, in "La política y el gasto para la trata de personas: una aproximación a la perspectiva de genero," in Rostros diversos de la trata de personas en México: Situaciones presentes y potenciales de las mujeres, niñas, niños y adolescentes, ed. Rodolfo Casillas R. Report by the Commission on Equity and Gender, Chamber of Deputies, LX Legislature, Mexico City, Mexico, 2009, 250–251.

[20] Bliss, *Compromised Positions*, 207.

continued, and by the late 1970s, an emergent sex workers' rights movement materialized to support intimate commerce.[21] At the center of this advocacy was a defense of sexual choice as labor rights, claims made by activists who likewise sold sex for money.[22] By itself, advocates insisted, prostitution was not an act of violence against women. They claimed, instead, that instances of coercion and abuse by clients often took place in unmonitored work zones. Individual choice operating within an expanded scope of labor rights and sexual freedom held sway even as conflicting viewpoints advocated for the eradication and criminalization of the same actions.

Tensions remained between sex workers' rights activists and culturally conservative groups who supported abolition as part of a broader moral agenda. But these conflicts did not influence Mexican feminism nor did they cleave into pro- or anti-prostitution lobbies as they had for second-wave western feminists during the so-called Sex Wars debates. The Sex Wars, an exchange of scholarly debates waged outside of Mexico and Latin America in the mid-1970s through the late 1980s, divided women's rights advocates in the Anglophone world into two structured positions: one held by radical feminists who viewed prostitution as sexual slavery and constitutive of patriarchy; and the other, among self-identified sex-positive feminists who embraced alternative sexualities to subvert patriarchy and pursue greater sexual freedom.[23] For radical feminists, the

---

[21] Marta Lamas argues that abolition during the mid-twentieth century differed from the meaning it holds today – that is, the practice of prostitution is criminalized under such regimes. In the mid-century context of Mexico, abolition meant the canceling of state-granted permits or inspection of sex workers. The state also divorced itself from the business of commercial sex by not keeping a registration book of prostitutes or by continuing medical inspections and social hygiene maintenance in brothels. Lamas, *El fulgor de la noche, El comercio sexual en las calles de la Ciudad de México* (Oceano: Mexico City, 2007), 18–19. Sophie Day also makes this point in "The Reemergence of 'Trafficking': Sex Work Between Slavery and Freedom," *Journal of Royal Anthropological Institute* 16, no. 4 (December 2010): 816–834.

[22] For a discussion on the history of sex workers' rights movement see Elvira Madrid Romero, Jaime Montejo, and Rosa Icela Madrid, "Trabajadores sexuales conquistan derechos laborles," *Debate Feminista* 50 (October 2014): 137–159, 147.

[23] For purposes of capturing the Sex Wars lobbies that roughly comprised three approaches, I have somewhat collapsed the views of "pro-positive sex feminism" and "anti-sex feminism" into the category of "radical feminism" following the work of Bernadette Barton, "Dancing on the Möbius Strip: Challenging the Sex War Paradigm," *Gender and Society* 16, no. 5 (October 2002): 585–602. Over time, scholars have assigned various labels in mostly binary fashion to describe the Sex Wars lobbies. For Sex Positive Feminists vs. Anti-Sex Work or Abolitionists, see Kari Lerum, "Twelve-Step Feminism Makes Sex Workers Sick: How the State and the Recovery Movement Turn Radical

prostitute was a "sex object" – a woman formed through sexual violence. Prostitution negated free will, making consent in transactional sex impossible.[24] In contrast, sex-positive feminists considered sex work as "erotic labor" and an act of sexual autonomy and experimentation.[25] They emphasized the agency of the sex worker who operated within structures of unequal power and male privilege over constructions of her as a victim of male oppression.[26]

In Mexico, though, the Sex Wars debate was of minor purchase. As the anthropologist and social theorist Marta Lamas points out, "[Mexican] feminists have not confronted one another in 'wars' like the 'Sex Wars,' at least not with the force and publicity elsewhere."[27] Although Lamas attributes the near-absence of the debate to the legality of prostitution and to a "less puritanical culture in Mexico," in actuality what slowed the Sex Wars divisions from overtaking feminist discourse and activism was the historical regime of regulated prostitution and an attendant sex workers' rights movement. By 2007, state-sanctioned prostitution fell under closer scrutiny. The soaring discourse of "human trafficking as prostitution and prostitution as modern day slavery" triggered feminists into reconsidering the relationship between sexual commerce and exploitation, and to see the utility of anti-trafficking law as a potential legal instrument to combat gender violence.

***

Women Into 'Useless Citizens'," *Sexuality & Culture* 2 (1998): 7–36; and for three descriptive categories, Pro-'Positive' Feminism, Anti-Sex Feminism, and Sex Radical Feminism, see Maggie O'Neill, *Prostitution and Feminism: Towards a Politics of Feeling* (Cambridge: Polity Press, 2001), 23–24.

[24] Andrea Dworkin, *Intercourse* (New York: Free Press, 1987); and Catherine MacKinnon, *Feminism Unmodified: Discourses on Life and Law* (Cambridge: Harvard University Press, 1987).

[25] Gayle Rubin, "Thinking Sex: Notes for a Radical Theory of the Politics of Sexuality," in *American Feminist Thought at Century's End: A Reader*, ed. L. S. Kaufmann (Cambridge: Blackwell Press), 143–179; Patrick Califia, "Feminism vs. Sex: A Neo-Conservative Wave," *Advocate*, February 21, 1980; and Wendy Chapkis, *Live Sex Acts: Women Performing Erotic Behavior* (New York: Routledge, 1998).

[26] Min Lui, "Human Trafficking and Feminist Debates: Feminist Debates on Human Trafficking," in *Migration, Prostitution, and Human Trafficking the Voice of Chinese Women*, ed. Min Liu (New Brunswick: Transaction Publishers, 2011), 37–39; and Alison Phipps, "Sex Wars Revisited: A Rhetorical Economy of Sex Industry Opposition," *Journal of International Women's Studies* 18, no. 4 (2017): 306–320, 307.

[27] Marta Lamas, "Feminismo y prostitución: la persistencia de una amarga disputa," *Debate Feminista* no. 51 (2016): 18–35, 28; and Prostitución, trabajo o trata? Por un debate sin prejuicios, *Debate Feminista* no. 50 (2014): 160–186.

Neo-Abolitionism emerged as a significant force in national politics during Mexico's militarized campaign against organized crime under the presidential administrations of Vicente Fox Quesada (2000–2006) and Felipe Hinojosa Calderón (2006–2012). The landmark 2000 presidential election, which ended the seventy-one-year political monopoly of the PRI (Partido Revolucionario Institucional or Institutional Revolutionary Party), raised expectations that the PAN-led government would champion the culturally conservative causes of the religious community. The newly elected president, Vicente Fox, who enjoyed widespread support among moderate Catholics and corporate and media magnates, did not disrupt this important PAN political constituency. During Fox's administration, hostility toward feminist advocacy intensified as they called for increased social services for reproductive health, the legalization of abortion, and an end to gender violence for which feminists held the state responsible.[28]

Under the succeeding president, Felipe Calderón (2006–2012), PAN's commitment to conservative morality strengthened and the marginalization of feminist advocacy furthered. Calderón, a former energy secretary under Fox and a member of the Christian Democrats in his youth, leveraged ultra-right support for a protracted military-led offensive against drug trafficking organizations. At the same time, Calderón pursued a conservative cultural agenda. Militarization and state-sanctioned violence against drug cartels ensued even as feminists among others denounced the ravaging of communities brought on by armed aggression. As they had under Fox, feminists continued to unleash opposition to the failure of the state to eradicate gender violence. Feminists implicated neoliberalism for producing conditions of extreme vulnerability for working-class women and immigrants and insisted upon governmental policies

---

[28] The term "feminicidio" is attributed to Marcela Lagarde y los Rios. See "Por la Vida y Libertad de las Mujeres. Fin al Feminicidio." *Fem* 28, no. 255 (2004): 26–24 and "Preface: Feminist Keys for Understanding Feminicide: Theoretical, Political, and Legal Construction," in *Terrorizing Women: Feminicide in the Americas*, eds. Rosa-Linda Fregoso and Cynthia Bejarano (Durham: Duke University Press, 2010), xi–xxv. For a discussion of the Pan-feminist tensions, see Tania Hernandez Vicencio, "El Partido Acción Nacional y la democracia cristiana," *Perfiles Latinoamericanos* 37 (enero–junio 2011): 128–129, 113–138; and Tania Hernández Vicencio, "Avances y retos del Partido Acción Nacional," *Espiral* 10, no. 28 (September–December 2003): 57–61, 47–85. On the early fight to end femicide see, Julia Estela Monárrez Fragoso, "La cultura del feminicidio en Ciudad Juarez, 1993–1999," *Revista Frontera Norte* 12, no. 23 (2000): 87–117; and for femicide globally see, Dora Inés Munévar M. , "Delito de femicidio. Muerte violenta de mujeres por razones de género," *Estudios Socio-Jurídicos* 14, no. 1 (January–June 2012): 135–175.

to remedy deep gender inequality, including ending the culture of feminicide and the crime itself.

At approximately the same time, Mexico ratified the Palermo Protocol and committed its national legislative body to create new criminal categories and to develop a federal-level prosecutorial framework to prevent, investigate, and prosecute trafficking crimes. Ideological differences between Fox allies, feminists, and PAN chamber deputies (congresspersons) somewhat quiesced in the face of widespread public support for passing national-level anti-trafficking laws. As Mexican officials and members of civil society prepared to enact an interim anti-trafficking law, international-based diagnoses of the problem of human trafficking in their nation emerged. The US State Department's Trafficking in Persons Report (US TIP Report) identified Mexico to be "a source, transit, and destination country for persons trafficked for sexual exploitation and labor" and framed human trafficking in Mexico as a problem of forced labor migration and sex trafficking that originated in undocumented migration from Eastern Europe and Central America.[29] The report likewise noted the high incidence of female and child migrants from those same areas transferred into the Mexican sex trade. Apart from Eastern European countries, 16,000–20,000 child victims of sex trafficking from Central America and Mexico comprised a thriving sex tourism industry located mostly at northern border towns, resort cities, and in large metropolitan areas. Without formal legal protections, foreign-born victims of human trafficking, irrespective of age or gender, received no shelter or government help. Deportations occurred.

American officials did not hesitate to criticize Mexico for these failings. "[By] lacking a comprehensive anti-trafficking law, Mexico has no national law enforcement strategy to address human trafficking," the TIP Report stated. "Much more needs to be done." For its perceived lackluster record, the US State Department downgraded Mexico to its Tier 2 Watch List.[30] This status categorized Mexico as a country whose government did not follow minimum standards to combat human

---

[29] United States Department of State, *U.S. Department of State 2004 Trafficking in Persons Report – Mexico* (Washington, DC: US State Department, 2004), accessed December 13, 2019, www.refworld.org/docid/4680d82818.html.

[30] Ibid. Mexico remained a Tier 2 Watch List nation until 2008, a year after the passage of its first national anti-trafficking bill. United States Department of State, *U.S. Department of State 2008 Trafficking in Persons Report – Mexico* (Washington, DC: US State Department, 2008), accessed May 18, 2020, https://2009–2017.state.gov/j/tip/rls/tiprpt/2008/index.htm.

trafficking as established by the US Trafficking Victims Protection Act of 2000 (TVPA). Had it been a Tier 3 country, that is, a nation whose government did not adhere to US guidelines to fight trafficking, the withholding of non-humanitarian aid would have occurred and American authorities would have instructed developmental banks and the International Monetary Fund to take the same action. Tier 1 nations meet with the TVPA's minimum standards against human trafficking.

In December 2004, under such pressures but with the help of representatives of civil society organizations and international agencies, PRI senators in a rare alliance with PAN party members issued a draft decree, "Protocol to Prevent and Punish Trafficking in Persons, Especially Women and Children."[31] This pronouncement put in place a provisional legal framework to define, investigate, and punish the crime of human trafficking (*trata de personas*). Several civil society organizations and individual members from the Inter-American Commission of Women of the Organization of American States, the Regional Coalition Against Trafficking in Women and Girls in Latin America and the Caribbean (CATWLAC), the Mexican National Human Rights Commission (CNDH), and the International Organization for Migration (IOM) assisted officials during this transition period. To prepare for national-level anti-trafficking legislation, officials focused on sharpening relevant federal penal codes and strengthened existing state-level measures addressing organized crime and forced prostitution. But as Mexican officials proceeded, they did not consider the implications of prior UN decisions over prostitution for its national context.[32] In the final version of the

---

[31] Mexico was among 147 signatories to adopt the Palermo Protocol in 2000. In 2003, the Palermo Convention was ratified thus paving the way for signatories to officially pass their own national anti-trafficking laws. Secretaría de Gobernación. Decreto promulgatorio del Protocolo para prevenir, reprimir y sancionar la trata de personas, especialmente mujeres y niños, que complementa la Convención de las Naciones Unidas contra la delincuencia organizada transnacional, adoptado por la asamblea general de las Naciones Unidas 2003: Diario Oficial de la Federación, 2003, accessed May 18, 2020, www.dof.gob.mx /nota_detalle.php?codigo=697012&fecha=10/04/2003. The anti-trafficking protocol was signed as one of three components of the Convention against Transnational Organized Crime, which Mexico also signed. The others were the Protocol against the Smuggling of Migrants by Land, Sea and Air and the Protocol against the Illicit Manufacturing of and Trafficking in Firearms, their Parts and Components and Ammunition.

[32] Articles 206 and 206 BIS of the Federal Criminal Code (Código Penal Federal) were amended on June 12, 2003. These two articles address smuggling and trafficking, but do not distinguish between the two crimes. Nuevo Código Publicado, Diario Oficial de la Federación, August 14, 1931, last reformed June 21, 2018, Chapter 6, Procuring and Trafficking in Persons, 58.

Palermo Protocol, UN negotiators rejected the binary perspectives redolent in the Sex Wars debate: that prostitution was an act of individual consent or sexual slavery. Negotiators, instead, determined human trafficking in capacious terms as "the exploitation of the prostitution of others," "other forms of sexual exploitation," "the abuse of power," or "a position of vulnerability." In the absence of a precise view of human trafficking, the Palermo Protocol left Mexico and other signatory parties to puzzle through the meaning of exploitation, abuse, and vulnerability for itself.[33]

Hastened by United States and domestic pressures to set up an anti-trafficking interim law, Mexico's 2004 draft decree adopted the Palermo Protocol's definition of human trafficking as a process involving three interdependent elements – action (what is done), means (how it is done), and purpose (why it is done). Each component is necessary to make up a crime of human trafficking, except in cases involving children where consent of the minor-age victim is always irrelevant.

'Trafficking in persons' shall mean the recruitment, transportation, transfer, harboring or receipt of persons, by means of the threat or use of force or other forms of coercion, of abduction, of fraud, of deception, of the abuse of power or of a position of vulnerability or of the giving or receiving of payments or benefits to achieve the consent of a person having control over another person, for the purpose of exploitation. Exploitation shall include, at a minimum, the exploitation of the prostitution of others or other forms of sexual exploitation, forced labor or services, slavery or practices similar to slavery, servitude or the removal of organs.

The consent of a victim of trafficking in persons to the intended exploitation set forth in subparagraph [a] of this article shall be irrelevant where any of the means set forth in subparagraph [a] have been used.

The recruitment, transportation, transfer, harboring or receipt of a child [defined as under eighteen years of age] for the purpose of exploitation shall be considered 'trafficking in persons' even if this does not involve any of the means set forth in subparagraph [a] of this article.[34]

---

[33] Jo Doezema, "Now You See Her, Now You Don't: Sex Workers at the UN Trafficking Protocol Negotiations," *Social and Legal Studies* 14, no. 1 (2005): 61–89, 66–67; and for a deft discussion on UN lobbies, the prostitution question, and the UN protocols see Anne Gallagher, "Human Rights and the Neo- UN Protocols on Trafficking and Migrant Smuggling: A Preliminary Analysis," *Human Rights Quarterly* 23, no. 4 (2001): 975–1004, 985–987.

[34] Article 3, UN General Assembly, Protocol to Prevent, Suppress and Punish Trafficking in Persons, Especially Women and Children, Supplementing the United Nations Convention against Transnational Organized Crime, November 15, 2000, accessed August 25, 2019, www.refworld.org/docid/4720706c0.html.

In adopting the international definition of human trafficking in its draft decree legislation, Mexican law remained consistent with a global language that defined human trafficking as a complex tripartite crime that victimizes persons irrespective of age, sex, and national origin through coercion. When Mexico ratified the Palermo Protocol, it likewise inherited the convention's framework connecting human trafficking as an outcome of organized crime. As a result, Mexico privileged criminal justice solutions and border-security strategies through militarization to exact severe punishment on sex-traffickers and prostitutes. Criminalization and militarization channeled "rescued victims" to human rights organizations for their rehabilitation.[35]

The interim anti-trafficking law remained intact until Mexico replaced it with its first national-level anti-trafficking legislation in 2007, the Law to Prevent and Punish Trafficking in Persons (Ley para Prevenir y Sancionar la Trata de Personas). But this law did not come into force until February 2009, beset by many delays. It integrated several of the elements of the draft decree of 2004, including the three-part definition of human trafficking suggestive of the Palermo Protocol, adding organ trafficking to its list of crimes.

The crime of trafficking in persons is committed by anyone who promotes, solicits, offers, facilitates, procures, transfers, delivers or receives, for himself or for a third party, a person, by *means* [author's emphasis] of physical or moral violence, deceit or the abuse of power to subject him to sexual exploitation, forced labor or services, slavery or practices similar to slavery, or the removal of an organ, tissue or components thereof.[36]

When this crime is committed against people under the age of eighteen years old, or against those who are not capable of comprehending the significance of the act committed, or those who are not capable of resisting it, the verification of the means of trafficking will not be required.[37]

In addition, Mexico's anti-trafficking laid out harsh penalties to those who victimized minors or those with diminished capacity to resist. It is worthwhile noting that the legislative text of Mexico's first anti-trafficking law comprised ten pages, brief when measured against the comprehensive

---

[35] Ezeta, Fernanda y Monica Salazar, *Consecuencias invisibles del rescate. El caso del Table dance* (México: Colectivo contra la Trata de Personas, A.C., 2005), 45–47; and Janie A. Chuang, "Rescuing Trafficking from Ideological Capture: Prostitution Reform and Antitrafficking Law and Policy," *University of Pennsylvania Law Review*, 158 (2010): 1655–1728.

[36] Article 5, Chapter II, "Of the Crime of Human Trafficking," The Law to Prevent and Punish Trafficking in Persons, 3.

[37] Ibid.

mandate for UN signatory states. Even so, the legislation was significant. It placed the crime of human trafficking in Mexican federal law for the first time, thus allowing for the prosecution and punishment of the crime to occur. The legislation likewise granted the president the authority to create an Inter-secretarial Commission, an agency responsible for institutionalizing a national anti-trafficking program, including facilitating public policies aimed at prevention and punishment of trafficking crimes and protection for victims of the crime. To aid the Commission, Mexican officials reauthorized several organizations to continue anti-trafficking efforts. The Commission reinstalled the 2004 Program to Support Victims of Human Trafficking or PROTEJA (Programa de Apoyo a Victimas de Trata de Persons), a binational, anti-TIP shelter project funded by USAID (United States Agency for International Development).[38] Importantly, the Bush Administration agency required the eradication of prostitution for USAID grantees. To receive funding, recipients must have in place an official policy opposing prostitution and sex trafficking. They must also conform to the policy "Prohibition on the Promotion and Advocacy of the Legalization or Practice of Prostitution or Sex Trafficking," colloquially known as "The Prostitution Pledge."[39] USAID, through its support of several key agencies including PROTEJA, regularly assisted Mexico's anti-trafficking efforts. Through PROTEJA, American officials reinforced the perspective that prostitution is a crime of human trafficking.[40]

Over the next four years, confusion and ineffective enforcement foiled Mexico's original anti-trafficking law. Mostly, the meaning of exploitation and the crimes recognized as human trafficking perplexed lawmakers at the state level. The lack of clarity led to uneven enforcement throughout the country. To make matters worse, only 19 states out of the 32 including the Federal District created a specific anti-trafficking law, and of these, just 6 passed special measures on prevention and protection of victims.[41] Social conservatives, mainly Catholics and evangelical Christians, key constituencies in Calderón's election to the presidency,

---

[38] Article 5, Chapter III, De la Política Criminal del Estado Mexicano en materia de prevención y sanción de la Trata de Personas, 5.

[39] Ronald Weitzer, "Movimiento para criminalizar el trabajo sexual en Estados Unidos," *Debate Feminista* No. 50 (2014): 187–219, 193.

[40] Jiménez Portilla, "Apuntes sobre la emergencia," 45.

[41] Seven states (21.88 percent) lack legislation on trafficking: Aguascalientes, Baja California Sur (typifies it as not serious in the penal code), Campeche, Chihuahua, Colima, Guanajuato and Zacatecas. Oficina de las Naciones Unidas contra la Droga y el Delito, Diagnóstico Nacional sobre la Situación de Trata de Personas en México (México: 2015), 36.

leveraged the inconsistent enforcement of Mexico's initial anti-trafficking legislation to push for its replacement. Their alternative vision coincided with neo-abolitionism and aligned with Calderón's understanding of human trafficking in his National Development Plan, 2007–2012 (PND). In the PND, Calderón defined human trafficking as slavery and one among many wrongs, including the trafficking of arms and drugs, at the center of transnational organized crime activity.[42]

In 2012, Mexico abrogated its first anti-trafficking law replacing it with a new anti-trafficking law, the General Law to Prevent, Punish and Eradicate Crimes in Trafficking in Persons and for the Protection and Assistance to Victims of these Crimes (Ley General para Prevenir, Sancionar y Erradicar los Delitos Materia de Trata de Personas y para la Protección y Asistencia a las Víctimas de estos Delitos). The new law defined human trafficking as modern day slavery, completely transforming the understanding and prosecution of trafficking in persons.[43] The General Law abandoned the international communities' tripartite definition of human trafficking by eliminating means, a way to determine if exploitation had taken place. In the absence of means, it was no longer necessary for prosecutors to prove that force or deception or the abuse of power to gain the consent of a person had occurred to secure a conviction of human trafficking. The third element, purpose, identified eleven categories of exploitation from which twenty-six crimes, nine involving sexual matters, emerged.[44] Human trafficking included slavery, servitude, the prostitution of others or any other form of sexual exploitation, and labor exploitation. The new law likewise introduced punishment for actions approximating human trafficking such as wittingly purchasing sex from a trafficked person and knowingly providing a location used for trafficking activity. Given this enlarged scope of criminality and the elimination of means as one of three internationally established elements that comprises the definition of human trafficking, the General Law opened up countless possibilities in which a person,

---

[42] PND, Estrategia, 15.1, 70.

[43] The 2012 reformed law is entitled Ley General para Prevenir, Sancionar y Erradicar los Delitos en Materia de Trata de Personas y para la Protección y Asistencia a las Víctimas de estos Delitos, Ley para Prevenir y Sancionar la Trata de Personas, Última Reforma, DOF, June 14, 2012. From here on referred to as the General Law.

[44] Comisión Nacional de los Derechos Humanos (CNDH), Diagnóstico sobre la Situación de la Trata de Personas en México 2019, 12. From hereon referred to as CNDH 2019 Diagnóstico.

either as a potential perpetrator or victim, could end up in human trafficking.

The General Law marked the political ascendancy of neo-abolitionism in Mexico. Through both secular and religious activism, neo-abolitionists successfully formed political alliances with the Calderón government and PRI politicians around a shared vision that prostitution is a severe form of exploitation antithetical to human dignity and freedom. Calderón's understanding of and approach to human trafficking, as delineated in his PND, differed considerably from Mexico's existing anti-trafficking law. Calderón not only looked toward militarized solutions to combat human trafficking, he defined it as "the illegal transfer of persons through borders, unregulated procurement, prostitution, pedophilia and child pornography which have given rise to modern versions of slavery and dehumanization, starting with criminal groups who endanger the security of human beings." Human trafficking, in Calderón's view, was modern day slavery and a crime that required international cooperation and a strong national police force to protect Mexicans from cartel violence associated with the crime.

One of the main civic organizations that influenced Calderón and emerged as an important ally once he became president in 2006 was House on the Rock. In 1993, Rosi Orozco and her husband Alejandro Lucas Orozco founded House on the Rock, and with it, built a para-ecclesiastical interdenominational movement of evangelical revivalism based on a theology of prosperity and social action of its members. The church holds family and evangelization as priorities while adhering to a "law of secrecy," an in-group practice that prohibits the sharing of church doctrine to the outside world. House on the Rock is one of Mexico's most prominent mega-churches with an estimated membership of over 17,000 followers whose aim is to influence public policies based on its neo-Pentecostal vision. Calderón and his wife, Margarita Zavala, associate with House on the Rock.[45]

---

[45] Angélica Eliú Patiño Reséndiz, "Religión y Poder: Un estudio sobre el poder político-religioso en la comunidad evangélica. El caso de 'Casa Sobre la Roca,'" (Master's thesis, Autonomous Metropolitan University, Iztapalapa, 2016), 21; and Rodolfo Montes, *La cruzada de Calderón: Su herencia católica, Casa sobre la Roca y el nuevo mapa religioso de México* (New York: Penguin Random House Grupo Editorial México, 2012), 60–62. Several sources confirm the close relationship between the Calderóns and House on the Rock. Among them, Montes, La cruzada de Calderón; nos. 1-6; 18–24; Bernardo Berranco V. "Casa sobre la Roca en Gobernación," *La Jornada* 7 December 7, 2011, accessed May 18, 2020, www.jornada.com.mx/2011/12/07/opinion/027a1pol.

Rosi Orozco's relationship with Calderón and Zavala began through their shared activities at House of the Rock a few years before Calderón became the PAN presidential nominee in 2005. As a regular attendee at House on the Rock events and a purported convert to neo-Pentecostalism, Calderón enjoyed the organizational facility of House on the Rock to mobilize campaigns in support of candidates running for public office. The relationship benefitted Calderón as he was elected president of Mexico in 2006 with robust backing from the Christian right. Rosi Orozco profited as well: she won a seat in the Chamber of Deputies as a PAN member in 2009. Once in office, Orozco laid the groundwork for new anti-trafficking law that aligned with neo-abolitionism and Calderón's vision of human trafficking as slavery.[46] As Calderón was appointed president of the Special Commission to Combat Trafficking in Persons in 2011, Orozco brokered an alliance with PRI deputies to abrogate the existing anti-trafficking law for a new General Law. She also advocated harsher laws governing organized crime.[47] On the day the law went up for a vote in the Mexican Congress, Orozco evoked the memory of Martin Luther King, Jr., in a plea for greater freedom for sex trafficking victims in Mexico. "Today I say to you . . . as Martin Luther King said: we have a dream; it is a dream deeply rooted in the dreams of each of the victims and their families. We have a dream that one day Mexico will rise up and live the true meaning of freedom, of understanding that all men

---

[46] "Que reforma y adiciona diversas disposiciones de la Ley para prevenir y sancionar la Trata de Personas, a cargo de la diputada Rosi Orozco, del Grupo Parlamentario del PAN, Gaceta Parlamentaria, número 2899-II, jueves 26 de noviembre de 2009, accessed May 18, 2020, http://gaceta.diputados.gob.mx/Gaceta/61/2009/nov/20091126-II.html. Orozco's anti-trafficking advocacy began early. When Mexico's first anti-trafficking law took effect in February 2009, Orozco several months later successfully petitioned the Congress to amend the original legislation. Orozco proposed that the Intersecretarial Commission, which had yet to be installed by the President, include a representative from House of Deputies and one from the Senate. Although Orozco's term as PAN Deputy expired before the Commission was installed in 2012, PAN representatives and the neo-abolitionist perspective were well represented on the Commission. Adriana Dávila Fernández, a PAN Senator, remains the Commission's long-standing president having been initially appointed to the post in 2012.

[47] For this alliance see Decreto por el que se expide la Ley General para Prevenir, Sancionar y Erradicar los Delitos en Materia de Trata de Personas y para la Protección y Asistencia a las Víctimas de estos Delitos; y abroga la Ley para Prevenir y Sancionar la Trata de Personas, DOF el 14 de junio de 2012, 1. For Orozco's 2011 advocacy see Que expide la Ley General para prevenir, combatir y sancionar la Trata de Personas; y abroga la Ley para prevenir y sancionar la Trata de Personas. Presentada por la diputada Rosi Orozco, del Grupo Parlamentario del PAN, el 10 de marzo de 2011. Gaceta Parlamentaria, número 2992-11, martes 20 de abril de 2010.

and women are created equal; therefore, human beings cannot be for sale under any circumstance or condition."[48] To elevate the urgency of passing a new anti-trafficking law, Orozco muddled African American civil rights history and placed it alongside an allusion to chattel slavery. Orozco (mis-)appropriated referent history and referent pain and injustice to promote neo-abolitionism in Mexico. In 2012, Mexico passed the General Law and defined human trafficking as slavery.

There are real consequences of neo-abolitionism. Using trafficking law to punish crimes of gender violence spurred feminists into a new discussion about sex workers' rights and prostitution as sexual slavery redolent of the Sex Wars. When the influential scholar-activist Marcela Lagarde contended that prostitution was rape and a human rights violation against women and later coupled it with feminicide, it prompted deliberation about the relationship between contemporary slavery and severe forms of gender violence.[49] To encompass feminicide, though, is an extreme example of the elastic usefulness of Mexico's definition of human trafficking as contemporary slavery. These logics, nonetheless, extended to a suite of governmental organizations originally designated to investigate feminicide. State agencies in Ciudad Juárez for example, broadened their scope of authority to take on cases of trafficking in persons and those linked to gender violence and the disappearance of women. According to the anthropologist Luz Jiménez Portilla, "[t]he institution originally created to deal with feminicide in Ciudad Juárez became the body responsible for dealing with cases of trafficking in persons and those linked to gender violence and the disappearance of women. Thus, the definition of

---

[48] Decreto por el que se expide la Ley General, Capitulo 5, "Dictamen de las Comisiones Unidas de Derechos Humanos, y de Justicia, con proyecto de decreto que expide la Ley General para prevenir, sancionar y erradicar los Delitos en materia de Trata de Personas y para la Protección y Asistencia a las Víctimas de Estos Delitos; abroga la Ley para prevenir y sancionar la Trata de Personas," DOF 27 abril 2012, 5. Orozco has written extensively on abolitionism and rescue. See Orozco with Rita María Mellado-Prince Contreras, "Dignidad y libre desarrollo de la personalidad," *El Cotidiano* (May–June 2018): 9–16; *Una hoja en blanco: Historias de triunfo de sobrevivientes de la trata de personas* (Madrid: Grafo House Publishing, 2019); and *Explotación sexual: Esclavitud Como Negocio Familiar*: Volume 31 (Createspace: 2016); and *Del cielo al infierno en dia* (Mexico City: Ediciones Selectas Diamante: 2011).

[49] Marcela Lagarde, *Los cautiverios de las mujeres: madresposas, monjas, putas, presas y locas* (Universidad Autónoma de México, cuarta edición, 2005, primera reimpresión, 2006); and Marcela Lagarde y de los Ríos, "Preface: Feminist Keys for Understanding Feminicide: Theoretical, Political, and Legal Construction," in *Terrorizing Women: Feminicide in the Américas*, eds. Rosa-Linda Fregoso and Cynthia Bejarano (Durham: Duke University Press, 2010), xvi–xx.

trafficking was equated with other expressions of extreme violence against women."[50] Similarly, the discourse of "human trafficking as prostitution and prostitution as modern day slavery" works to curtail criticism about ever harsher and more violent state controls against the putative twin threats of undocumented migration and sexual slavery from Central America. Even more troubling is the view that measures designed to control and prevent migration from the Northern Triangle (e.g., for-profit immigration detention centers; deportation holding cells) are cast as part of a legitimate effort to protect immigrants from traffickers and thus safeguard their human rights. The paradoxes of neo-abolitionism are clear. According to the sociologist Kamala Kempadoo, New Abolitionism sustains a "double-talk" of condemning modern slavery as a violation of human rights, and in the same breath, continues to call for harsher criminalization measures and immigration restriction to suppress the flow of trafficked persons from crossing into wealthier nations.[51]

***

At present, the long-standing system of regulated prostitution exists along-side, but in tension with, a recent movement promoting its end. For however quickly neo-abolitionism took hold in Felipe Calderón's adminis-tration and continued under his successor, Enrique Peña Nieto, the institu-tion of regulated prostitution remains relatively intact, although beleaguered by constant cultural battles with abolitionists and a cadre of feminists. An ardent defense of sex workers' rights and labor rights prevails in organizations such as Brigada Callejera de Apoyo a la Mujer "Elisa Martínez" A.C. (Street Brigade in Support of Women) and Asociación en Pro Apoyo a Servidores, A.C. (Association in Support of Sex Workers or APROASE) despite official harassment and the indefensible arrests of sex workers' rights advocates for violations of human trafficking law. Under the current president, Andrés Manuel López Obrador, policy-makers are reconsidering the General Law and some are beginning to call for its abrogation. Recent PAN party infighting over allegations of the misuse of public funds and property to assist trafficking victims, especially the public quarrels between Rosi Orozco and the current president of the Inter-Secretarial Commission, Adriana Davíla Fernández, prompted retrospec-tion about unchecked support for programs to rescue and redeem

[50] Jiménez Portilla, "Apuntes sobre la Emergencia," 43–45.
[51] Kamala Kempadoo, *Trafficking and Prostitution Reconsidered: New Perspectives on Migration, Sex Work, and Human Rights* (Boulder: Paradigm Publishers, 2012), xvi.

trafficking victims. Yet, local governance may prove just as critical in settling the political and legal battles over prostitution and human trafficking. Constitutional authority gives Mexico's thirty-one individual states and the Federal District of Mexico City (DF) broad discretion to determine their own policies regarding prostitution and public health safeguards. Likewise, state-level laws afford wide legal latitude to support the regime of regulated prostitution. Tijuana in Baja California, Nuevo Laredo in Tamaulipas, Ciudad Juarez in Chihuahua, and Mexico City are among the most profitable and well-known cities where sex tourism continues to cater to a mostly male clientele from Mexico, the United States, Canada, and Europe. These cities, perhaps not ironically, also accommodate thriving *zonas de tolerancia* and have done so for over a century. If history is instructive, then the lesson is familiar for Mexico: that local-level, time-honored institutions overcome nationally imposed systems of moral control but at substantial human expense.

7

Undermining Labor Power

The False Promise of the Industry-led Antislavery Initiatives

Elena Shih, Jennifer (JJ) Rosenbaum, and Penelope Kyritsis

7.1 INTRODUCTION

The past few decades have seen a sharp and persistent rise in market-based solutions to address contemporary social concerns. Corporations have responded to an increased demand for ethical business practices by adopting commitments and programs that signal their dedication to improving labor rights conditions for the people who are sewing their clothes, picking their cocoa, or cleaning their hotel rooms. These industry-led initiatives – which are commonly understood to fall under the banner of corporate social responsibility (CSR) – are founded on the premise that there is no conflict between the goals of maximizing profit and social uplift for their workers; this is captured succinctly in the CSR mantra of "doing well by doing good."

More recently, CSR initiatives have displayed a growing interest in efforts to combat "modern day slavery," a social and legal category that has emerged since the introduction of global human trafficking protocols.[1] As scholar organizers who are deeply connected to racial justice and working class struggles globally, we push back against the widespread adoption of the antislavery discourse. We stand in solidarity with voices that have claimed the modern day slavery movement simultaneously co-opts and erases Black suffering endured during and in the aftermath of the transatlantic slave

---

[1] Julia O'Connell Davidson, *Modern Slavery: The Margins of Freedom* (London: Palgrave, 2015); Orlando Patterson, "Trafficking, Gender and Slavery: Past and present," in *The Legal Understanding of Slavery: From the Historical to the Contemporary*, ed. Jean Allain (Oxford: Oxford University Press, 2012), 322–359.

trade;[2] that it evokes the colonial practices and ideology of the "white [wo]men's burden";[3] and that the emotive capacities of the term facilitate a moral panic and "exploitation creep"[4] away from the legal definitions of forced labor and human trafficking.

Despite these trenchant criticisms, the language of "modern day slavery" has taken off and within the past five years has been adopted by academic, legal, and private sector institutions. For instance, in 2015, Thomson Reuters Foundation initiated the "Stop Slavery Award" to recognize companies for their efforts to eliminate forced labor in their supply chains. These awards follow cues from recent laws – including the 2010 California Supply Chain Transparency Act, 2015 UK Modern Slavery Act, and 2017 French Duty of Vigilance Law – that aim to increase supply chain transparency between multinational corporations and their manufacturing producers in the Global South. Equally they celebrate a global turn toward engaging the private sector in human rights issues that have historically been tasked to governments and civil society. In the past five years, the award has recognized Adidas, Apple, Nestlé, and Walmart, among dozens of other companies for their recently launched efforts to combat slavery. The Stop Slavery Award program joins the US State Department Trafficking in Persons Report Heroes Award, the UK Top 100 Corporate Modern Day Slavery Award, and the Free the Slaves Anti-Slavery Hero Award among others that exemplify the trend toward public recognition of anti-trafficking efforts. These awards banquets, and their related publicity and staff, are now a several hundred-million-dollar industry fundamentally illustrative of what Carol Leigh has labeled the "anti-trafficking industrial complex."[5]

In 2017, the same year that Adidas was awarded the Stop Slavery Award, Indonesian labor activist and SBGTS-GSBI union president Kokom Komalawati led ongoing protests in a multi-year-long battle with an Adidas subcontractor seeking severance pay for workers.

[2] Lyndsey P. Beutin, "Black Suffering for/from Anti-trafficking Advocacy," *Anti-Trafficking Review* 9 (2017): 14–30.

[3] Kamala Kempadoo, "The Modern-day White (Wo)Man's Burden: Trends in Anti-trafficking and Anti-slavery Campaigns," *Journal of Human Trafficking* 1, no. 1 (2015): 8–20.

[4] Janie A. Chuang, "Exploitation Creep and the Unmaking of Human Trafficking Law," *American Journal of International Law* 108, no. 4 (2014): 609–649.

[5] See Carol Leigh, "Anti-Trafficking Industrial Complex Awareness Month, second edition (2017), accessed May 18, 2020, https://modernslavery.yale.edu/sites/default/files/pdfs/anti-trafficking_industrial_complex_awareness_month_2nd_edition_with_images_carolleigh_stori_o.pdf.

Protests followed the 2012 retaliation against the newly formed trade union's leadership and the subsequent termination of 1,300 mostly women workers who were fired from the Adidas subcontractor PT Panarub Dwikarya Benoa factory (PDK) after a strike demanding the right to freedom of association, a back-payment of the legal minimum wage, and improvement of the health and safety conditions in the factory, in which women also suffered from verbal and physical violence. In 2016, the ILO Committee on Freedom of Association concluded in its interim report that the dismissal of the PDK workers was unjustified and an abuse of the workers' fundamental right to freedom of association, according to ILO standards.[6]

This chapter examines the startling juxtaposition between corporate approaches to supply chain management often celebrated under the label of combatting "modern day slavery", and the ongoing labor struggles within the same supply chains that these approaches not only fail to address, but in fact, invisibilize. This chapter is situated at the intersection of the literature that assesses the effectiveness of corporate social responsibility with regards to labor rights and the critical study of "antislavery" campaigns and discourses. While the corporate social responsibility and "antislavery" endeavors have been roundly studied and critiqued, the implications for worker power that emerge at the intersection of these two regimes remain an under-explored area of study. Building on existing research and case studies, this chapter seeks to elaborate on ways in which initiatives that purport to protect workers' rights – which have increasingly embraced "antislavery" as a focal point – actively disempower the very people they seek to protect. It additionally asks how the public lauding of CSR's antislavery efforts whitewashes brand images and actually displaces efforts to enforce labor standards across supply chains. Finally, it offers an alternative approach to corporate-driven supply chain management, advocating instead an approach to reduce labor abuse in global supply chains centered in collective worker action and international labor standards.

---

[6] International Labour Office, "Interim Report- Report No 380, October 2016," accessed May 18, 2020, www.ilo.org/dyn/normlex/en/f?p=NORMLEXPUB:50002:0::NO::P50002_COMPLAINT_TEXT_ID:3302041.

7.2 A GENEALOGY OF CORPORATE SOCIAL RESPONSIBILITY

Contemporary efforts that demand corporate transparency are not novel, but have roots in corporate social responsibility efforts dating back to the early 1950s. These earliest articulations argued that business ethics and social obligation were important for long-term superior outcomes for a firm or business.[7] At the same time, Howard Bowen's foresight offered three areas of critical reservation that remain relevant over half a century later, that it:

(1) might be manipulated by businesses to maintain positions of power;
(2) might be unfeasible in a competitive market with rising costs passed onto consumers or workers, and
(3) might violate legal obligations to stockholders.

This chapter is particularly interested in the first of these reservations, and explores how CSR has tended to take on paternalistic functions that fortify corporate power at the expense of worker power.

Historically, the CSR concept arose as a result of industrialization and corporate legitimation during the postwar "golden age" of capitalism, despite the fact that industrialists had been using certain similar techniques since the Progressive era. In the 1970s, definitions proliferated, including a new philosophical shift to "corporate social responsiveness," epitomized by the ability to respond to social pressures.[8] In general, one of the main issues with the term CSR has been the lack of consensus over its definition.[9] Alexander Dahlsrud's analysis of thirty-seven different definitions of CSR in literature from 1980 to 2003 grouped definitions into five

---

[7] Archie B. Carroll, "Corporate Social Responsibility: Evolution of a Definitional Construct," *Business and Society* 38, no. 3 (1999): 268–295; Howard R. Bowen, *Social Responsibilities of the Businessman* (Iowa City: University of Iowa Press, 2013, r.p. 1953), 5.

[8] William C. Frederick, "From CSR1 to CSR2: The Maturing of Business-and-Society Thought," *Business & Society*, 33, no. 2 (1994): 150–164.

[9] Ruth Aguilera, Cynthia A. Williams, John M. Conley, and Deborah E. Rupp, "Corporate Governance and Social Responsibility: A Comparative Analysis of the UK and the US," *Corporate Governance: An International Review*, 14, no. 3 (2006): 147–158; David P. Baron, "Private Politics, Corporate Social Responsibility, and Integrated Strategy," *Journal of Economics & Management Strategy*, 10, no. 1 (2001): 7–45; Andrew Crane, Abagail McWilliams, Dirk Matten, Jeremy Moon, and Donald S. Siegal, eds., *The Oxford Handbook of Corporate Social Responsibility* (Oxford: Oxford University Press, 2008); Genevieve LeBaron and Jane Lister, "Benchmarking Global Supply Chains: The Power of the 'Ethical Audit' Regime," *Review of International Studies*, 41, no. 5 (2015): 905–924.

dimensions, including the environmental dimension, the social dimension, the economic dimension, the stakeholder dimension, and the voluntariness dimension.[10] A simple definition can be summarized broadly as the "activities making companies good citizens who contribute to society's welfare beyond their own self-interest," although the question of self-interest has never left the field of debate around CSR. The rise of multinational corporations during the era of vociferous globalization in the mid-1990s helped institutionalize the concept of CSR.[11] This institutionalization manifested in a burgeoning mid-to-upper managerial profession, and growing numbers of CSR divisions in corporations through Western Europe and the United States.[12]

A series of corporate scandals and crises in the 1990s and 2000s, such as the Enron scandal and Nike's association with sweatshops, increased the public relations emphasis of CSR, and shifted the conversation from mainly environmental impacts to a more central focus on corporate impacts on human society. The emergence of human trafficking since the 2000 UN Palermo Protocol, and more recent articulations of modern day slavery within the past decade have become the latest social concern. Labor abuse has grown to be an increasing area of interest for the CSR industry, and in the wake of global antislavery efforts, has taken the form of demands for increased transparency across global supply chains, among other forms. Efforts by groups like the Worker Driven Social Responsibility Network have directly taken on the notion that labor rights can be achieved without binding accountability to workers and worker organizations.

7.3 ARTIFICIAL DISTINCTIONS

Researchers have long critiqued the "antislavery" movement for relying upon and feeding into a set of sensationalistic narratives that foreground extreme suffering and abuse, instead of attending to (and challenging) structural inequality factors. The disproportionate focus on sex trafficking in the early years following the 2000 UN Palermo Protocol led to the

[10] Alexander Dahlsrud, "How Corporate Social Responsibility is Defined: An Analysis of 37 Definitions," *Corporate Social Responsibility and Environmental Management* 15, no. 1 (2008): 1–13

[11] Steven K. May, George Cheney, and Juliet Roper, eds., *The Debate Over Corporate Social Responsibility* (Oxford: Oxford University Press, 2007).

[12] Archie Carroll, "Corporate Social Responsibility: The Centerpiece of Competing and Complementary Frameworks," *Organizational Dynamics* 44 (2015): 87–96, 95.

cultivation of fictive, racialized, and gendered representations of victim-hood that conflate all forms of sexual labor with "trafficking." Rather than aiding the people that were targeted by such interventions, this construction of victimhood led to the proliferation of policies focused on criminalization, thus exacerbating the vulnerability of sex workers and others like migrant workers also vulnerable to state prosecution.[13] While the "antislavery" discourse has evolved beyond its initial narrow focus on sexual exploitation to encompass a wider range of economic activities, it remains deeply invested in stereotypical narratives of extreme suffering and abuse, which as noted by Nicola Mai and Rutvica Andrijasevic, "conveniently distract the global public from their increasing and shared day-to-day exploitability as workers because of the systematic erosion of labor rights globally."[14] A rich body of scholarship posits that unfree labor represents only the "tip of the iceberg," urging us to view the types of labor abuse that amount to "modern slavery" not as isolated or fixed forms of abuse, but rather as occupying the extreme end of the same labor exploitation continuum.[15] Critics have further argued that the focus on extreme abuse amounting to "modern slavery" have given rise to a framing that views exploitation as being exceptional, randomly occurring outside of the normal workings of the global economy.[16] But, as scholars have argued, labor abuse, including forced labor, is a very predictable and logical outcome of the way that the global economy is structured.[17]

Contemporary neoliberal globalization engendered the rise of increasingly complex global supply chains, through which brands and retailers coordinate production across a multitude of suppliers around the world. The rise of global supply chains coincided with the increasing power and

---

[13] Elizabeth Bernstein, "Militarized Humanitarianism meets Carceral Feminism: The Politics of Sex, Rights, and Freedom in Contemporary Antitrafficking Campaigns," *Signs: Journal of Women in Culture and Society*, 36, no. 1 (2010): 45–71; Elena Shih, "Not in My 'Backyard Abolitionism': Vigilante Rescue against American Sex Trafficking," *Sociological Perspectives*, 59, no. 1 (2016): 66–90.

[14] Rutvica Andrijasevic and Nicola Mai, "Editorial: Trafficking (in) Representations: Understanding the Recurring Appeal of Victimhood and Slavery in Neoliberal Times," *Anti-Trafficking Review* 7 (2016): 1–10.

[15] Klara Skrivankova, *Between Decent Work and Forced Labour: Examining the Continuum of Exploitation* (York, UK: Joseph Rowntree Foundation, 2010).

[16] Genevieve LeBaron, Neil Howard, Cameron Thibos, and Penelope Kyritsis, *Confronting Root Causes: Forced Labour in Global Supply Chains* (Sheffield: SPERI, 2018).

[17] Andrew Crane, Genevieve LeBaron, Jean Allain and Laya Behbahani, "Governance Gaps in Eradicating Forced Labor: From Global to Domestic Supply Chains," *Regulation & Governance*, 13, no. 1 (2017): 86–106.

concentration of multinational corporations at the top of supply chains, which have, in an effort to maximize profit and accumulate wealth, exerted pressure for very low costs in other portions of their supply chains. As argued by Mark Anner, the contemporary supply chain model of fast, high-turnover production – characterized by a "price squeeze," with buyers constantly seeking to lower the price paid to suppliers, as well as a "lead time squeeze," with buyers demanding ever-shorter turnaround times for orders – has a profound impact on labor beyond wage levels.[18] Workers experience this "sourcing squeeze" in many different ways, including unsustainable quotas, forced or unpaid overtime, wage theft, gender-based violence and harassment, non-payment of benefits, and harassment and discrimination, to name a few of these dynamics. Countries are incentivized to compete for these production jobs through limiting labor and environmental regulation and their enforcement. Crucially, this business model has cultivated a context in which suppliers have a financial incentive to crack down on workers who attempt to organize, unionization being a powerful vehicle through which labor can bargain for higher wages and better working conditions. Yet corporate "antislavery" endeavors rarely account for the supply chain dynamics that are at the root of labor exploitation. Nor do they seek to protect workers' associational rights in a meaningful way. Instead, they promote and fuel a narrative that positions extreme forms of labor abuse ("modern slavery") as an exception to otherwise "clean" or "untainted" supply chains. As Elizabeth Bernstein argues, the sharp demarcation of "clean" vs. "tainted" supply chains relegates the small handful of instances that constitute "modern slavery" to a black box, while "morally redeeming" the sets of labor relations that fall beyond the purview of the modern slavery" threshold by categorical contrast.[19]

Beyond distorting our understanding of the dynamics that render workers vulnerable to various grades of labor exploitation, the "antislavery" discourse has conveniently provided a smokescreen for corporations, deflecting attention away from their responsibility in fostering these labor conditions throughout their supply chains. Such logics have informed industry-led solutions to address labor rights exploitation,

[18] Mark Anner, "Squeezing Workers' Rights in Global Supply Chains: Purchasing Practices in the Bangladesh Garment Export Sector in Comparative Perspective," *Review of International Political Economy* 27, no. 2 (2019): 320–347.
[19] Elizabeth Bernstein, "Redemptive Capitalism and Sexual Investability," in *Perverse Politics? Feminism, Anti-Imperialism, Multiplicity*, eds. Ann Shola Orloff, Raka Ray, and Evren Savci (Bingley, UK: Emerald Group, 2016), 45–80.

which have done a tremendous disservice to workers in the global economy.

7.4 FLAWED BY DESIGN

The past two decades have witnessed a swell of industry-led programs that purport to combat labor exploitation within the global economy. When it comes to protecting the rights of workers throughout global supply chains, CSR initiatives have largely emerged from the notion that it is the responsibility of brands and retailers at the top of supply chains to influence the labor practices of their suppliers via social auditing schemes, ethical certification programs, and supplier codes of conduct. While codes of conduct and auditing standards have long prohibited the use of forced labor, "modern slavery" has become an increasingly salient issue for corporate actors in recent years.

Despite the considerable funds being poured into programs through which corporations can signal their dedication to improve the labor conditions and protect workers in their supply chains from "modern slavery," extensive research has documented that these programs have failed to live up to their rhetoric. For example, Genevieve LeBaron's *Global Business of Forced Labour* projects that workers at the bottom of the tea and cocoa supply chains are subject to myriad forms of labor exploitation and abuse, including forced labor.[20] Workers reported experiencing physical violence, sexual violence, verbal abuse, threats of violence, and debt bondage, among other forms of abuse. This is despite the fact that LeBaron's study sample included tea plantations and cocoa farms that are covered by several industry initiatives to address and prevent forced labor in global supply chains, including Fairtrade International, Rainforest Alliance, the Ethical Trade Partnership, and UTZ.[21] Overall, the study found that certification had little to no impact on labor standards in the tea industry, with some of the worst cases of exploitation occurring on ethically certified plantations. In the case of cocoa, the study documented extensive confusion among producers related to the certification process, with 95 percent of workers interviewed unaware of whether their worksite was certified or not.

The limitations of CSR are by no means limited to the tea and cocoa industries. Evidence-based research by the Asia Floor Wage Alliance and Global Labor Justice revealed sexual violence and harassment; and

---

[20] See chapter by LeBaron, this volume.   [21] See chapter by LeBaron, this volume.

industrial discipline practices, including physical violence, verbal abuse, coercion, threats, retaliation, and routine deprivations of liberty – including forced overtime on the Asian fast fashion supply chains of H&M, Gap, and Walmart, along with systematic repression of collective worker attempts to expose and remedy the problems.[22] An investigation by the Worker Rights Consortium (WRC) documenting labor rights conditions in Ethiopia's burgeoning garment sector found a raft of labor rights abuses in factories producing for H&M, PVH (the parent company of Calvin Klein and Tommy Hilfiger), and the Children's Place.[23] The WRC conducted off-site interviews with workers from four garment facilities, who reported facing draconian wage deductions, degrading verbal abuse, quid pro quo sexual harassment, forced and unpaid overtime, and pregnancy discrimination, among other rights violations. The WRC's investigation also found wages as low as twelve cents an hour, with an average of eighteen cents an hour. These wages are possible, in part, because Ethiopia is unique among significant apparel-exporting countries in having no statutory minimum wage for workers in the private sector, including garment workers. Not only do each of the brands and retailers sourcing from the country have voluntary codes of conduct and participate in ethical certification schemes that prohibit the abuses outlined earlier, but several of these brands have officially embraced "living wage" as the appropriate wage standard for workers in their global supply chains.[24] It is difficult to see how these brands reconcile their living wage promises with their decision to expand production in a country with no minimum

---

[22] Asia Floor Wage Alliance and Global Labor Justice, *Gender Based Violence in the GAP Garment Supply Chain: Workers Voices from the Global Supply Chain* (2018), accessed May 18, 2020, www.globallaborjustice.org/wp-content/uploads/2018/06/GBV-Gap-May-2018.pdf; Asia Floor Wage Alliance and Global Labor Justice, *Gender Based Violence in the H&M Garment Supply Chain: Workers Voices from the Global Supply Chain* (2018); accessed May 18, 2020, www.globallaborjustice.org/wp-content/uploads/2018/05/GBV-HM-May-2018.pdf;

Asia Floor Wage Alliance and Global Labor Justice, *Gender Based Violence in the Walmart Garment Supply Chain: Workers Voices from the Global Supply Chain* (2018), accessed 18 May 2020, www.globallaborjustice.org/walmart-report/.

[23] Worker Rights Consortium, *"Ethiopia is a North Star": Grim Conditions and Miserable Wages Guide Apparel Brands in their Race to the Bottom*, December 31, 2019, accessed May 18, 2020, www.workersrights.org/wp-content/uploads/2019/03/Ethiopia_isa_North_Star_FINAL.pdf.

[24] On its corporate website, H&M states that "All textile workers have the right to a fair living wage," and as a member of the Fair Labor Association, PVH has the obligation to take meaningful action to ensure that its suppliers are paying their workers a living wage. H&M, "Fair and Equal," accessed May 18, 2020, https://hmgroup.com/sustainability/fair-and-equal.html.

wage and use suppliers who pay eighteen cents an hour. Unfortunately, these examples are not exceptional; they are merely a few data points pertaining to the longstanding trend of CSR failing to protect workers in global supply chains.[25]

A key flaw of industry-led labor rights compliance initiatives, and recent supply chain accountability laws, lies in their voluntary nature. This applies to brands and retailers' supplier codes of conduct – which essentially give them complete discretion to create and enforce their own rules, all the while branding themselves as "socially responsible" – as well as third-party initiatives. In the case of social auditing and ethical certification schemes, such as Worldwide Responsible Accredited Production, Social Accountability International, Fairtrade and others, it is self-selecting suppliers that apply for and pay for certification. In an effort to outsource responsibility for labor rights compliance, brands and retailers increasingly require such certifications as a prerequisite for a commercial relationship. This leads to a host of conflicts of interest: the suppliers have an incentive to conceal labor violations from auditors in order to maintain artificially low production costs, while the auditors rely on issuing certifications to generate revenue, which in turn gives them a financial incentive to underreport labor violations. And with the mushrooming of the third-party private auditing industry, Carolijn Terwindt and Miriam Saage-Maass argue, the competition among auditors "creates incentives that push towards keeping auditing standards, costs and efforts low."[26] Absent the risk of reputational harm should labor rights scandals be exposed by journalists or watchdog organizations, there are no meaningful consequences for brands, retailers, and suppliers to fail to live up to their labor rights commitments. It is therefore unsurprising that CSR initiatives have been largely unsuccessful in detecting, reporting, and providing adequate remedy for labor rights abuses in global supply chains.

In addition to this crisis of standards without enforcement, critics have attributed the weakness of CSR initiatives to their systematic failure to

---

[25] AFL-CIO, *Responsibility Outsourced: Social Audits, Workplace Certification and Twenty Years of Failure to Protect Worker Rights* (2013), accessed May 18, 2020, https://aflcio.org/sites/default/files/2017-03/CSReport.pdf; Remi Edwards, Tom Hunt, and Genevieve LeBaron, *Corporate Commitments to Living Wages in the Garment Industry* (Sheffield: SPERI, 2019); Clean Clothes Campaign, *Fig Leaf for Fashion: How Social Auditing Protects Brands and Fails Workers* (Sep 2019), accessed May 18, 2020, https://cleanclothes.org/file-repository/figleaf-for-fashion.pdf/view.

[26] Carolijn Terwindt and Miriam Saage-Maass, *Liability of Social Auditors in the Textile Industry* (Berlin: ECCHR, 2016).

address the root causes that render workers vulnerable to labor abuse in the first place. Labor abuse does not occur in a vacuum; it happens at the nexus of workers' intersecting vulnerabilities – which can be rooted in economic destitution, societal discrimination, and/or a degraded labor rights landscape – and the downward pressure exerted by leading brands and retailers, which stand to profit from various forms of labor exploitation. The "Confronting Root Causes" report analyzes the various dynamics that trigger a "demand" for exploitative forms of labor, including the concentration of corporate power and ownership, which creates significant downward pressure on working conditions, partly by lowering the "share of the pie" available to workers as wages; outsourcing, which fragments responsibility for labor standards and undermines the oversight and accountability; and irresponsible sourcing practices, which lead to heavy cost and time pressures on suppliers.[27] These dynamics no doubt benefit brands and retailers at the top of global supply chains, but have profoundly damaging impacts on labor. As LeBaron, Lister, and Dauvergne have argued, "for nearly two decades, workers' rights and trade union organizations, scholars, and auditors themselves have documented the flaws of the audit regime; yet, corporations have done little to transform it. The problem is not one of finessing the institutional design or audit methodology, but rather relates to corporate power, politics, and profits."[28]

7.5 A DIFFERENT FORM OF CORPORATE GREENWASHING: ORGANIZING AGAINST GENDER-BASED VIOLENCE IN THE ERA OF MARRIOTT HUMAN TRAFFICKING TRAININGS

Organizations serious about climate change have exposed how Marriott International – the world's largest and richest hotel chain – engages in greenwashing. The Sierra Club has highlighted how public-facing programs like Marriott's "Make a Green Choice" Program, which encourages hotel guests to forego hotel housekeeping to "reduce water, energy, and chemical usage," mask a prioritization of corporate profits over actual investments that would significantly limit its carbon footprint.

---

[27] Genevieve LeBaron, Neil Howard, Cameron Thibos, and Penelope Kyritsis, *Confronting Root Causes: Forced Labour in Global Supply Chains* (Sheffield: SPERI, 2018).

[28] Genevieve LeBaron, Jane Lister, and Peter Dauvergne, "Governing Global Supply Chain Sustainability through the Ethical Audit Regime," *Globalizations* 14, no. 6 (2017), 958–975.

Meanwhile, hotel housekeepers bear the impact of reduced scheduling – in many cases resulting in loss of healthcare benefits related to hours worked – while being expected to clean dirtier rooms on the same schedule. "We want to save the planet, and we want to make it more sustainable, but we don't want to do it on the backs of working families," said Pedro Cruz, a senior representative for the Sierra Club's Labor and Economic Justice Program.[29] Read in tandem with Marriott's Anti-Modern Day Slavery efforts, such startling juxtapositions mask a refusal to address systemic labor issues.

In 2017, Marriott wheeled out a human trafficking identification training program that, as of May 2019, alleges to have trained 500,000 of the company's 730,000 workers globally.[30] Partnering with the Polaris Project, and ECPAT-USA, they use training materials that aim to educate hotel workers on how to identify victims of human trafficking that enter Marriott hotels. Joining a chorus of victim identification training programs, with cosmetologists, and medical professionals, these trainings operate with a widespread assumption that increased civilian vigilance is crucial for detecting human trafficking. However, such trainings have been criticized for how they "see" human trafficking based on proxy indicators of poverty, migration, and sex work and encourage forms of racial vigilantism that lead to gender and racial stereotyping.[31]

Since Marriott broadcasted its plan, other businesses in the tourism and hospitality sector have followed. Hotel chains Motel 6 has recently adopted a similar training program. Amidst the backdrop of incalculable investment in anti-trafficking efforts however, there exist ongoing labor concerns voiced by hotel workers – including about rampant gender-based violence against hotel workers by other staff and guests – continue to be pushed to the side.

At the same time that Marriott was coordinating its global anti-trafficking trainings, Marriott refused to meet with the International

[29] Chloe Zilliac, "Are Hotel Greening Programs Hurting Housekeepers?," *Sierra: The National Magazine of the Sierra Club*, January 12, 2020, accessed May 18, 2020, www.sierraclub.org/sierra/are-hotel-greening-programs-hurting-housekeepers.

[30] "Marriott International Has Trained 500,000 Hotel Workers to Recognize the Signs of Human Trafficking," *Marriot International News Center*, January 18, 2019, accessed May 18, 2020, https://news.marriott.com/news/2019/01/18/marriott-international-has-trained-500-000-hotel-workers-to-recognize-the-signs-of-human-trafficking.

[31] Shih, "Not in My 'Backyard Abolitionism'."

Union of Food, Agricultural, Hotel, Restaurant, Catering, Tobacco and Allied Workers' Associations (IUF) to partner toward a global accord to end sexual harassment in Marriott's 6,400 hotels in 126 countries.[32] IUF's surveys indicated that a large majority of hospitality workers – up to 89 percent in some countries – have experienced sexual harassment on the job in the course of their working lives. At the International Labor Conference in Geneva in May 2018 during global negotiations on an international labor standard combatting violence and harassment at work, long-time Marriott employees told of their personal experiences of sexual harassment and assault by guests, of management's "blame the victim" mentality and failure to take adequate measures to protect workers, and of the lasting trauma such incidents inflict. Workers also spoke of management efforts to undermine union organizing by pressuring workers to resign their membership and by firing activists and supporters. The meeting, convened to highlight the vital link between sustainable tourism, decent work, and gender equality, forcefully underlined the importance of freedom of association for efforts to eliminate sexual harassment at the workplace. With several hundred workers uniting under a banner for calls for "just tourism," such approaches understand that the global precarity that drives human trafficking is structurally tied to gender and economic vulnerability, not simply the threat of commercial sex.

To date, Marriott has refused to sign a global accord on sexual harassment with IUF. Understanding Marriott's anti-trafficking awareness trainings within their reticence to address systemic labor inequities within their own staff reflects the myopic interests of modern day slavery and anti slavery campaigns. The pervasive dismissal of gender-based violence and sexual harassment within Marriott's own working arrangements have taken a backseat to the more global concern to "rescue" alleged victims of trafficking.

In 2018, Marriott workers in the United States also filed a class action lawsuit alleging that the Marriott Employees Federal Credit Union failed to inform members – who are employees at Marriott International and other companies – about the true costs of its "mini-loans" in violation of US law.[33] The complaint alleges the credit union charged more in fees for

---

[32] IUF, "Global Sexual Harassment Campaign," *International Union of Food, Agricultural, Hotel, Restaurant, Catering, Tobacco and Allied Workers' Union* (2018), accessed May 18, 2020, www.workersofmarriott.org/campaigns/global-sexual-harassment-campaign/.

[33] Payne et al. v. Marriott Employees Federal Credit Union. Filed: September 18, 2018, accessed May 18, 2020, § 2:18CV4009, www.classaction.org/news/marriott-employees-

every dollar loaned than any other credit union of its type and that this is "part-and-parcel of the unequal bargaining relationship between Marriott and its employees." In other words, without living wages and reliable schedules, Marriott employees rely on predatory loans which Marriott then deducts from their already poverty wages.

Corporate social responsibility enables Marriott and corporations like it to replace a labor rights approach to responsible business practices with a consumer-facing approach. Such efforts garner public relations acclaim without requiring accountability, obscuring failures to attend to and negotiate with trade unions. This echoes the fallibility of CSR approaches in the agricultural and manufacturing sectors.

7.6 MODERN DAY ANTISLAVERY EFFORTS MASK FAILURES TO ADDRESS GLOBAL BUSINESS MODELS BUILT ON LABOR EXPLOITATION

This chapter has sought to bring together two strands of critique – the critical studies of the "antislavery" endeavors and the critique of CSR initiatives – to elaborate on the politics that emerge at their intersection. In pursuing and fueling sensationalistic narratives that isolate instances of "modern slavery" from all other forms of abuse along the labor exploitation continuum, the "antislavery" frame has conveniently obscured the dynamics within our global economy that shape workers' vulnerability to exploitation, including forced labor. Specifically, this chapter has elaborated on the ways in which powerful corporations have benefitted from the artificial distinction between "clean" and "tainted" supply chains to justify pursing CSR initiatives that leave current power dynamics within the global economy intact, and further increase the demand for exploitable labor. The failure of CSR initiatives to live up to their rhetoric of social uplift and labor rights protection is foregrounded by the various case studies that demonstrate persistent and widespread labor rights abuse despite the various voluntary codes of conduct, social auditing programs, ethical certification schemes, and, ever increasingly, "antislavery programs" purporting to protect workers from abuse. Global brands in agriculture, fast fashion, and hotels receive awards and public acclaim for their efforts to end "modern day slavery" in the same moment as

federal-credit-union-facing-class-action-lawsuit-over-allegedly-predatory-mini-loan-practices#embedded-document.

workers collectively demanding wages, violence-free workplaces, and other fundamental labor rights are retaliated against for making demands and forming unions.

This chapter argues that these are not coincidental, but that the widespread championing of antislavery commitments allows companies to obfuscate deeply entrenched labor inequalities within their global workforce. Absent commitment to international labor standards with meaningful enforcement mechanisms and the engagement with worker organizations, such initiatives merely provide a smokescreen for corporations to continue business as usual. Not only do such initiatives obscure the widespread repression of workers' rights to organize and bargain collectively, but they also cement power relations in the global economy, which rely on the dilution of worker power in the pursuit of profit maximization and wealth accumulation.

The case studies articulated above underscore the dire need for labor rights alternatives to corporate whitewashing schemes, to center freedom of association and collective bargaining. Placing the moment of Marriott's engagement with trafficking in tandem with the corporation's refusal to recognize and address its workers' grievances and highlighting Adidas's acceptance of an award while Indonesian women workers persist in a multi-year campaign against retaliation exposes which voices and lives are prioritized by the recent global panic to end human trafficking.

Rather than be complicit with such strategies of corporate green-/ whitewashing, our essay asks readers to consider: how might we understand solutions to human trafficking differently if we understood global labor relations through a worker-centered lens? Furthermore, how does the current prevailing approach of efforts like Marriott's human trafficking awareness training programs displace worker organizing? In the absence of meaningful shifts in corporate practices – which necessarily require a disruption of power relations within supply chains and the global economy – antislavery initiatives are structurally unable to protect workers in global economy from labor abuses. Beyond their ineffectiveness to remedy and mitigate labor rights abuses, the proliferation of "antislavery" initiatives actively undermine worker power: they obfuscate the anti-union practices occurring in the global economy, all while preserving the business models driving the heightened repression of workers attempting to enact power through unions or other forms of worker organizing.

8

A Market in Deception? Ethically Certifying Exploitative Supply Chains

Genevieve LeBaron[1]

8.1 INTRODUCTION

Buying products that are certified as ethical by organizations like Fairtrade and Rainforest Alliance makes us feel better about the goods we consume. But what evidence do we have that these programs actually work to eradicate forced labor in global supply chains, as major companies increasingly claim? Is life really better for workers in ethically certified supply chains? Does the extra money we pay for bananas, coffee, tea, chocolate, and other products covered in little frog logos and fair trade logos really end up in workers' pockets? Does this money create robust monitoring systems that ensure forced labor isn't used on certified worksites? There is very little research that sheds light onto these questions and the effectiveness of ethical certification as a tool to verify and raise labor standards. So, tired of wavering between expensive tea cartons adorned in ethical certification logos, and cheaper, uncertified, plain-looking tea cartons, I decided to find out what working conditions are like at the bottom of ethically certified supply chains.

[1] The data in this paper comes from my UK Economic and Social Research Council grant (ES/N001192/1). Data collection for the project was supported by a team of researchers and interpreters, including: E. Gore, D. Ottie-Boakye, O. Opoku Afrane, P. Ekka, H. K. H., A S. Arunkumar, R. Goswami, M. Rahman, N. Howard, P. Roberts, H. Dutta Sarkar, V. Ampiah, and J. Nyarko. I am grateful for their assistance. I am hugely indebted to the members of the Gilder Lehrman Center's Modern Slavery Working Group at Yale University for their feedback on earlier drafts of this chapter and for inspiring my thinking about these themes, especially David W. Blight, Gunther Peck, J. J. Rosenbaum, Janie Chuang, and Andrew Crane. The historians in the group, especially Zoe Trodd, Jessica R. Pliley, and Grace Peña Delgado, gave me helpful suggestions and references.

In 2016, I started a research project to investigate working conditions in global agricultural supply chains, including on ethically certified worksites. This large multi-year research project is called the Global Business of Forced Labour project and was funded by the United Kingdom's (UK) Economic and Social Research Council.[2] My research focused on the patterns of forced labor within cocoa and tea supply chains, with production located in Ghana and India respectively, and led by UK-based companies. One of the key questions I had going into the project was whether and to what extent ethical certification schemes like Fairtrade, Rainforest Alliance, UTZ, and Trustea successfully create worksites free from forced labor and labor exploitation more broadly. As part of the research, my team interviewed 1,154 workers across 96 cocoa and tea worksites in India and Ghana, including on both ethically certified and noncertified plantations and farms.

My research uncovered widespread forced labor and labor abuse within the cocoa and tea industries, including on certified worksites. All of the workers interviewed within my study reported having experienced some form of labor abuse, including verbal abuse, threats of violence, debt bondage, the under-provision of legally required goods and services, being required to perform unpaid labor, and underpayment or withholding of wages. In the worst cases, the forms of abuse reported by workers amount to forced labor.[3] Even more surprisingly, I found that whether or not a worker was working on an ethically certified worksite had almost no bearing on whether or not they were likely to experience labor abuse. Working conditions were very similar on certified and noncertified worksites and fell well below the standards set by ethical certification schemes. I found that producers violated ethical certification scheme standards around wages, basic necessities like water and housing, and child and

---

[2] You can read more about the project on its website: http://globalbusinessofforcedlabour .ac.uk/.

[3] I discuss the definition of forced labor used within the Global Business of Forced Labour project here: Genevieve LeBaron, *The Global Business of Forced Labour: Report of Findings* (SPERI & University of Sheffield, 2018), 13–15. Briefly put, we use the international legal definition, which comes from the ILO's 1930 Convention: "All work or service which is exacted from any person under the menace of any penalty and for which the said person has not offered himself voluntarily." However, we identify and seek to overcome a number of limits with this definition, including that the threshold between "forced labor" and labor that is highly exploitative but not "forced" is not easy to determine in practice. As well, while the ILO excludes situations of economic coercion, such as potential for destitution or starvation, from its definition of forced labor, our worker interviews reveal this to be a crucial underpinning cause of some of the most abusive and exploitative labor relations.

forced labor. In fact, some of the worst cases of forced labor and abuse that my research uncovered occurred on ethically certified tea plantations.

My research findings raise serious and urgent questions about the use of ethical certification schemes as a tool to combat forced labor in global supply chains. As public and policymaker concern about forced labor grows, industry groups are ramping up their efforts to market products as ethically certified and "slavery-free." But if these standards are not credible – if the extra money consumers are paying for these "ethically certified" products is not actually going to improve conditions for workers, and if working conditions on the ground do not actually meet the standards set by ethical certifiers – then we need to critically question the role and value of these certification schemes within the global economy and their growing use as a tool to fight forced labor.

In this chapter, I present data that shows ethical certification schemes are a largely ineffective tool to combat labor exploitation in global supply chains, and that pattern of labor exploitation across certified and non-certified worksites is broadly similar. I argue that ethical certification labelling is misleading consumers about the labor conditions involved in the goods they are buying. I explore the contradictions of selling "ethical" products that give the impression that goods have been made through labor standards that they are known to fall short of, and consider the challenge of modernizing historically successful strategies to combat slavery-made goods for use in the present.

The chapter unfolds as follows. First, I describe companies' growing use of ethical certification as a strategy to tackle forced labor in global supply chains. Then I present an overview of the study and its methodology, as well as main findings. Finally, I argue that ethical certification is doing more to cover up labor abuse than it is doing to fix it, and in doing so, is creating a misleading impression of labor standards within supply chains. I explore the contradictions of selling deceptively marketed "ethical" products and of rendering market-based strategies like boycotts – which have been successful tools to combat slavery made-goods in previous eras of global capitalism – fit for the present day.

8.2 ETHICAL CERTIFICATION AS A TOOL TO FIGHT MODERN SLAVERY

In the face of mounting public and government pressure to address the problems of forced labor, human trafficking, and "modern slavery" in global supply chains, big brand companies and retailers like Walmart,

Nestlé, Tesco, and Unilever have intensified their efforts to ethically certify supply chains. Ethical certification is a form of private voluntary initiative that sets standards around labor and environmental conditions, such as wages and chemical usage, in production processes. Producers can apply for certification from organizations like Fairtrade and Rainforest Alliance, who confirm that the company, farm, or co-op meets their standards. They can then sell their tea, coffee, cotton, fish, or other commodities as ethically certified goods, commanding higher prices.

Ethical certification organizations claim that by buying and selling certified products, consumers and businesses can contribute to a more just and sustainable global economy that benefits workers. For instance, Rainforest Alliance's website encourages consumers to "Shop Smart", noting that "choosing products with the little green frog seal is an easy way to help protect forests, conserve wildlife, and support communities around the world."[4] Fairtrade's website notes, "Fairtrade is a simple way to make a difference to the lives of people who grow the things we love. We do this by making trade fair."[5]

In recent years, as consumers, activists, and policy-makers have sought to address severe labor exploitation in supply chains, ethical certification schemes like Fairtrade and Rainforest Alliance have become a popular strategy to prevent and address forced labor in their supply chains. Companies have confirmed this in Modern Slavery Statements published in the wake of the 2015 UK Modern Slavery Act and similar legislation, where reporting around the measures they are taking to eradicate and guard against forced labor in their global supply chains often revolves heavily around ethical certification, as well as overlapping private verification methods like social auditing. Some industry leaders have even made commitments to move toward "full certification" of various products. For instance, tea brand Tetley announced in 2010 a "commitment to purchase all of the tea for its branded tea bad and loose tea products from Rainforest Alliance Certified™ farms" and Tata Global Beverages, which owns Tetley tea brand, noted in a recent Slavery and Human Trafficking statement that "in FY 2016/17, 86 percent of all Tetley branded Black, green [camellia Sinensis] and red [rooibos] tea, including flavored and decaffeinated varieties, sold by us is Rainforest Alliance

---

[4] "About the Rainforest Alliance," Rainforest Alliance, accessed May 18, 2020, www.rainforest-alliance.org/about.

[5] "What Fairtrade Does," Fairtrade Foundation, accessed May 18, 2020, www.fairtrade.org.uk/What-is-Fairtrade/What-Fairtrade-does.

Certified™, and we are working towards full certification."[6] As multi-national companies have adopted ethical certification as a key strategy to mitigate risks of illegal labor practices in their supply chains in recent years, the market share of certified products has expanded across a range of industries, including palm oil, soy, sugarcane, tea, forestry, cotton, coffee, and bananas.[7]

Like most corporate social responsibility programs, ethical certification schemes do not rely on government labor inspectors. Rather, they rely on in-house and third-party social auditors to check whether or not worksites are meeting labor standards. As well, some schemes allow worksites to self-report whether or not they are meeting certification standards. Where auditors are used, audits can be of varying quality; social auditing has been heavily criticized by researchers as consisting of brief "snapshot" inspections that are fraught with financial conflict of interest and easily cheated.[8] Social auditing is a highly profitable global industry; one large auditing, inspection, and certification firm SGS generated 6.7 billion CHF in revenue (around US $6.5 billion) in 2019.[9] As well, a whole industry of highly-paid consultants are involved in advising companies about which ethical certification schemes to join, and provide assurance and advisory services about dealing with and reporting on modern slavery in supply chains, including through ethical certification schemes.[10]

While the growth of ethical certification is widely believed to be a positive trend that benefits workers, to date, there has been very little research exploring the effectiveness of ethical certification as a tool to fight forced labor in supply chains. Indeed, in spite of the ample scholarship from the disciplines of business, political science, geography, and other fields analyzing corporate social responsibility (CSR) and ethical certification schemes, there has been very little investigation of on-the-ground

---

[6] Tata Global Beverages, "Slavery and Human Trafficking Statement 2016/2017," (2017), 2, accessed May 18, 2020, http://tataglobalbeverages.com/docs/default-source/default-document-library/slavery-and-human-trafficking-statement-2016–17.pdf?sfvrsn=0.

[7] Julia Lemond, Jason Potts, Gregory Sampson, Salvador Garibay, Matthew Lynch, Vivek Voora, Helga Willer, and Joseph Wozniak, *The State of Sustainable Markets 2017: Statistics And Emerging Trends* (ITC: Geneva, 2017).

[8] Genevieve LeBaron, Jane Lister, and Peter Dauvergne, "Governing Global Supply Chain Sustainability through the Ethical Audit Regime," *Globalizations* 14, no. 6 (2017), 958–975.

[9] SGS, Our Value to Society: 2018 Integrated Annual Report, accessed 18 May 2020, www.sgs.com/-/media/global/documents/financial-documents/financial-reports/2018/sgs-2018-annual-report.pdf.

[10] Luc Fransen and Genevieve LeBaron, "Big Audit Firms as Regulatory Intermediaries in Transnational Labor Governance," *Regulation & Governance* 13 (2018), 260–279.

effectiveness of these schemes related to labor conditions. Studies have tended to focus on the influence of governance and uptake factors like influence of supply chain structure, company culture, and activist and consumer pressure and perceptions on company involvement, or questions around outcomes in relation to factors like farmer welfare, access to market, prices, or union rights. However, effectiveness in relation to forced labor or even labor standards more broadly is a notable gap within the literature. In light of this gap, I decided to investigate how well ethical certification is working to create worksites that are free from labor exploitation, using the tea and cocoa supply chains as case studies.

8.3 THE GLOBAL BUSINESS OF FORCED LABOR: RESEARCH APPROACH

From 2016 to 2019, I led a research project investigating the business dynamics and patterns of forced labor and labor exploitation in global tea and cocoa supply chains called The Global Business of Forced Labour project. The research involved extensive field work and data collection, conducted by a fourteen-person international research team. A full overview of my research methodology is outlined in the open-access overview report of the project's key findings.[11] In this section of the chapter, I will give a brief overview of the data I collected that is relevant to the question of whether ethical certification is an effective tool to combat forced labor in global supply chains.

The main goal of the project was to systematically map and compare the business models of forced labor, as these manifest in cocoa and tea supply chains. In doing so, I analyzed the patterns surrounding forced labor and exploitation in tea and cocoa supply chains, including how variation in certain businesses dynamics impacted labor standards. For instance, I included tea plantations of different sizes, covered under different certification schemes, producing for both export and domestic consumption, and of varying distances from major cities; all of these have been documented as significant factors influencing labor standards within previous research and can shed light into the patterns of businesses

---

[11] Genevieve LeBaron, *The Global Business of Forced Labour: Report of Findings* (SPERI & University of Sheffield, 2018). For further discussion of research methods to investigate forced labor, see Genevieve LeBaron, ed., *Researching Forced Labour in the Global Economy: Methodological Challenges and Advances* (Oxford: Oxford University Press, 2018).

that use exploitation and forced labor. As well, I evaluated the effectiveness of antislavery laws and CSR initiatives in preventing and addressing forced labor.

Because there is so little reliable secondary data on forced labor in global supply chains, I had to create my own primary dataset. The key components of this dataset are in-depth interviews with 61 tea workers and 60 cocoa workers; a digital survey of 536 tea workers from across 22 tea plantations; a digital survey of 497 cocoa workers from across 74 cocoa communities; 19 interviews with international business actors, including executives of MNCs, ethical certification, and social auditing firms; 25 interviews with domestic business actors, including owners and managers of tea plantations and cocoa farms, as well as buyers, packagers, exporters, and industry associations; 28 interviews with international organization officers and government representatives from India, Ghana, the United Kingdom, and the United States; 40 interviews with experts from civil society, trade unions, and academia; and export data that linked these industries to the UK market. Importantly, given the focus of this chapter, the dataset included worksites that had been certified by leading ethical certifiers like Fairtrade, Rainforest Alliance, UTZ, and Trustea.

Before turning to the findings, I want to briefly explain two key motivations for my approach. First, the empirical evidence base on contemporary dynamics of forced labor is incredibly thin, and much of the data that does exist has gathered only very limited information from workers, or focused on small groups of workers. This type of data, of course, can helpfully shed light into the experiences and dynamics of forced labor, but it is less useful in giving us a sense of the patterns. Why does forced labor occur in some portions of the supply chain and not others? Or among some types of businesses but not others? To have the necessary traction to explore these sorts of questions, a larger sample size of workers is required. Interviewing workers – and especially a large sample of them – is a surprisingly rare practice within research on labor standards in global supply chains; often, researchers are more focused on standard setting processes and their legitimacy than the actual labor dynamics and experiences of workers on the ground. Second, there is very little reliable data on the businesses that perpetrate exploitation and forced labor, since so much of the attention to date has been on the big brand companies at the top of the supply chain. To really understand the dynamics of profitability and exploitation surrounding forced labor, it is important to understand the businesses at the bottom of the supply chain, as well as the top, which is why I investigated such a diverse range of business actors.

Finally, I wanted to collect data that give a holistic view of working conditions within the tea and cocoa industries, and the place of forced labor within this landscape. Too often, research on forced labor takes a binary approach that is more focused on turning workers into either a one or a zero (where 1 = yes, the person is a modern slave; and 0 = no, the person is not a modern slave) than on understanding the nuances of working conditions and experiences. I have sought in this project to develop a methodology that can capture the prevalence and distribution of forced labor across work-sites, but can also shed light into broader dynamics of labor exploitation and into how severe and more minor forms of abuse overlap and are interrelated. I use mixed quantitative and qualitative methods to collect extensive data about workers and businesses, including measures relevant to the categories of "forced labor" and labor standards more broadly. This included data on the prevalence and distribution of forced labor in sectors and supply chains; financial details, including wages (promised and actual), deductions from pay, and credit and loan dynamics; and the size, profitability, and geography of business and supply chain actors. The method and instruments I have developed for this study seek to uncover the slippery overlaps between forced labor and lesser forms of labor abuse at the level of daily life.

Both minor and severe forms of exploitation are relevant to our interest in the effectiveness of ethical certification schemes, since the schemes set standards around both. For instance, they set standards around the provision of basic needs, underpayment, minimum wages, levels of indebtedness and debt bondage, and credit and lending – violations of which can lead to minor forms of abuse, or sometimes more severe instances of abuse, especially when combined with other forms of coercion. As well, they set standards around severe labor exploitation such as forced labor and the worst forms of child labor.

8.4 FINDINGS: THE IMPACT OF ETHICAL CERTIFICATION ON LABOR STANDARDS

I'll briefly explain the overall findings of the research project, to give context for my findings about ethical certification schemes. Overall, I found that workers in both the tea and the cocoa supply chains are subject to multiple types of labor exploitation and abuse, including forced labor. These include physical violence; sexual violence; verbal abuse; threats of violence; threats of dismissal; debt bondage; the under-provision of legally mandated goods and services including housing, sanitation, water, food, and medical care; non- and under-payment of wages; and requirements to complete unpaid labor as a condition of employment. Although we did not include language like "slavery" or "bondage" within our interview questionnaire, focusing instead on short fact-based questions about workers' conditions, workers used this language to describe their conditions. One tea worker explained, "I am working as a bonded laborer like a slave."[12] Another worker described, "the management do not treat the workers as humans."[13]

I also found that these dynamics are not "hidden" as is so often emphasized within the literature on modern slavery, and media and civil society accounts of forced labor, modern slavery, and human trafficking. Rather, there are predictable, stable patterns with respect to how employers profit from forced labor and abuse. Businesses use labor abuse and forced labor to make money in two key ways.

First, they use it to reduce their costs of doing business. In the tea industry, we found that employers systematically under-pay wages and under-provide legally mandated services essential to workers, such as water, housing, and sanitation facilities. Given the remote location of many tea plantations, and the history of bonded labor in India's tea industry, employers are legally required to provide basic services for permanent workers and their families on large plantations. However, nearly half of the tea workers within our research (47 percent) did not have access to potable water, over a quarter (26 percent) did not have access to a toilet, and nearly a quarter (24 percent) did not have access to reliable electricity. As well, workers explained that they experience fraudulent charges for these services; for instance, they are charged for electricity but do not actually receive it. In the cocoa industry, employers – usually smallholder farmers – seek to cut production costs through a complex system of financial calculations to under-pay workers and create situations of debt bondage. This includes fines for not carrying out mandatory unpaid labor (which workers reported is often a condition of their employment), fees for obtaining jobs on the cocoa farm, and deductions (e.g., for the cost of pesticides). In both industries, in the worst cases, these widespread forms of exploitation to lower costs were also sometimes accompanied by physical violence, threats, verbal abuse, or sexual violence. Sometimes, under-provision took place as retaliation for workers' attempts to exert rights or for taking part in a protest. As one tea worker explained, "Benefits were usually given, but

---

[12] Interview with Tea worker 1.   [13] Interview with Tea worker 30.

we started to protest on September 6, after that, for about 4–6 months they did not provide any of these benefits . . . there were power outages, no firewood. There was a lot of torture."[14]

Second, we found employers also use forced labor and exploitation to generate revenue. In the tea industry, this primarily took the form of seeking to generate revenue by lending money or providing services to workers and charging usurious interest rates on debts. In both industries, situations of debt bondage are closely linked to the under-provision of basic services and needs like drinking water, medical care, and housing. Most workers within our research reported needing to borrow money for food or medical care, since these were under-provided by employers, and in emergencies, they often borrowed at very high interest rates. As well, in the cocoa industry, employers generate revenue by forcing workers to carry out additional labor beyond the agreed terms and conditions of their normal work, such as working for free on the employer's other farmlands. Sometimes, unpaid labor required by employers could last for periods as long as three months. Failure to perform this involuntary labor results in deductions from workers' wages, fines, threats, or even dismissal. In the worst cases, these widespread forms of exploitation to generate revenue were also sometimes accompanied by physical violence, threats, verbal abuse, or sexual violence. In one example, an employer provided medical services for workers suffering from cholera, then required workers to work extra hours to pay off the "debt" for the cost of medical care (although this should be provided at no cost). As one worker explained, "The people of the plantation were suffering from cholera and then the manager by the name X provided them medical help and asked the workers to work 1 hour extra per day. They were made to work for 1 to 2 hours extra per day for 1 to 2 months . . . the workers were asked to work extra so that the financial condition of the plantation could be recovered. Many people died."[15]

As a result of these dynamics, worker wages are very low in both industries. Our research found that workers are living below the poverty line, in spite of being in full-time work. The World Bank's poverty line for lower middle-income countries such as Ghana and India is US $3.20 (£2.35) per day. The wages of the tea workers in my study were as low as 25 percent of the poverty line amount, and for cocoa workers, wages were around 30 percent of the poverty line amount. Their low wages, lack of savings, and high rates of indebtedness contribute to the severe

---

[14] Interview with Tea worker 50.   [15] Interview with Tea worker 1.

constraints that workers experience in exiting exploitative tea plantations and cocoa farms.

8.4.1 Comparing Labor Standards Across Certified and Noncertified Tea Plantations

It would be reasonable to expect that ethically certified worksites have higher labor standards than those that are not ethically certified. After all, ethical certification schemes set labor standards around wages, unions, and basic services that often go above legal minimums. However, our research found that certification makes no real difference to workers' wages, working conditions, or living standards in the tea industry – in spite of the fact that all of the certification schemes within our study set standards across these three areas.

Living standards on certified and noncertified tea plantations were broadly similar, and on some measures, certified plantations actually fared worse when it came to providing the services for basic needs that are legally required of tea plantations. I included within my survey and interviews several questions related to the provision of services for basic needs, and, as described above, found that these were being routinely under-provided by employers. Although ethical certification schemes set standards around the provision of services and basic needs – such as the provision of decent, private, secure, and structurally sound housing – my data suggests that certified worksites are falling short of these standards. For instance, over 40 percent of workers on certified plantations in my study did not have reliable electricity, nearly 25 percent did not have housing, nearly half lacked access to potable water, and a third lacked access to a toilet. As Figure 8.1 makes clear, across all four key measures of provision for basic needs, workers on certified plantations fared worse than those on noncertified plantations. Many plantations are remote and in rural areas with limited services, so if employers fail to fulfill their duties to provide things like health care and electricity, these may not be available at all, leaving tea workers at the base of highly profitable global supply chains lacking basic necessities.

Certified plantations don't fare much better at realizing standards when it comes to worker wages, as demonstrated by Figure 8.2. Across both regions within my study, workers on certified and noncertified plantations received nearly identical wages. In Kerala, where wages are generally much higher than they are in Assam, tea workers received an average of 312 Rs per day so long as they were able to meet the ambitious daily quota of tea,

Under-provision of Services for Basic Needs

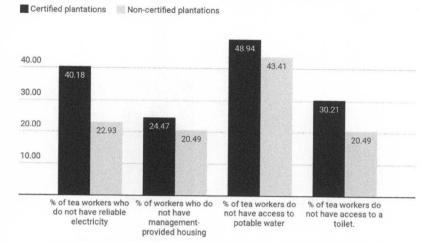

FIGURE 8.1 Under-provision of services for basic needs on certified and non-certified tea plantations
Source: The author.

Average Daily Wages (Rs)

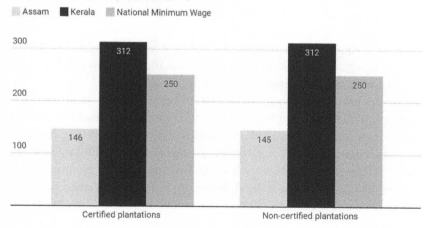

FIGURE 8.2 Average daily wages on certified and non-certified tea plantations
Source: The author.

which ranged between 21 to 27 kg of tea per day in the off season and 81 to 150 kg in the high season. In Assam, workers received a daily average of 146 Rs on certified plantations and 145 Rs on noncertified plantations, so

Wage Violations

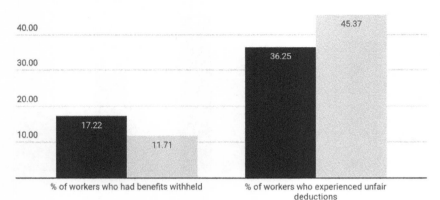

FIGURE 8.3 Wage violations on certified and non-certified tea plantations
Source: The author.

long as they meet the quota targets which range from 15 to 30 kg of tea per day in the off season and 81 to 150 kg in the high season. These levels fall below India's national minimum wage of 250 Rs per day, and there-fore, fall significantly below the wage standards set by three of the four ethical certification schemes within our study, which require that where there are multiple wage standards, the higher of legally mandated wages be paid (in this case, 250 Rs). They also fall dramatically below a living wage in India, which is calculated to be around 625 Rs per day.[16]

Finally, patterns of wage violations on certified and noncertified tea plantations were also similar, and on some metrics, certified plantations fared worse than noncertified plantations. As mentioned, our research found that plantation business models are configured to minimize costs by under-paying workers. This took several forms, ranging from penalties and deductions for failing to meet daily quotas, fraudulent deductions for services like electricity (which were not in fact provided), deductions for services or benefits that plantations are legally required to provide free of charge, to the non-payment of wages altogether. Figure 8.3 summarizes patterns of wage violations across certified and noncertified plantations

---

[16] This living wage figure is based on calculations by Asia Floor Wage Alliance.
While the living wage calculations are based on the garment sector, they are the closest reliable calculations.

within our study. Unfair deductions were a problem across both sets of plantations, with certified plantations doing slightly better – only 36.25 percent of workers on certified plantations reported unfair deductions, compared to 45.37 percent of workers on noncertified plantations. However, this still falls short of standards set by certification schemes included within the study. As well, 17.22 percent of workers on certified plantations reported that their benefits were withheld by plantation management. In my interviews with workers, they explained that this included payment for Provident Fund (which a worker is supposed to receive after retirement), but which is sometimes not provided. As well, some workers reported that benefits were withheld as a punishment for reporting or protesting unfair treatment.

In short, although all of the certification schemes within my study set standards around workers' wages and living standards in the tea industry, I found that these were frequently violated by employers. Workers on ethically certified tea plantations also reported wide-ranging problems regarding their health and safety, including inadequate provision of safety equipment (e.g., for use while spraying pesticides), and serious health problems related to undertaking hazardous work. For instance, five of the workers interviewed in Kerala (aged between 31 and 47) reported heart attacks or serious heart problems.[17] As well, workers on ethically certified plantations reported similar patterns of verbal abuse, threats, coercion, and intimidation as we discovered on noncertified plantations. Workers also reported physical violence from plantation managers, as well as threats, and sexual violence, just as they did on noncertified plantations. Finally, they reported retributory, punitive, and discriminatory actions by management for their involvement in unions, strikes, or other collective action, just as on noncertified plantations. In the worst cases, these dynamics came together to create situations of forced labor.

In summary, my research found very little difference between labor practices and workers' living conditions on ethically certified and noncertified tea plantations, and these fell below certification standards and the law. It is definitely not the case that certification leads to worksites free from exploitation; by contrast, there is a profound gap in implementation between certification standards and the realities of labor conditions in tea supply chains.

---

[17] Tea workers 40, 44, 47, 31, and 29.

8.5 FINDINGS: CERTIFYING EXPLOITATION

Sales of ethically certified products are lucrative and growing. To take just one example among many, the value of Fairtrade International's retail sales went from US $1,032 million to US $8,099 million in 2015.[18] Certification is generating profits for retailers, certifiers, and brands – as well as for highly paid consultants, auditors, and others involved in "monitoring" and "verifying" compliance with ethical certification schemes. But there's very little evidence that it's working to actually achieve ethical working conditions. The question is, why not? And, what is it doing instead?

8.4.2 Why Is Certification Falling Short?

The reasons that ethical certification falls short varys across certification scheme, sector, and part of the world. But stepping back, there are four clear shortcomings across ethical certification schemes that explain why they are not reliable tools to detect, address, and prevent forced labor in supply chains. These include ethical certification schemes frequently creating loopholes around vulnerable workers, which means they tend to exclude those most vulnerable to forced labor; the inability of producers to afford the financial costs of meeting standards; limited verification; and audit fraud and deception. I'll briefly summarize these key issues, as they surfaced within my research.

In the first case, the design of many ethical certification schemes is not fit for the purpose of detecting and addressing forced labor in supply chains, notwithstanding their increasingly common use for this purpose. A common problem is that ethical certification schemes tend to exclude the most vulnerable workers within supply chains; these range from temporary and agency workers, certain forms of hired labor, to informal and home workers. For instance, in the cocoa industry, most ethical certification programs exclude hired and waged workers, focusing instead only on farmers. As one representative of an ethical certification organization explained, "the hired labor of smallholders is still an area we can't reach. Because you imagine, how much work it is to inspect groups of 4,000 smallholders and then to meaningfully control how they treat their

---

[18] Julia Lemond, Jason Potts, Gregory Sampson, Salvador Garibay, Matthew Lynch, Vivek Voora, Helga Willer, and Joseph Wozniak, *The State of Sustainable Markets 2017: Statistics And Emerging Trends* (ITC: Geneva, 2017), 31.

hired labor ... we don't have a system for that."[19] That hired workers – including those included within my study – are excluded from ethical certification programs is a major concern, given the widespread dynamics of exploitation and forced labor they reported.

A second challenge is that producers are often unable to meet the financial costs of the ethical standards set by certification schemes. This was a frequent problem reported by producers within my study. For instance, cocoa producers reported selling beans made with the same labor standards to certified and noncertified buyers, and acknowledged that these standards fell short of the expectations of certifiers. One farmer we interviewed explained that he could not meet certification standards because selling ethically certified beans does not pay enough to meet the costs of the standards. He explained that when he sold certified beans, he receives just 12 GHS per bag of cocoa more than he receives for the uncertified beans, which is insufficient to meet the much higher costs of the standards – such as, for instance, not using child labor. Another farmer explained that he received just 14 GHS more per certified bag of cocoa and this wasn't enough to cover the costs of meeting ethical certification standards. As he explained, "If I made the comparison, the expenses [of running the cocoa farm] is more than the premium."[20] While ethically certified products tend to cost more, only a very small amount of the extra cost paid by consumers finds its way to the bottom of the supply chain.

A third reason that certification schemes are falling short relates to limited verification. As a voluntary CSR program, private certification schemes are not enforced by government inspectors, but rather by private social auditors. Once producers have passed an initial audit by an ethical certification scheme (which varies in stringency and quality across schemes), most rely on self-reporting by producers to verify standards. This means that ethical certifiers are not actually checking whether or not their standards are being upheld on the ground. As one certifier explained, "We are working with around 118,000 cocoa farmers so we have not been able to visit any farms as of now but groups like [certified cooperative] for instance, they have workers who are mandated to visit farmers and check plantation on our behalf but us [certification scheme] workers personally we haven't been able to visit ever farmer's farm due to their numbers."[21] This creates the possibility that producers or their cooperatives will misrepresent their own practices.

---

[19] Interview with Certifier 3.   [20] Interview with Cocoa seller 2.
[21] Interview with Certifier 5.

While some ethical certification schemes do conduct external audits, these tend to cover only a small proportion of producers. For instance, one ethically certified co-op representative told us that they audit a sample of only 5 percent of the farms within the co-op.[22] Given how limited on-the-ground verification is, it isn't surprising that certification standards are so widely violated by employers.

Finally, ethical certification schemes are plagued by audit fraud and deception. Workers reported that when external audits do take place, employers tended to alter their working practices to meet certification standards, but then reverted to breaking standards once the certification scheme auditors had left. As one worker described, "For safety equipment, when the [certifier] team visits, in that period alone, there is a strict process of enforcement – like wearing this strip with safety equipment. But only when [the certifier] visits."[23] Workers on ethically certified worksites reported that employers are cheating audit processes, by creating misleading pictures of working conditions during their short annual visits.

8.4.3 Misleading Consumers, Civil Society, and Policy-makers

The reality is that although ethical certification schemes are being touted as a solution to the problem of forced labor in supply chains, they are currently an ineffective tool to improve labor standards. They are falling short when it comes to creating worksites on which workers are guaranteed minimum wage, have basic needs met, and are protected from abuse, sexual violence, debt bondage, and other bad and illegal practices by employers. That ethical certification schemes do not guarantee safe, fair, and ethical working conditions for workers would no doubt come as a surprise to many consumers and policy-makers. Indeed, consumers who buy ethically certified products are trying to ensure that they do not support companies whose products are made by exploited workforces, so they would surely be disappointed to discover that the extra money they are paying is not actually ending up in workers' pockets. Similarly, policy-makers reading about the expansion of ethical certification within businesses' modern slavery reporting no doubt also expect that if this tool is being used to address forced labor, it is fit for purpose.

Ultimately, ethical certification is doing more to cover up labor abuse in global supply chains than it is doing to fix it. As ethical certifiers rubber stamp and lend their logos to abusive employers, rack in the sales of their

[22] Interview with Cocoa buyer 4.   [23] Interview with Tea worker 51.

products, and advertise themselves as offering an alternative to unequal and exploitative trade in global supply chains, they are profiting from the impression that they can rid supply chains of labor abuse. They are well aware that abuse continues to take place within these supply chains. The certifiers I spoke to within my research were open about this. They repeatedly claimed that ethical certification "is no guarantee. We don't use the word guarantee."[24] Another explained, in relation to child labor, "I mean, [certification scheme] doesn't guarantee that there would not be any child labor in your systems ... We can't guarantee that there is no child labor but we are making efforts to make sure that there would not be any child labor in our supply chain."[25] Those ethical certifiers do not "guarantee" that the standards they advertise are actually met within supply chains should raise big questions for those buying and supporting their products and organizations. No matter how well-intentioned, these programs are at best badly managed and executed, and at worst, they are brokering in deception to mollify consumers and protect corporate profits. It isn't totally clear which is the case, and perhaps, it is a bit of both. Regardless, given the sizable gap between ethical certifiers' standards and the actual labor conditions on certified worksites – as exemplified by my study of tea plantations – ethical certification schemes are creating a misleading impression of labor standards within supply chains. As businesses discuss their growing use of ethical certification within the context of modern slavery statements and reporting, and civil society groups champion ethical certification as a strategy to promote slavery-free supply chains, a false sense of security and good feelings are building about the ethical standards associated with products that is completely unwarranted.

8.6 UPDATING HISTORIC MARKET-BASED ANTISLAVERY ACTIVISM FOR THE PRESENT DAY

The research I've presented in this chapter raises some important questions, like: what can be done to stop the sale of deceptively marketed "ethical" products? Can ethical certification schemes be strengthened, and if so, how? Which market-based mechanisms would work better to combat forced labor in global supply chains? Does this mean that fair trade campaigns are no longer useful tools in the fight against slavery, as they have been for hundreds of years? These are big, sweeping, and

[24] Interview with Certifier 5.   [25] Interview with Certifier 5.

complex questions that I hope my research will prompt activists, consumers, researchers, policy-makers, and others to discuss together and reflect on strategies to combat forced labor in global supply chains. Here, I want to share some reflections on the historic contribution of fair trade movements within the struggle against slavery and on why strategies used by activists in earlier eras of global capitalism, prior to the legal abolition of slavery, may be less effective today.

As historians have documented, the fair trade movement goes back over 200 years and was a crucial force in early abolitionist struggles against slavery. In the early 1790s, hundreds of thousands of British citizens boycotted goods made by slaves in the West Indies, most famously sugar. Sales of slave-made sugar dropped dramatically. A few decades later, the American Free Produce society emerged in 1826 and pushed for alternatives to goods made through slavery, such as sugar and cotton. As historian Carol Faulkner describes: "Advocates of 'free produce' touted the superiority of free over slave labor, creating businesses and associations that offered producers and consumers economic alternatives to slavery."[26]

African American abolitionists, women abolitionists, and other proponents of free trade, or trade that did not rest upon slavery promoted boycotts as a powerful and practical response to slavery. Free trade activists called for moral purity and abstinence; they asked for consumers to live without goods until the producers of those goods stopped making them with slave labor. As one influential British Quaker, Elizabeth Heyrick, wrote in 1824: "When there is no longer a market for the productions of *slave labour*, then, and not *till then*, will the slaves be emancipated."[27] Free produce stores popped up in cities like Philadelphia, giving consumers the ability to shop and take part in burgeoning consumer society without upholding "slaveholders" power over the mind, soul, body, and produce of the slave.[28]

It is challenging to know in retrospect whether the verification systems that free trade activists used were more effective than those used today. But their task was in some ways simpler than ours is today. Back then, because slavery was legal in many countries it was easier to determine whether goods were made with slavery or not based on their place of origin. If a country hadn't abolished slavery, and if the industry was

---

[26] Carol Faulkner, "The Root of the Evil: Free Produce and Radical Antislavery, 1820-1860," *Journal of the Early Republic* 27, no. 3 (2007), 377–405.

[27] As quoted in Faulkner, "The Root of the Evil," 381.

[28] As quoted in Faulkner, "The Root of the Evil," 388.

known to depend on slave labor (which was concentrated in certain industries), then the product was a good candidate for boycott. For instance, West Indies sugar was slave-grown, while East Indies sugar was produced by "free" labor. Thus, when abolitionists pushed for the boycott of slave-made sugar, they could offer the alternative of non-slave made sugar. Where alternatives couldn't be procured, some sellers would resist selling the good entirely. For instance, Quaker merchant James Wright advertised in 1792 that he wouldn't be selling sugar until he could procure it through "channels less contaminated, more unconnected with slavery, less polluted with human blood."[29]

The global economy – and global trade and production, in particular – has changed dramatically since the eighteenth century when this form of fair trade activism first arose. Today, because slavery and overlapping forms of forced labor are illegal, it is much harder to determine which products are made with illegal labor practices and which are not. It is no longer as easy as saying, let's boycott all of the sugar coming from a certain part of the world. As well, the list of products that would need to be boycotted has grown much longer. The US Department of Labor creates a list each year of the goods made with forced and child labor (the TVPRA list). The 2018 list includes 148 goods, from garments to cotton, from bricks to poultry, from coffee to flowers, from cereal to tea, and from gold to silk.[30] Reading through this list, it is hard to think of a single item that one could purchase from a grocery store or shopping mall that isn't dependent on forced and child labor. These practices now pervade large swathes of the economy.

Another challenge is the division and compartmentalization of production processes. While in previous eras of global capitalism, entire products were made by the same workforce, today, products often contain parts made by dozens of different workforces sometimes spanning multiple national borders. For instance, *The New York Times* reported in 2012 that an Apple iPhone contains glass produced in Taiwan and Japan, circuits from Korea, microelectronics from Morocco, semiconductors from Germany and Malaysia, metal from Asia and Africa, and is assembled across 18 factories in China.[31] The rise of subcontracting, and

---

[29] James Wright, Letter in the *General Evening Post*, March 6, 1792, accessed May 18, 2020, http://gallery.nen.gov.uk/asset72644_1318-abolition.html.

[30] U.S. Department of Labor, *2018 List of Goods Produced by Child Labor or Forced Labor* (Washington DC: US DOL, 2018).

[31] Charles Duhigg and Keith Bradsher, "How the U.S. Lost Out on iPhone Work," *The New York Times*, January 21, 2012.

splintering of production around the world, means that it is far harder than it used to be to determine whether a product is slavery-free because the parts within it are often made by several different workforces. Furthermore, within those workforces, workers may even have several different employers, since some could be contract workers provided by recruiters, agents, or other intermediaries, subject to debt-bondage before they've even arrived on the factory floor.

What's more, consumers do not have the same level of choice between companies. The growth and monopolization of corporations, and concentrations of corporate ownership, means that today companies tend to source products from many parts of the world and sell them under different brand names. For example, a single consumer goods conglomerate company – "Unilever" – owns a range of tea brands, including Lipton, Tazo, PG Tips, Pukka, Bushells, and Pure Leaf. To make its tea products, Unilever buys and blends tea from many different parts of the world. Even if one were to boycott all of a single tea company's brands, the reality is, vast swathes of the global tea market are controlled by just three massive mega-companies who operate in competitive markets and have huge overlap in their sourcing base since tea producers often sell to more than one company. The nature of global sourcing and the size of contemporary multinational corporations thus introduce significant hurdles to traditional models of free trade activism.

To put it simply, it's far more complicated than it used to be to achieve change in business practices through boycotts. Long gone are the days that a single company or regional product can be boycotted, in favor of an easily identified slave-free alternative. Indeed, today, boycotting a single brand of product rarely has the result that its intended, since the alternative brand is often owned by the same monopoly company, or another company with similarly demanding shareholders pushing for short-term growth and profit. These developments have profound implications for our use of brand-based and fair trade activism today, and require some creative thinking by activists, workers, and unions to overcome.

That's not to say that boycotts can no longer be a successful tool in the fight against labor exploitation in the globalized world. Indeed, the Delano grape strike in the 1960s – which involved collaboration between the Agricultural Workers Organizing Committee, United Farm Workers, and consumers who boycotted non-union grapes – is a powerful example of a grassroots effort combining community organizing, boycotts, and union efforts to improve conditions for exploited workers. Its lessons have been chronicled in history books by Frank Bardacke, Miriam Pawel, Matt

Garcia, and others.[32] Even more recently, the Fair Food Program launched in Florida by the Coalition of Immokalee Workers show that worker-driven consumer boycotts can help workers to negotiate directly with buyers and win agreements that throw large corporations' commercial weight behind zero tolerance policies on modern slavery and gender-based violence.

One key continuity that cuts across both of these successful examples of market-based solutions to forced labor in supply chains is that it is workers – not high paid consultants, for-profit social auditors, companies, or anyone else – who are tasked with identifying which goods are slavery-free and which are not. Workers are best equipped to speak to the labor standards on any given production site and associated with any given products. They are also best equipped to monitor labor standards, as they do in the Fair Food Program and similar worker-driven social responsibility initiatives. Taking free trade initiatives forward and rendering them more fit for the contemporary global economy will require close and innovative collaboration with the workers making the goods that we buy, and empowering them to combat abuse – not sidelining them and leaving them unprotected, as is currently the case in too many antislavery and fair trade initiatives in supply chains.

8.7 CONCLUSION

This book asks what is working and not working in the struggle to fight modern slavery. I have argued that ethical certification schemes are not working. Not only are some ethically certified worksites little better than noncertified worksites when it comes to labor standards, as my research on the tea industry makes clear, but also ethical certification schemes are giving misleading impressions of the endemic labor abuse, poverty, and exploitation that continues to be associated with many products in the global economy. After over twenty years of nudging these schemes toward greater effectiveness and better performance, it is time to regulate their market in deception. Indeed, a key step in eliminating slavery from the

---

[32] See for instance Frank Bardacke, *Trampling Out the Vintage: Cesar Chavez and the Two Souls of the United Farm Workers* (London: Verso, 2012); Miriam Pawel, *The Union of Their Dreams: Power, Hope, and Struggle in Cesar Chavez' Farm Worker Movement* (New York: Bloomsbury Press, 2010); Matthew Garcia, *From the Jaws of Victory: The Triumph and Tragedy of Cesar Chavez and the Farm Workers Movement* (Berkeley: University of California Press, 2014).

marketplace is eliminating the market in deception by holding ethical certification organizations accountable for their claims.

We need supply chain and market-based strategies that actually work to address forced labor on the ground. Considering how market-based strategies like boycotts – which have been successful tools to combat slavery made-goods in previous eras of global capitalism – can be made fit for the present day is a promising starting point. The successful examples of worker-led boycotts in grapes and tomatoes are inspiring stories to turn to in designing new initiatives with workers at the center.

9

Preventing Human Trafficking

The Role of the IOM and the UN Global Compact on Migration

Janie A. Chuang

9.1 INTRODUCTION[1]

The year 2020 marks the twentieth anniversary of the United Nations Trafficking Protocol[2] – a treaty that offered an early framing of the problem of human trafficking as a transnational crime, best addressed through aggressive prosecution of traffickers.[3] Since the treaty's adoption, global anti-trafficking law and policy have evolved significantly. The once near-exclusive focus on the prosecution prong of the "3Ps" approach to trafficking – prosecuting traffickers, protecting victims, and preventing trafficking – has given way to an increased emphasis on victim protection. Prevention, however, remains the neglected prong, with efforts typically limited to public awareness campaigns to warn vulnerable populations, potential consumers of trafficked goods, and potential perpetrators regarding the risks and manifestations of trafficking.

We are now at a critical inflection point in our understanding of the trafficking phenomenon and how best to prevent it. With too few traffickers prosecuted and too few victims protected, more robust efforts to prevent trafficking are clearly necessary. In 2018, governments worldwide identified a total of 85,613 victims, brought 11,096 prosecutions, and

---

[1] A longer version of this chapter was first published as 'Preventing Trafficking Through New Global Governance Over Labor Migration' *in Georgia State University Law Review*, Vol. 34, No. 4.

[2] Protocol to Prevent, Suppress and Punish Trafficking in Persons, Especially Women and Children, supplementing the United Nations Convention against Transnational Organized Crime, November 15, 2000, in force December 25, 2003, 2237 UNT.S. 319, Art. 3.

[3] Protocol to Prevent, Suppress and Punish Trafficking in Persons, Arts. 2, 4.

obtained 7,481 convictions.[4] Considering that purportedly 40.3 million people are in "modern slavery" worldwide,[5] prosecution and post-hoc protection strategies have hardly made a dent in the problem.[6] That is particularly so for nonsexual labor trafficking, which despite constituting 80 percent of all forced labor/trafficking cases worldwide,[7] accounted for only 4 percent of prosecutions, 3 percent of convictions, and 13 percent of victims identified by global law enforcement authorities in 2018.[8]

Efforts by advocates to draw attention to nonsexual labor trafficking have underscored how trafficking is not simply the product of deviant, criminal behavior that, once rooted out, can be eliminated. Rather, deeply embedded societal structures that facilitate, and even reward, exploitation are also to blame – in particular, weak labor and migration frameworks that perpetuate precarity for migrant workers in their search for economic opportunities.[9] Because migrant worker exploitation and trafficking differ in degree, not in kind, addressing worker exploitation more broadly can prevent the abuses from escalating into trafficking.[10]

Recent developments in the international migration field present an opportunity to address structural contributors to trafficking by establishing norms and institutions to foster safe labor migration. In 2015, large-scale mixed movements of refugees and migrants prompted the UN General Assembly to recognize the need for States to cooperate, share responsibility, and to take action to address the phenomenon.[11] This ultimately resulted in the UN General Assembly adopting, in 2018, two

---

[4] United States Department of State, *Trafficking in Persons Report 2019* (Washington, DC: Government Printing Office, 2019), 38.

[5] The 40.3 million includes 15.4 million in forced marriage, and 24.9 million in forced labor. International Labour Organization, *Global Estimates of Modern Slavery* (International Labour Organization, 2017), 9.

[6] United States Department of State, *Trafficking in Persons 2019 Report*, 2–3.

[7] Of the estimated 24.9 million people in "forced labor" (a statistic often correlated with "trafficking"), 20.1 million were in nonsexual forced labor, while 4.8 million were in "forced sexual exploitation." International Labour Organization, *Global Estimates of Modern Slavery*, 9–10.

[8] United States Department of State, *Trafficking in Persons Report 2019*, 38. The statistics cited included a breakout of the total prosecutions, convictions, and victims identified in cases involving nonsexual labor trafficking in 2018: 11,096 (457) prosecutions; 7,481 (259) convictions; 85,613 (11,009) victims identified.

[9] Janie A. Chuang, "Exploitation Creep and the Unmaking of Human Trafficking Law," *American Journal of International Law*, 108 (2014): 609–649.

[10] Hila Shamir, "A Labor Paradigm for Human Trafficking," *UCLA Law Review*, 60 (2012): 76–136, citation on 110.

[11] G. A. Res. 71/1, "New York Declaration for Refugees and Migrants" (September 19, 2016).

global compacts: a Global Compact on Refugees (Refugee Compact), and a Global Compact for Safe, Orderly, and Regular Migration (GCM).[12] The Refugee Compact builds upon established refugee law and policy to improve States' responses to large movements of refugees and protracted refugee situations. By contrast, the GCM is the international community's first attempt to develop a framework for achieving a shared vision of safe, orderly, and regular global migration.

Unlike for refugees, who are the subject of a robust regime of laws, policies, and institutions, migrant workers are the focus of only a handful of international treaties. Not only do these treaties suffer from notoriously low ratification rates, but the few States that have ratified them are primarily countries of origin rather than the destination countries where migrant workers are in most immediate need of protections. Moreover, no international institution has been established to facilitate global efforts to address labor migration, unlike for just about every other issue of significant global concern – for example, the World Trade Organization (trade), World Intellectual Property Organization (intellectual property), and the UN Office of the High Commissioner for Refugees (refugees), among others.

At long last, the GCM is seeking to begin filling these normative and institutional gaps – suggesting the possibility of new global governance over migration. In addition to establishing a set of objectives for safe and orderly migration, the GCM assigns the International Organization for Migration (IOM) to the role of secretariat and coordinator for UN efforts to assist States with GCM implementation,[13] in effect elevating the IOM to lead global migration agency.[14] This chapter offers initial thoughts on the possible impact the GCM might have on global efforts to prevent and address trafficking, with a particular focus on the role of the IOM. Based on arguments I have made elsewhere,[15] my analysis takes as a given that a normative, rights-based approach to migrant work is necessary to

---

[12] UN General Assembly Resolution 71/1, "New York Declaration for Refugees and Migrants" (September 19, 2016); Rep. of the UN High Comm'r for Refugees, "Global Compact on Refugees," UN Doc. A/73/12 (Part II) (August 2, 2018); Intergovernmental Conference to Adopt the Global Compact for Safe, Orderly and Regular Migration, "Global Compact for Safe, Orderly and Regular Migration," UN Doc. A/CONF.231/3 (July 30, 2018).

[13] "Global Compact for Safe, Orderly, and Regular Migration," para. 17.

[14] UN General Assembly, Resolution adopted by the General Assembly on July 25, 2016: 70/296. Agreement concerning the Relationship between the United Nations and the International Organization for Migration, UN Doc. A/RES/70/296, Art 2(3) (August 5, 2016).

[15] Chuang, "Exploitation Creep."

prevent migrant worker exploitation and abuse from escalating into trafficking. From that perspective, this chapter explores the possibility that, in advising States on GCM implementation, the IOM could take a more proactive role in advancing workers' rights in furtherance of the longer-term goal of preventing trafficking.

Part I assesses the GCM's potential for advancing the rights of migrant workers. Whether and to what extent migrant workers are sufficiently protected against exploitation will turn on how States balance three competing concerns: (1) concerns over border security, (2) the desire to derive labor market benefits from economic migration, and (3) the imperative to protect migrants' rights. Empowered to guide States in their efforts to implement the GCM, the IOM will play a crucial role in helping to translate GCM norms into state practice. Section 9.3 analyzes the IOM's operational history and structure for insights into how the IOM might balance the GCM's competing concerns. The IOM's checkered history and its unique status as a non-normative UN-related organization suggest an inclination to prioritize States' concerns over border security and labor market access above concerns regarding migrant welfare. Yet, the IOM's recent efforts to promote ethical recruitment standards suggest potential for a more proactive stance toward migrant workers' rights protections. Section 9.4 explores these efforts, situating them within broader debates over whether and to what extent rights tradeoffs are necessary (or acceptable) to maximize the development potential of migration. In advising States on GCM implementation, how the IOM responds to pressures from development actors to trade migrant workers' rights for access to labor markets will surely test the IOM's professed commitment to ethical recruitment frameworks. That could prove to be a bellwether of the IOM's broader approach to balancing migrant worker welfare interests against States' interests in border security and labor market access. In this environment, close scrutiny and strong advocacy by rights advocates will be necessary to fully realize the GCM's – and the IOM's – potential to advance migrant workers' rights and prevent trafficking.

9.2 THE GCM AND LABOR MIGRATION NORM DEVELOPMENT

The latest available statistics indicate that, in 2017, there were an estimated 258 million international migrants globally (3.4 percent of the world's population), of which 164 million were migrant workers.[16] In 2018, migrants remitted approximately $689 billion worldwide, of which $529 billion were sent to developing countries, equivalent to over four times the amount of official development assistance.[17] With remittances accounting for as much as 40 percent of a country's GDP,[18] it is hardly surprising that out-migration for labor has become a de facto development policy. Not only do struggling economies benefit from the revenues derived from remittances, but there is the added benefit of reduced local unemployment rates. At the same time, favored countries of destination have come to rely heavily on migrant labor – particularly to fill the so-called "3D" (dirty, dangerous, difficult) jobs that local workers find less desirable.

Despite their significant contributions to these economies, migrant workers worldwide suffer from a lack of meaningful labor protections, and experience a wide range of exploitation and abuse, including trafficking. The absence of international labor recruitment regulations has enabled a rapidly growing private labor recruitment industry to enjoy impunity for a wide range of abusive practices. In most destination countries, because migrant workers enjoy limited labor protections, employers can exert inordinate control over whether and under what conditions migrant workers labor. For example, under most temporary guestworker programs, migrant workers' visas are tied to specific employers – meaning that when a worker leaves the employment, even if as a result of abusive treatment, the worker's visa is immediately rendered invalid.[19] Moreover, the threat of retaliatory termination of employment or deportation can compel migrant workers to endure abusive working conditions in silence. These structural features of cross-border labor migration can enable, if not encourage, exploitation that reaches trafficking or "modern day slavery" extremes.

---

[16] International Organization for Migration, "Global Migration Trends," accessed November 7, 2019, www.iom.int/global-migration-trends; International Labor Organization, *ILO Global Estimates on International Migrant Workers: Results and Methodology* (International Labour Organization, 2018), 5.

[17] KNOMAD (the Global Knowledge Partnership on Migration and Development), "Remittances Data," accessed November 7, 2019, www.knomad.org/data/remittances.

[18] KNOMAD reports the following amounts of remittances as a percentage of GDP for 2018, for example: Tonga (40.7%), South Sudan (35.3%), Kyrgyz Republic (33.2%), Haiti (30.9%), Tajikistan (29%), Nepal (28%), El Salvador (20.7%).

[19] Daniel Costa & Philip Martin, *Temporary Labor Migration Programs* (Economic Policy Institute, 2018), 2.

The glaring lack of labor migration norms and institutions reflects a long-standing and deeply-rooted bias against "economic migrants" in the international system. Border control aptly described as "the last bastion of sovereignty," States have been deeply reluctant to commit to legal obligations toward non-nationals within their territories.[20] As Professor Tendayi Achiume states, "non-nationals are definitionally *political strangers* with no cognizable claims to shaping the trajectory of the nation-state."[21] Sovereignty entails, after all, a nation-state's ability to define its political community, and hence the terms of admission and inclusion for non-nationals. The singular exception to this broad privilege to exclude is the obligation that most nation-states have accepted – under the UN Convention on the Status of Refugees and its Protocol – with respect to refugees, or those whose migration is compelled by fear of certain forms of persecution by their home governments. "Economic migrants," on the other hand – whose migration is viewed far less sympathetically, as motivated primarily by the desire for a better life – have no claim to States' beneficence unless they are deemed trafficked. (And even then, trafficked persons' claims to the protections of the destination country typically are contingent on their cooperation with efforts to pursue their traffickers, unlike refugees, whose status as refugees triggers State protections.) States' adherence to a fundamental distinction between refugees and economic migrants accounts for why the existing normative and institutional architecture of global migration governance focuses almost exclusively on *refugee* populations.

Merely a decade ago, economic migration was viewed as best addressed at the regional level and through bilateral arrangements. Engagement at the international level was limited to a series of global dialogues and consultative processes – for example, the UN High Level Dialogue on International Migration and Development, and the Global Forum for Migration and Development (GFMD). These fora enabled countries and other stakeholders to develop a "better common understanding of contested aspects of migration that are at the center of [international] debates, buil[d] trust between participating Member States and develo[p] ideas and data."[22] These dialogues and consultative processes fostered greater

---

[20] Catherine Dauvergne, *Making People Illegal: What Globalization Means for Migration and Law* (London: Cambridge University Press, 2009), 2.

[21] Tendayi Achiume, "Migration as Decolonization," Stanford Law Review, 71, (2019): 1509–74, quotation on 1505.

[22] UN General Assembly, Making Migration Work for All, Report of the Secretary-General, UN Doc. A/72/643 (December 12, 2017), para. 79.

confidence and willingness to engage in multilateral action. That foundation combined with the need to address large-scale movements of people – for example, from/through the Middle East and North Africa to Europe, Central America to the United States, and Bangladesh/Myanmar to other Southeast Asian countries – incentivized the international community to finally treat economic migration as an issue of urgent international concern.[23] After all, large-scale movements can have significant and widespread political, economic, social, developmental, humanitarian, and human rights ramifications across borders. A global approach is necessary to prevent and address the negative repercussions, particularly for developing countries, which tend to be disproportionately affected.[24]

The GCM was thus born of the recognition that international cooperation regarding economic migration is necessary to address the world's migration crises. The GCM thus signifies an important turning point, albeit with some notable limitations. The GCM is a non-binding instrument – an unfortunate but necessary concession in order to bring States to the negotiating table. Despite explicitly affirming "the sovereign right of states to determine their national migration policy and their prerogative to govern migration within their jurisdiction in accordance with international law,"[25] some states (including the United States) withdrew, claiming sovereignty concerns.[26] As to the substance of the instrument, the GCM is built around a set of twenty-three "Objectives for Safe, Orderly and Regular Migration," each accompanied by a list of actions States can take to realize each objective. The Objectives are wide-ranging and attempt to balance States' concerns over border security, their desire to derive economic gains from migration, and the imperative to reduce migrant vulnerability to harm and exploitation.

GCM Objective 10 targets trafficking specifically, and includes a list of ten suggested actions to realize that goal. These focus on law enforcement measures to suppress negative phenomena related to trafficking – for example, monitoring irregular migration routes and cross-border intelligence-sharing to disrupt financial flows associated with trafficking. The proposed actions also feature a few strategies to empower both actual and potential victims – for example, awareness-raising campaigns to educate

---

[23] UN Dep't of Econ. & Soc. Affairs, International Migration 2019, UN Doc. ST/ESA/SER. A/438, at iv (2019).
[24] "New York Declaration for Refugees and Migrants," para. 7.
[25] "Global Compact for Safe, Orderly and Regular Migration," para. 15.
[26] Austria, Australia, Brazil, Bulgaria, Chile, Hungary, Israel, Latvia, Poland, and Slovakia refused to sign the GCM.

migrants of the risks of trafficking, and improved access to justice for victims and those at risk of becoming victims. Indeed, the recommended actions go further than the UN Trafficking Protocol requires, in at least two crucial respects. First, the GCM recommends that States "avoid criminalization of migrants who are victims of trafficking in persons for trafficking-related offenses."[27] Second, it recommends that States "ensure that the victim receives appropriate protection and assistance, not conditional upon cooperation with the authorities against suspected traffickers."[28] Both are guarantees that human rights advocates had unsuccessfully sought to have included in the UN Trafficking Protocol.

But perhaps even more significant for anti-trafficking efforts are the non-trafficking-specific provisions of the GCM that, if meaningfully implemented, would significantly reduce vulnerability to trafficking by targeting structural contributors to migrant worker exploitation. Many migrant workers throughout the world labor under conditions that do not rise to the level of trafficking, yet suffer significant rights violations for which meaningful access to protection and redress is limited if not non-existent. Such exploitation, if left unchecked, can readily worsen and become trafficking. Attending to the structures that enable these "lesser" abuses to occur, therefore, can reduce migrants' vulnerability to trafficking.

Take, for instance, GCM Objective 6, which seeks to "facilitate fair and ethical recruitment and safeguard conditions that ensure decent work." Objective 6 targets abusive labor recruitment practices, which can foster situations of debt bondage and forced labor. The suggested actions include, for example, prohibiting recruiters and employers from charging or shifting recruitment fees or related costs to migrant workers; allowing migrant workers to change employers; and ensuring migrants safe access to effective complaint and redress mechanisms in case of workplace violations.[29] If meaningfully implemented, these suggested actions would address major structural contributors to migrant worker exploitation and trafficking. The ability to charge recruitment fees provides unscrupulous employers (and recruiters) tremendous leverage to prevent migrant workers from leaving even extreme situations of exploitation. Many migrant workers cannot afford to pay the fees up front, so often obtain loans (at exorbitant interest rates and with family assets put

---

[27] "Global Compact for Safe, Orderly and Regular Migration," Objective 10, para. 26(g).

[28] "Global Compact for Safe, Orderly and Regular Migration," Objective 10, para. 26(g), emphasis added.

[29] "Global Compact for Safe, Orderly and Regular Migration," Objective 6(c), (g), (j).

up as collateral) that they pledge to reimburse with their earnings. To avoid harsh penalties for defaulting on the loans, migrant workers often refrain from complaining about workplace abuses because doing so could result in retaliatory termination, retaliatory deportation, and/or blacklisting from future jobs. Moreover, if terminated, the worker may not be able to seek employment from a new employer if – as is the case for most guestworker programs around the world – the worker's visa is tied to a specific employer such that leaving that employer immediately renders the visa invalid, and the worker out of status. Implementing Objective 6 by prohibiting recruitment fees, eliminating employer-tying of visas, and providing anti-retaliation protections would therefore go a long way to reducing migrant worker vulnerability to trafficking.

None of these suggested actions are new recommendations. Rather, they encapsulate what rights advocates have long sought (with limited success) to have included in laws and regulations governing migrant work. For example, rights advocates in the United States have sought to protect migrant workers who report labor violations from retaliatory deportation and termination, only to have proposed legislation languish in the US Congress.[30] US rights advocates have also sought a prohibition on recruitment fees. While they have succeeded with respect to workers employed by federal contractors that provide goods and services to the US government,[31] they have made few inroads toward achieving a prohibition on recruitment fees for US guestworker programs writ large – partly due to strong objections from business associations. Groups such as the US Chamber of Commerce have argued, for example, that only "unreasonable" (as opposed to all) recruitment fees should be prohibited, and, in any event, that the term "recruitment fees" be narrowly construed to exclude many of the fees typically charged to workers (e.g., visa processing, transportation).[32] On an even more

---

[30] Protect Our Workers from Exploitation and Retaliation Act (POWER Act), H.R. 5908 – 115th Congress (2017–2018).

[31] Federal Acquisitions Regulations, Subpart 22.17 – Combating Trafficking in Persons.

[32] See, for example, Letter from US Chamber of Commerce to the General Services Administration, FAR Case 2015–2017, Combating Trafficking in Persons – Definition of "Recruitment Fees" (81 Fed. Reg. 29244) (July 11, 2016); Letter from US Chamber of Commerce to General Services Administration, Comment on the Senior Policy Operating Group to Combat Trafficking in Persons Draft Definition for "Recruitment Fees" (FAR Case 2014–001 – Ending Trafficking in Persons) (March 18, 2015). The US government released a broad definition of "recruitment fees" three years after the prohibition was promulgated. Federal Register, Vol. 83, No. 244, 65466 (December 20, 2018), Federal Acquisition Regulation: Combating Trafficking in Persons – Definition of "Recruitment Fees."

discouraging trajectory, employer-tying remains the norm in guestworker programs in the United States and many countries abroad, particularly in Gulf States utilizing a *kafala* system. Israel banned employer-tying in the domestic work sector in 2010, only to reinstate it a year later in response to strong lobbying by elderly and disabled groups concerned about caregiver turnover.[33] In a similarly regressive move, in 2012, the United Kingdom introduced employer-tying of visas for domestic workers as part of a broader effort to restrict entry of low-skilled migrants – which resulted in markedly increased rates of abuse as compared to the previous period, when domestic workers were free to change employers.[34]

Although the GCM suggests States undertake targeted action in all of these areas, ensuring that States actually do so will require overcoming significant resistance, not only by States, but also by powerful non-state actors to whom States have long outsourced labor migration governance. The goal of improving migrant worker welfare will inevitably be weighed against the competing concerns of facilitating access to migrant labor markets and maintaining border control. Given its assigned role under the GCM, the IOM is well-positioned to influence State actions on such matters. But determining how the IOM might strike the balance between competing concerns requires a closer look at the IOM's operational history and structure, as explored further below.

9.3 LABOR MIGRATION MANAGEMENT AND THE IOM

Until its elevation to lead migration agency under the GCM, the IOM existed largely on the periphery of the international system. Despite its extensive operations, the IOM has rarely been examined in academic literature, in part due to (mis)perceptions of its historical insignificance as a glorified travel agency, and in part due to its opacity as an institution. Its newly elevated status, however, has drawn a spotlight on the organization, illuminating two aspects of the IOM's structure and operational history that have raised concerns regarding the human rights and labor

---

[33] Adriana Kemp and Rebeca Raijman, "Bringing in State Regulations, Private Brokers, and Local Employers: A Meso-Level Analysis of Labor Trafficking in Israel," *International Migration Review* 48, no. 3 (2014): 604–42, 617–18.

[34] Siobhan Mullally and Clíodhna Murphy, "Migrant Domestic Workers in the UK: Enacting Exclusions, Exemptions, and Rights," *Human Rights Quarterly* 36, no. 2, (2014): 397–427, 411–13; Kalayaan, *Slavery by Another Name: The Tied Migrant Domestic Worker Visa* (May 2013), accessed May 18, 2020, www.kalayaan.org.uk/wp-content/uploads/2014/09/Slavery-by-a-new-name-Briefing.pdf.

rights implications of the IOM's new role. The first is the IOM's checkered history with respect to its operations on the ground, which have both advanced and also severely constrained (if not violated) the rights of migrants. The second is the IOM's status as a UN "related organization" that, unlike UN specialized agencies that also deal with migrant populations (e.g., UNHCR, OHCHR, ILO), does not have a normative protection mandate. Both features call into question whether the IOM would prioritize migrant welfare in advising States on GCM implementation.

9.3.1 IOM's Operational History

Founded in 1951, the IOM has grown from a small, intergovernmental body of 16 Member States to an organization of 173 Member States (and a further 8 States with observer status). Unlike UN specialized agencies such as UNHCR and the ILO, the IOM is a decidedly *non*-normative organization, and thus is not required to engage in rights-based governance. Its Constitution simply establishes that the IOM is to provide migration services to its Member States and that in carrying out its functions, IOM is to cooperate with other entities concerned with migration, and to recognize the primacy of national law. To implement this mandate, the IOM maintains a small headquarters office in Geneva, while its approximately 10,000 employees primarily staff the IOM's 500 field offices and duty stations located in over 100 countries. The IOM works in four areas of "migration management": migration and development, facilitating migration, regulating migration, and forced migration.[35] Its diverse activities have included, for example, refugee resettlement, repatriation of trafficked persons and unsuccessful asylum seekers, labor recruitment, and implementation of immigrant detention programs, among others.

This wide range of activities is at least partly attributable to the IOM's funding model. Unlike UN specialized agencies, the IOM does not receive a regular budget within which to balance its activities. Instead, its funding relies on activity-based costing such that the IOM offices and staff survival depend on the acquisition of projects. As Dr. Fabian Georgi explains, projectization "creates an instrumental-rational logic that establishes the monetary value of a project as an independent and important factor in addition to its practical-use value or its normative

---

[35] International Organization for Migration, "About IOM," accessed November 7, 2019, www.iom.int/about-iom.

justification."[36] Projectization combined with the IOM's decentralized structure results in the IOM operating like a private company, or a "bureaucratic entrepreneur" whose first priority is survival.[37] This funding structure has created the perception that the "IOM as an agency will do anything as long as there's money with which to do it."[38] The IOM's heavy reliance on projects for mostly Western governments of industrialized countries – which have relied on the IOM for its "jack of all trades" flexibility and its logistical efficiency in project delivery – has fed the perception that the IOM is an "instrument of Northern foreign policy."[39]

The IOM's funding structure and its lack of a normative mandate have fostered the perception that the IOM is a "deeply ambivalent organization" that engages in diverse activities that are contradictory, if not controversial.[40] The IOM claims a humanitarian mission – working "to ensure the orderly and humane management of migration" and "to provide humanitarian assistance to migrants in need, including refugees and internally displaced people."[41] At the same time, the IOM's involvement in the "ordering of movement" has drawn criticism from human rights organizations for using coercive practices (e.g., immigrant detention, refugee repatriation) that arguably "constrain rather than advance the rights and well-being of migrants."[42] Indeed, the fact that the IOM receives funding to undertake activities within the purview of normative agencies such as the UNHCR has prompted human rights organizations to question whether States might strategically fund the IOM to undertake these activities to avoid more rigorous application of human rights standards.[43]

---

[36] Fabian Georgi, "For the Benefit of Some: The International Organization for Migration and its Global Migration Management," in *The Politics of International Migration Management*, eds. Martin Geiger and Antoine Pécoud, 45–72 (Basingstoke, UK: Palgrave Macmillan, 2010), 63.

[37] Martin Geiger and Antoine Pécoud, "The Politics of International Migration Management," in Geiger and Pécoud, *The Politics of International Migration Management*, 1–20.

[38] Georgi, "For the Benefit of Some," 63.

[39] Megan Bradley, "The International Organization for Migration (IOM): Gaining Power in the Forced Migration Regime," *Refuge: Canada's Journal of Refugees* 33, no. 1 (2017): 97–106, 103.

[40] Georgi, "For the Benefit of Some," 47.

[41] International Organization for Migration, "About IOM."

[42] Amnesty International & Human Rights Watch, "Statement by Amnesty International & Human Rights Watch to the Governing Council, International Organization for Migration (December 2–4, 2002)" accessed November 7, 2019, www.amnesty.org/down load/Documents/120000/ior420062002en.pdf.

[43] Human Rights Watch, "Human Rights Watch's Statement to the IOM Governing Council, November 29–December 2, 2005, 90th Session," page 7, accessed November 7, 2019, https:// governingbodies.iom.int/system/files/jahia/webdav/shared/shared/mainsite/about_iom/en/cou

Regarding labor migration specifically, the IOM's activities have reflected its entrepreneurial ethos and drawn concern regarding its normative commitment to migrant worker welfare. The IOM directly participated in labor recruitment in at least two pilot programs: working closely with governments to recruit Thai agricultural workers for work in Israel, and to recruit Guatemalan agricultural workers for work in Quebec. Both programs were mired in controversy. The IOM's involvement apparently did nothing to curtail the rampant human rights abuses suffered by the Thai migrant workers – including 122 deaths – detailed in a Human Rights Watch investigative report.[44] As to the Guatemala-Quebec program, the IOM essentially created a transnational labor migration corridor that ultimately rendered Guatemalan migrant workers "extremely vulnerable to manipulation and abuse."[45] The workers were allegedly mistreated not only by the IOM personnel directly but also by unscrupulous labor recruiters who emerged after the IOM was forced to end its involvement in the program in the wake of corruption scandals involving the Director of IOM-Guatemala.[46]

9.3.2 IOM's Non-normative Mandate

After several decades operating independently of the UN system, in 2016, the IOM chose to become a UN "related organization" – a status held by only two other institutions: the World Trade Organization, and the International Atomic Energy Association. The IOM could have become a specialized agency of the United Nations, which would have subjected the IOM to UN accountability mechanisms and the UN Charter's requirement of impartiality, and require the IOM to operate consistently with the normative protective mandates of UN agencies.[47] Choosing instead to

ncil/90/Human%20Rights%20Watch.pdf; Ishan Ashutosh and Alison Mountz, "Migration Management for the Benefit of Whom? Interrogating the Work of the International Organization for Migration," *Citizenship Studies*, 15, no. 1 (2011): 21–38, 22.

[44] Human Rights Watch, A Raw Deal: Abuses of Thai Workers in Israel's Agricultural Sector (2015), accessed November 7, 2019, www.hrw.org/report/2015/01/21/raw-deal/abuse-thai-workers-israels-agricultural-sector.

[45] Christina Gabriel and Laura Macdonald, "After the International Organization for Migration: Recruitment of Guatemalan Temporary Agricultural Workers to Canada," *Journal of Ethnic and Migration Studies* 44, no. 10 (2018): 1706–1724, 1720.

[46] Giselle Valarezo, "Offloading Migration Management: The Institutionalized Authority of Non-State Agencies over the Guatemalan Temporary Agricultural Worker to Canada Project, *Journal of International Migration & Integration* 16, no. 3 (2015): 661–677.

[47] Miriam Cullen, "The IOM's New Status and its Role under the Global Compact for Safe, Orderly and Regular Migration: Pause for Thought," *EJIL Talk!*, (March 29, 2019),

become a UN-related organization enabled the IOM to maintain its independence. The UN–IOM Agreement establishing the relationship, thus states that the IOM "shall function as an *independent*, autonomous and *non-normative* international organization in the working relationship with the United Nations."[48]

Notwithstanding its refusal to become a UN specialized agency, the IOM quickly branded itself as "UN Migration" – a move interpreted by some as an effort to establish equal position as the UNHCR, or "The UN Refugee Agency."[49] The IOM quietly assumed the role of lead migration agency not only in name, but in practice, as the United Nations transferred increasing responsibility for migration issues to the IOM that would otherwise be handled by the UN Secretariat or a UN specialized agency.[50] It therefore came as little surprise that the GCM would ultimately designate the IOM to serve as "the coordinator and secretariat" of a UN network on migration, established "to ensure coherent system-wide support" to GCM implementation, including its "capacity-building mechanism."[51] Assigning the IOM this responsibility was controversial, as it bypassed a number of UN specialized agencies that address labor migration-related issues within their portfolios and under *rights-protective* mandates (e.g., ILO, UN Office of the High Commissioner for Human Rights, and UNHCR). Tellingly, the UN Secretary General, in a report providing input on the first draft of the GCM, noted that strengthening the international community's work on migration issues would best be achieved if, in time, the "IOM [was] brought more fully into the United Nations system as a specialized agency, properly equipped for that role."[52]

Contrary to the UN Secretary General's expressed hope, however, the IOM remains decidedly non-normative and independent of the United

accessed November 7, 2019, www.ejiltalk.org/the-ioms-new-status-and-its-role-under-the-global-compact-for-safe-orderly-and-regular-migration-pause-for-thought/.

[48] UN General Assembly, Resolution adopted by the General Assembly on July 25, 2016: 70/296. Agreement concerning the Relationship between the United Nations and the International Organization for Migration, UN Doc. A/RES/70/296, Art 2(3) (August 5, 2016) (emphasis added).

[49] International Organization for Migration, "About IOM;" United Nations High Commissioner for Refugees, "UNHCR-The UN Refugee Agency," accessed November 7, 2019, www.unhcr.org; Martin Geiger and Martin Koch, "World Organization in Migration Politics: The International Organization for Migration," *Journal of International Organization Studies* 9 no. 1 (2018): 25–44, 32.

[50] Cullen, "The IOM's New Status."

[51] "Global Compact for Safe, Orderly and Regular Migration," para. 44.

[52] UN General Assembly, Making Migration Work for All, Report of the Secretary-General, UN Doc. A/72/643 (December 12, 2017), para. 73.

Nations. As the IOM Director General Antonio Vitorino explained at a March 2019 event:

> ... in the migration field, we do not have the equivalent normative source that other agencies can build on, like UNHCR, [for instance, the 1951 Refugee Convention, and its 1967 Protocol], or like the ILO Conventions on the rights of migrant workers in spite of fact that [they're] not widely ratified – in the migration policy field, there is no equivalent normative [base], so everything will depend much more on cooperation, international cooperation with IOM Member States, and international organizations and Member States. That's the issue. Life is what it is. And therefore if you see what is with the UN Global Compact – it's quite clear that there are no conditions for speaking of a normative role equivalent to the ones of other agencies.[53]

Yet, as scholars have noted, although the International Convention on the Protection of the Rights of Migrant Workers and Members of their Families ("UN Migrant Workers Convention") is indeed poorly ratified, many of its provisions echo rights guarantees contained in widely ratified international human rights treaties.[54] Moreover, the GCM's preambular language explicitly states that the GCM "rests" on international human rights treaties and ILO conventions on promoting decent work and labor migration, among other treaties.[55] Hence, whether contained in international treaties or in the GCM itself, there is indeed a normative base from which the IOM could draw if it chose to pursue a rights-based agenda.

9.4 MIGRANT WORKERS' RIGHTS VS. "MIGRATION AS DEVELOPMENT" APPROACHES

Close examination of global labor migration dynamics and the diverse roles the IOM has assumed in migration management underscore why its lack of a protection mandate matters. Global labor migration is marked by normative and governance gaps, particularly with respect to transnational labor recruitment practices. While States remain key players in labor migration, strategic non-state actors have also assumed prominent roles. Over the years, governments have increasingly outsourced cross-border labor

---

[53] Migration Policy Institute, A Conversation with António Vitorino, the Director General of the International Organization for Migration (March 6, 2019), video available at www.migrationpolicy.org/events/conversation-director-general-international-organization-migration.

[54] Ryszard Cholewinski, *"The Rights of Migrant Workers," International Migration Law: Developing Paradigms and Key Challenges* (The Hague: Asser Press, 2007): 255–74.

[55] "Global Compact for Safe, Orderly and Regular Migration," para. 2.

migration management – a 'de-responsibilization' of state agencies for labor migrants' rights and conditions – to these largely unregulated actors.[56] In doing so, they have fostered the creation of a highly competitive recruitment industry that has tended to prioritize private profit interests over migrant welfare.[57] That countries of origin and countries of destination view these migration pathways as mutually beneficial disincentivizes close scrutiny of the myriad ways that labor migration structures render migrants vulnerable to exploitation. Even where States attempt to minimize the risks migrants face, power imbalances between States – and between migrants differently situated within racialized and gendered labor markets, on the one hand, and the various actors who profit from the migration industry, on the other[58] – can readily undermine such efforts.

Given these dynamics, a rights-based approach is critical to ensure meaningful protection of migrant workers. Otherwise, the balance of interests underlying the GCM could readily tilt in favor of perpetuating the status quo, prioritizing interests in border control or labor market access over migrants' rights protections. The anti-trafficking field is already showing indications of a softening of rights standards, for example, with respect to efforts to address trafficking in labor supply chains, where proposed interventions have arguably diverted focus away from state responsibility and toward corporate social responsibility. Rather than sustained pressure on States to adopt laws and regulations to strengthen labor protections and accountability mechanisms, pressuring businesses to adopt voluntary standards and codes of conduct has become a dominant rubric in anti-trafficking advocacy.

In its new role as lead migration agency, the IOM could be well positioned to reinvigorate and promote a rights-based approach to labor migration governance as a means of preventing trafficking. Although the IOM's past involvement in creating (and perhaps profiting from) new transnational labor streams is troubling, the IOM recently has made a concerted effort to promote ethical recruitment standards. Upholding those standards will, however, require the IOM to navigate growing pressures from development institutions to permit rights tradeoffs for the sake of increasing labor mobility.

---

[56] Kemp and Raijman, "Bringing in State Regulations," 608.

[57] Valarezo, "Offloading Migration Management."

[58] Pauline Gardiner Barber and Catherine Bryan, "International Organization for Migration in the Field: 'Walking the Talk' of Global Migration Management in Manila," *Journal of Ethnic and Migration Studies* 44, no. 10 (2018): 1725–1742, 1726.

9.4.1 A Rights-based Approach

The GCM empowers the IOM to oversee a "capacity-building mechanism," to which Member States, the United Nations, and other relevant stakeholders, including the private sector and philanthropic foundations, are invited to contribute resources. The mechanism will include a "connection hub that facilitates demand-driven, tailor-made and integrated solutions" and a "global knowledge platform as an online open data source."[59] This effectively assigns the IOM the role of collector and gatekeeper of ideas, through which the IOM can identify, articulate, and disseminate rights standards. In its extensive operations on the ground, the IOM often serves as a hub for policy discussion and debate, integrating a wide range of state and non-state actors to "incite" them to think and act in similar ways.[60] These interactions enable the IOM to shape perceptions of migration. As Professor Pécoud explains, the IOM makes sense of local migration realities by translating them into international migration narratives while also translating these narratives into local expertise via training, capacity-building, cooperation with local stakeholders.[61]

The choice of perspectives with which the IOM might engage in developing the GCM's capacity-building mechanism can predetermine whether the mechanism produces knowledge that advances rights standards. The IOM's work on labor migration issues, past and present, suggests contradictory impulses, however, regarding whether and to what extent the IOM embraces a rights-based approach. On the one hand, IOM's entrepreneurial and market-based logic leads it to focus on controlling and facilitating migration. Its migration management approach could be viewed as an attempt to overcome the tension between protectionist border control and the economic need for a flexible migrant workforce. After all, full control of borders is not only impossible but potentially counter-productive too because it would undermine the necessary circulation of workers in the globalizing economy.[62] The IOM's migration approach thus aims to sort good from bad migration – the orderly and regular from the disorderly and irregular – such that migration can

---

[59] "Global Compact for Safe, Orderly and Regular Migration" para 43.

[60] Julien Brachet, "Policing the Desert: The IOM in Libya Beyond War and Peace," *Antipode* 48, no. 2 (2016): 272–292, 277.

[61] Antoine Pécoud, "What Do We Know about the International Organization for Migration?," *Journal of Ethnic and Migration Studies* 44, no. 1 (2018): 1621–1638, 1633.

[62] Antoine Pécoud, "Informing Migrants to Manage Migration?," in Geiger and Pécoud, *The Politics of International Migration Management*, 184–201, 196.

thereby be "for the benefit of all."[63] But as Professors Barber and Bryan observe, the IOM's policies have constructed "ideal migrants/immigrants as those servicing economic interests rather than humanitarian ones."[64]

On the other hand, the IOM's recent efforts to establish its International Recruitment Integrity System (IRIS) – "a global initiative that is designed to promote ethical international recruitment" – suggest a proactive effort to expand migrant workers' rights.[65] Collaborating with a coalition of government, private sector, and civil society actors, the IOM has established a benchmark for ethical recruitment known as the IRIS Standard, and is developing a voluntary certification scheme for ethical labor recruiters to "provide assurance of compliance with the IRIS Standard."[66] Granted, IRIS might be yet another product of the IOM's keen entrepreneurial ability to identify an opportunity and to stake a claim to expertise and a governance role in a growth area. The substance of the IRIS Standard reflects, however, a commitment to promote international human rights and labor standards as well as recruitment industry best practices.[67] The IRIS Standard calls upon recruiters to respect all applicable laws related to labor recruitment as well as the core labor standards recognized in the ILO Declaration on Fundamental Principles and Rights at Work (prohibiting trafficking, forced labor, child labor, and discrimination, and upholding freedom of association and collective bargaining rights).[68] The IRIS Standard further enumerates specific principles: prohibiting recruitment fees and related costs to migrant workers, and ensuring respect for freedom of movement, transparency regarding the terms and conditions of employment, confidentiality and data protection, and access to remedy.[69]

These principles find support in the GCM, which includes a number of suggested actions that clearly prioritize humanitarian interests over economic ones. For example, the IRIS Standard's prohibition on recruitment fees directly aligns with the terms of CGM Objective 6 (fair and ethical recruitment and decent work). Whether and to what extent the IOM relies

---

[63] Pécoud, "What do We Know," 1630.
[64] Barber and Bryan, "International Organization for Migration," 1728.
[65] International Recruitment Integrity System (IRIS), "Home," accessed November 7, 2019, https://iris.iom.int/.
[66] IRIS, "IRIS Standard," accessed May 5, 2020, https://iris.iom.int/iris-standard.
[67] IRIS, "IRIS Standard," Principle 1.
[68] IRIS, "IRIS Standard," General Principle A: Respect for Laws, and Fundamental Principles and Rights at Work.
[69] IRIS, "IRIS Standard," Principles 1–5.

on the IRIS Standard in advising States on implementing GCM Objective 6 will be a measure of the IOM's professed commitment to ethical labor recruitment.

9.4.2 The Migration-Development Nexus

Adopting a rights-based approach, however, will require the IOM to resist calls from development institutions to prioritize increased labor mobility even at the cost of certain migrant workers' rights. The development field is currently in an "optimistic" period regarding the so-called "migration-development nexus"[70] ("MDN") – which views the remittances migrants send home as underutilized and crucial tools for reducing poverty and promoting long-term economic growth.[71] MDN proponents frame migration as a solution to development, and thus seek increased labor mobility – usually through proliferation of temporary migration (or "guestworker") programs ("TMPs"). TMPs typically impose, however, rights restrictions on participating migrants – the lower the skill level, the greater the restrictions.[72]

For MDN proponents, rights restrictions are an acceptable tradeoff for increased access to remittance-generating jobs in foreign labor markets. Not only can remittances "bank the unbanked," but they also produce macro-economic benefits such as increased foreign currency reserves, an improved national credit rating, and an expanded tax base.[73] Moreover, migration also yields "social remittances" in the form of new ideas, values, skills, and practices that migrants gain while working abroad and share with their communities upon their return home.[74] Migration

---

[70] Hein de Haas, "Migration and Development: A Theoretical Perspective," *International Migration Review* 44, no. 1 (2010), 227–264, 227.

[71] Martin Geiger & Antoine Pécoud, "Migration, Development and the 'Migration and Development Nexus'," *Population, Space and Place* 19 (2013): 369–374, 369; Hein de Haas, "The Migration and Development Pendulum: A Critical View on Research and Policy," *International Migration* 50, no. 3 (2012): 8–25, 8; Ruby Khan, "Remittances; A Development Mantra or a Dutch Disease for a Developing Country," *International Journal of Research in Economics and Social Sciences* 9, no. 10 (October 2019) 1–17, 1–3; Kerry Preibisch, Warren Dodd, & Yvonne Su, "Pursuing the Capabilities Approach within the Migration-Development Nexus," *Journal of Ethnic and Migration Studies* 42, no. 13 (2016) 2111–2127, 2111.

[72] Martin Ruhs & Philip Martin, "Numbers vs. Rights: Trade-Offs and Guest Worker Programs," *International Migration Review* 42, no. 1 (2008): 249–265, 251.

[73] Kerry Preibisch, Warren Dodd, & Yvonne Su, *Irreconcilable Differences? Pursuing the Capabilities Approach within the Global Governance of Migration* (Washington DC: Solidarity Center, 2014), 7.

[74] Preibisch, Dodd, & Su, *Irreconcilable Differences*, 9.

offers a cost-effective, "bottom-up" solution that gives individuals and their communities direct access to funds and a greater role in promoting development in their country.[75] This is a welcome alternative to top-down, state-centered macroeconomic solutions imposed and mediated by (sometimes corrupt) government bureaucracies.[76]

Critics of the MDN paradigm note, however, that available empirical evidence offers scant support for such enthusiastic claims to long-term development gains.[77] Moreover, as Professor Rosser explains, "countries ignore at their own peril the economic challenges inherent when an economy is injected with extra capital divorced from national production," including inflation and increased inequality between families that receive remittances and those that do not.[78] Indeed, reliance on remittance incomes can disincentivize local work and fuel increased migration.[79] This can result in brain and brawn drain, siphoning off people with the talent and energy required to pursue the political and economic reforms necessary for meaningful structural development. Indeed, critics argue, the MDN paradigm overlooks features of the global political economy that drive people to migrate – for example, growing inequality between countries and within communities, development failures, and poor governance.[80] It thus absolves states of their responsibility to pursue necessary reforms to address these causal factors, and instead shifts the burden to migrants to engage in "self-help" development.[81] Migrants and markets, instead of States, become responsible for bringing about development.[82]

Notwithstanding the criticisms, development actors have pressed for establishing more temporary migration programs worldwide in order to maximize the development gains from remittance-producing migration. Take, for example, the new organization, Labor Mobility Partnerships

---

[75] Geiger & Pécoud, "Migration, Development," 371; Ezra Rosser, "Immigrant Remittances," *University of Connecticut Law Review* 41, no. 1 (2008): 1–62, 52.

[76] Geiger & Pécoud, "Migration, Development," 371; Kerry Preibisch, Warren Dodd, & Yvonne Su, *Irreconcilable Differences*, 7; Rosser, "Immigrant Remittances," 52.

[77] Geiger & Pécoud, "Migration, Development," 379; De Haas, "The Migration and Development Pendulum," 10, 16–17.

[78] Rosser, "Immigrant Remittances," 21–22.

[79] Geiger & Pécoud, "Migration, Development," 370.

[80] Preibisch, Dodd, & Su, "Pursuing the Capabilities Approach," 2115–16; De Haas, "The Migration and Development Pendulum," 10.

[81] De Haas, "The Migration and Development Pendulum," 8, 10; Geiger & Pécoud, "Migration, Development," 371.

[82] De Haas, "The Migration and Development Pendulum," 10, 19–20; Rosser, "Immigrant Remittances," 51–52.

(LaMP) launched by the Center for Global Development, a prominent think tank working to alleviate poverty. LaMP "aims to be the first organization which actively works to increase rights-respecting labor migration, with a long-term goal of unlocking billions in income gains from people filling needed jobs."[83] LaMP shares the IOM's "triple win" view of migration – namely, that with productive policies in place, an increase in migration can create new opportunities and benefits for host countries, origin countries, and migrants alike.[84]

While rights advocates would agree that labor migration could pose a triple win under certain conditions, the perspective LaMP articulates below offers a major point of contention:

If more legal channels for labor mobility were opened, the incomes of developing country citizens could increase fourfold while global GDP could as much as double. These potential gains make labor mobility one of the most powerful tools for poverty alleviation currently on the current development agenda.

Despite this fact, the international community provides little support to migrant sending and receiving countries struggling to connect potential migrants (who need jobs) to potential employers (who need workers). The available support *often promotes international standards which may have little to do with local circumstances and needs.*

This leaves many countries with critical unanswered demand for support in an era when labor mobility is increasing and desperately needed[85] (emphasis added).

In other words, adherence to international rights standards is a problematic barrier to labor mobility. This perspective invokes the "numbers versus rights" debate in migration policy. As Professors Ruhs and Martin explain, "there is a trade-off, i.e., an inverse relationship between the number and rights of migrants employed in low-skilled jobs in high-income countries."[86] Increasing migrant numbers comes at the sacrifice of migrants' rights. The questions of whether and how to accept such conditions as a matter of

---

[83] Center for Global Development (website), "Labor Mobility Partnerships (LaMP): Helping Connect International Labor Markets," accessed November 7, 2019, www.cgd ev.org/page/labor-mobility-partnerships-lamp-helping-connect-international-labor-markets.

[84] Michael Clemens, Cindy Huang, Jimmy Graham, and Kate Gough, *Migration is What You Make It: Seven Policy Decisions that Turned Challenges into Opportunities* (Center for Global Development, 2018).

[85] "Labor Mobility Partnerships (LaMP): Helping to Connect International Labor Markets," Center for Global Development, accessed May 18, 2020, www.cgdev.org/pa ge/labor-mobility-partnerships-lamp-helping-connect-international-labor-markets.

[86] Ruhs & Martin, "Numbers vs. Rights," 251.

migration policy are deeply divisive, and the responses reflect fundamentally divergent perspectives on migrant workers.[87]

On the one hand are those (including rights advocates) who view migrant workers as, in a sense, victims of broader forces that push and pull them over national boundaries (e.g., inequality, climate change). As such, migrant workers are deserving of special rights protections, especially considering the significant economic and social costs of migration – for example, the psychological impact of family separation that migrants' families must endure. For rights advocates, the willingness to sacrifice migrants' rights in pursuit of uncertain economic gains signifies a hollowed-out view of "development" that fails to appreciate the importance of expanding human capabilities as a measure of development progress.[88] On the other hand are those (including MDN proponents) who perceive migrant workers as rational economic actors who can – and do – willingly accept rights tradeoffs in order to gain access to jobs abroad.[89] Hence, accepting rights tradeoffs is a pragmatic choice that also honors migrants' decisions to become "agents of development."

Adopting the latter view, LaMP's policy prescriptions focus on which rights to afford or deny to migrant workers in order to maximize labor mobility. LaMP has argued, for example, against a prohibition on recruitment fees (or "zero-fee recruitment") – contrary to the IRIS Standards, the GCM's suggested measures, and the preference of rights advocates.[90] According to LaMP, zero-fee recruitment (1) ignores migrants' willingness to pay recruitment fees as an "investment" that can yield "vast gains"; (2) ignores the fact that there are real costs associated with recruitment services; and (3) relies solely on governments' ability to regulate and enforce transactions over which, in practice, they exert little control.[91] LaMP acknowledges that migrants take on debt in order to

---

[87] Compare Martin Ruhs, *The Price of Rights* (Princeton: Princeton University Press, 2013), 154–186 (proposing a set of rights tradeoffs) and Preibisch, Dodd, & Su, "Pursuing the Capabilities Approach," 2120–23 (criticizing the policy focus on the "rights versus numbers" debate).

[88] Preibisch, Dodd, & Su, "Pursuing the Capabilities Approach," 2112; Geiger & Pécoud, "Migration, Development," 372.

[89] Philip Martin, Merchants of Labor: Recruiters and International Labor Migration (Oxford: Oxford University Press, 2017) 139; Ruhs, The Price of Rights, 39–52; Ruhs & Martin, "Numbers vs. Rights," 259.

[90] Rebekah Smith & Richard Johnson, "Introducing an Outcomes-Based Migrant Welfare Fund," LaMP Blog, January 16, 2020, accessed May 18, 2020, https://lampforum.org/2020/01/16/introducing-an-outcomes-based-migrant-welfare-fund/.

[91] Smith & Johnson, "Introducing an Outcomes-Based Migrant Welfare Fund."

pay (often exorbitant) recruitment fees, providing recruiters (and employers) leverage to engage in abusive practices. But instead of prohibiting recruitment fees, LaMP proposes creating an "outcomes-based migrant welfare fund" that would fund recruitment of workers as well as "the necessary government institutions for protections and oversight."[92] The fund would begin with an infusion of funds from social investors, but eventually become self-financing through contributions from the migrant workers, who pay a percentage of their salary to the fund if they "successfully find and sustain quality employment."[93] The recruiters would have "outcomes-based contracts," with payments for their services contingent on the quantity and quality of jobs they secure for workers.

From a rights perspective, LaMP's proposal perhaps has surface appeal for attempting to disincentivize recruitment abuse by making payment of recruitment fees contingent on satisfactory outcomes. But the proposal raises too many questions to inspire confidence in its workability. Who determines, and by what standards, whether an outcome is satisfactory? Are there protections against unsatisfied workers from being blacklisted by future recruiters? The realities of how unequal bargaining power between employer/recruiter and migrant worker manifests invites skepticism toward any proposal that does not meaningfully protect workers' power to demand better working conditions.

But even beyond issues of practical application, LaMP's proposal contradicts a core principle of ethical recruitment frameworks such as that embraced by IRIS: that no worker should have to pay for a job. Under the "Employers Pay" principle that IRIS promotes, employers should cover the costs of recruitment, in exchange for access to flexible and affordable labor markets.[94] Indeed, the GCM recommends States prohibit recruitment fees "in order to prevent debt bondage, exploitation and forced labor."[95] Prohibiting recruitment fees deprives unscrupulous recruiters and employers of their leverage to maintain substandard if not abusive labor conditions. Sacrificing zero-fee recruitment can only create and sustain migrants' vulnerability to trafficking.

---

[92] Smith & Johnson, "Introducing an Outcomes-Based Migrant Welfare Fund."
[93] Smith & Johnson, "Introducing an Outcomes-Based Migrant Welfare Fund."
[94] IRIS, IRIS Standard, Principle 1 (Prohibition of Recruitment Fees and Related Costs to Migrant Workers).
[95] "Global Compact for Safe, Orderly, and Regular Migration," para 22(c) (under Objective 6: facilitate fair and ethical recruitment and safeguard conditions that ensure decent work).

In advising States on GCM implementation, the IOM could stave off this and other rights tradeoffs offered in exchange for increased labor mobility. Ethical recruitment is but one of a number of areas for which the IOM could tilt the balance of competing interests toward migrants' rights protections. The GCM is rife with suggested actions for States to take to reduce vulnerability to exploitation and abuse – many, if not all, of which find normative grounding in international human rights and labor laws. Eliminating employer-tying of visas and establishing anti-retaliation protections, for example, would address significant structural contributors to the problem of human trafficking. These and other features of global labor migration are deeply embedded in the practices and policies of both destination and origin countries. Realizing the GCM's transformative potential will therefore require rights advocates to closely scrutinize the IOM's efforts to guide States' implementation of the GCM. Doing so with an eye to ensuring that States incorporate these and other worker protections could meaningfully advance overdue efforts to prevent human trafficking in the long term.

Integrated and Indivisible

The Sustainable Development Agenda of Modern Slavery Survivor Narratives

Zoe Trodd, Andrea Nicholson, and Lauren Eglen

10.1 INTRODUCTION

In 2015, the global community of 193 countries set a target to end slavery by 2030. This goal includes both forced labor (United Nations [UN] Sustainable Development Goal [SDG] 8.7) and forced marriage (SDG 5.3). As yet there is no blueprint for achieving these objectives, nor any indicators set for SDG 8.7 except one around child labor.[1] To build long-term evidence-based strategies for abolition requires the answer to a fundamental question: what key factors account for slavery's prevalence in countries, regions, and industries? In answering this question, we take up the challenge to see the SDGs as "integrated and indivisible."[2] We do this through the lens of slavery survivors' own accounts. To date, the policy community has rarely sought input from survivors on definitions, or antislavery policies and programs. Non-governmental organizations (NGOs), government bodies, intergovernmental organizations, and service providers often use excerpts or third-person summaries of survivor narratives in program reports and awareness-raising campaigns, but as they work to achieve the SDG target of ending slavery, they are missing the antislavery ideas of formerly enslaved people themselves. Survivors' voices are not yet at the heart of antislavery strategy.

---

[1] United Nations Statistics Division, Development Data and Outreach Branch, SDG Indicators, accessed May 18, 2020, https://unstats.un.org/sdgs/metadata/?Text=&Goal=8&Target=8.7.
[2] United Nations Sustainable Development Goals, Transforming our World: The 2030 Agenda for Sustainable Development, preamble, accessed May 18, 2020, https://sustainabledevelopment.un.org/post2015/transformingourworld.

In highlighting the possibilities for a systematic design of new antislavery strategies based on the accounts and ideas of formerly enslaved people, this chapter draws from a major new collection of contemporary slavery survivor narratives created by the chapter authors and other members of a research team based in the Rights Lab at the University of Nottingham: VOICES.[3] By releasing narratives from the form of short and often third-person excerpts to analyze them in their full and first-person form, we access an important new set of antislavery and development ideas. Focusing on India, we undertook an analysis of these narratives to identify commonalities and patterns relating to the 169 SDG targets, and the relationships between them. This analysis included a more detailed evaluation of a subset of slavery survivor narratives, those by survivors of forced marriage. The results let us begin to answer a key question from the point of view of slavery survivors themselves: which SDG target achievements (beyond 8.7 and 5.3 themselves) are more likely to prevent or end enslavement?

10.2 FORCED MARRIAGE AS A FORM OF MODERN SLAVERY

We coded all 162 India narratives in the VOICES database, approximately 160,000 words. The dates on which the narratives were given ranged from 1999 to 2018. We focused on India as a case study because the *Global Slavery Index* (GSI) of 2018, compiled by the Walk Free Initiative as a country-level breakdown of its *Global Estimates of Modern Slavery* (GEMS) of 2017 with the International Labor Organization (ILO), estimates India as the country with the highest absolute number of enslaved people in the world (7,989,000, which is an estimated prevalence of 6.1 per 1000 population).[4] These high global figures for India are reflected in our database: we have gathered more survivor narratives from India than any other country. India therefore gives us the largest dataset for analysis. According to the GSI, men,

---

[3] See University of Nottingham, VOICES: Narratives by Survivors of Modern Slavery, accessed May 18, 2020, www.antislavery.ac.uk/narratives. As of January 2020, the publicly available version of our database contains 1,000 narratives, with more awaiting transcription, translation, or a permissions process. All narratives discussed in this chapter are publicly available at the site. Although some survivor narratives appear under a pseudonym in the database, for example to preserve anonymity for the safety of the survivor, all the narratives quoted and discussed in the chapter use the narrators' real names.

[4] Walk Free Initiative, Global Slavery Index 2018: India, access May 18, 2020, www .globalslaveryindex.org/2018/findings/country-studies/india/.

women, and children within India are subjected to the two major forms of global modern slavery identified in the GEMS: forced labor (including forced sexual exploitation of adults and commercial sexual exploitation of children) and forced marriage.[5]

Mirroring the estimated global proportions of 2017 by the ILO and Walk Free, that 15 million of the world's 40 million enslaved people are in forced marriage and 25 million are in forced labor, 35 percent of the India narratives (50 total) were primarily narratives of child and forced marriage (rather than of forced labor).[6] Child and forced marriage is prevalent in India. It is estimated that the country has the highest absolute number of child marriages in the world: 15.5 million children are married before the age of 18.[7] Though young boys are also subjected to child marriage in India, girls are disproportionately affected. Child marriage contributes to a cycle of poverty, ill health, illiteracy, and powerlessness for children. Children subjected to marriage are more likely than other children to experience reduced levels of sexual and reproductive health, lower levels of education, physical and sexual violence and abuse, and posttraumatic stress. Child marriage results in higher levels of both infant and maternal mortality than adult marriage.[8]

---

[5] For the methodology of the Global Estimates, see International Labour Office and Walk Free Foundation, *Methodology of the Global Estimates of Modern Slavery: Forced Labour and Forced Marriage* (Geneva: 2017), accessed May 18, 2020, www.ilo.org/global/topics/forced-labour/publications/WCMS_586127/lang–en/index.htm.

[6] The Global Estimates find that 15.4 million of the 40.3 million victims of modern slavery (38 percent) were in forced marriage (and 24.9 million were in forced labor). International Labour Office and Walk Free Foundation, *Global Estimates of Modern Slavery: Force Labour and Forced Marriage* (Geneva, 2017), 11, accessed May 18, 2020, www.ilo.org/global/publications/books/WCMS_575479/lang–en/index.htm.

[7] Eighteen percent of girls are married by 15 and 27 percent by 18, see *Girls Not Brides, Child Marriage Atlas*, accessed May 18, 2020, www.girlsnotbrides.org/where-does-it-happen/.

[8] Juliette Myers and Rowan Harvey, *Breaking Vows: Early and Forced Marriage and Girls' Education* (Plan International, 2011), accessed May 18, 2020, https://plan-uk.org/file/breaking-vows-efm-3462225pdf/download?token=RlE5iobL; International Planned Parenthood Federation, *Ending Child Marriage: A Guide for Global Policy Action* (London 2007), accessed May 18, 2020, www.ippf.org/sites/default/files/ending_child_marriage.pdf; Judith Bruce and Shelley Clark, *The Implications of Early Marriage for HIV/AIDS Policy* (2004), accessed May 18, 2020, www.popcouncil.org/uploads/pdfs/EMBfinalENG.pdf; UNICEF, "Child Marriages: 39,000 Every Day" *Press Centre*, March 7, 2013, accessed May 18, 2020, www.unicef.org/media/media_68114.html; Girls Not Brides, "Health," accessed May 18, 2020, www.girlsnotbrides.org/themes/health/; Robert Jensen and Rebecca Thornton, "Early Female Marriage in the Developing World," *Gender & Development* 11, no. 2 (2003): 9–19; International Center for Research on Women, "Child Marriage and Domestic Violence," (2006), accessed May 18, 2020, www.icrw.org

Child marriage has been a topic of contention in Indian governance for over 140 years. In 1978 the government of Indira Gandhi amended the Child Marriage Restraint Act of 1929 to increase the minimum age of marriage from 15 to 18 for females, and 18 to 21 for males, ages that have been maintained to today in the subsequent Prohibition of Child Marriage Act (PCMA) of 2006. The PCMA also established punishments for those failing to prevent child marriage and implemented Child Marriage Prohibition Officers to investigate and intervene. In 2013, the age of consent for sexual activity was raised to match that of the legal age of marriage under the Criminal Law (Amendment) Act, in the hope of reducing the maternal, reproductive, and sexual health issues that arise from child pregnancy. India is now a member of the South Asian Initiative to End Violence Against Children, and the UNICEF Global Programme to Accelerate Action to End Child Marriage is active in the country.[9] However, despite governmental, intergovernmental, and local NGO attempts to reduce child marriage, the practice continues across India, especially in the central and western states (Jharkhand, Uttar Pradesh, West Bengal, Madhya Pradesh, Andhra Pradesh, Karnataka, Chhattisgarh, and Tripura).[10] Marriage brokers and child marriage perpetrators are seldom prosecuted, so that the financial rewards from brokering a marriage continue to outweigh the legal risks. Victims themselves are often unaware of their rights.

The parameters of slavery, including whether its definition include forced marriage, remain contested. Child marriage exists where at least one of the parties is below the age of majority.[11] The presumed inability of children to consent to a marriage essentially creates a forced marriage in all cases (a marriage that is not capable of being freely and fully consented to, due to the status as child). However, throughout this

/files/images/Child-Marriage-Fact-Sheet-Domestic-Violence.pdf; Eliana Riggio Chaudhuri, *Thematic Report: Unrecognised Sexual Abuse and Exploitation of Children in Child, Early and Forced Marriage* (ECPAT International and Plan International, 2015), accessed May 18, 2020, www.ecpat.org/wp-content/uploads/2016/04/Child%20Marriage_ENG.pdf.

[9] Girls Not Brides, *Child Marriage: India,* accessed May 18, 2020, www.girlsnotbrides.org/child-marriage/india/.

[10] UNICEF India, "End Child Marriage," accessed May 18, 2020, http://unicef.in/Whatwedo/30/Child-Marriage.

[11] Convention on the Rights of the Child, Article 1: a child means every human being below the age of eighteen years unless under the law applicable to the child, majority is attained earlier. Prohibition of Child Marriage Act 2006, Article 2(a).

chapter we refer to both forced and child marriage in order to differentiate between ages. Taking a wider approach to definition, child and forced marriage has been identified as a form of slavery.[12] From a legal perspective, and following the Slavery Convention of 1926 and its clarification in the *Bellagio-Harvard Guidelines* of 2012, forced and child marriage only becomes slavery where control tantamount to possession exists, although forms of exploitation might exist at a lower threshold.[13] The mechanism of a survivor's enslavement, and the presence, level, or type of abuse, are not definitive of slavery,[14] thus domestic labor and/or sexual exploitation (whether domestic or commercial) as a result of forced and child marriage is not a determinant of forced marriage as slavery. Sexual exploitation is not evident in every case of forced and child marriage, and so is not in itself a condition of a finding of slavery, although sexual exploitation could itself amount to slavery. The picture is further muddied in relation to child marriage, as the power attaching to guardianship "mimics the exercise of many of those powers attaching to a right of ownership and approaches possession," potentially lowering the threshold for controlling acts amounting to possession.[15] While there is a close relationship between child marriage, exploitation, and slavery, with domestic servitude often inherent in child marriage,[16] these connections do not necessarily make all child marriages slavery. Given domestic labor was found in all of the child

---

[12] International Labour Office and Walk Free Foundation, *Global Estimates of Modern Slavery*; Jody Sarich, Michele Oliver, and Kevin Bales, "Forced Marriage, Slavery, and Plural Legal Systems: An African Example," *Human Rights Quarterly*, 38, no. 2 (2016): 450–476; and Suzanne Miers, "Contemporary Forms of Slavery," *Canadian Journal of African Studies/Revue Canadienne des Études Africaines*, 34, no. 3 (2000): 714–747.

[13] Report of the Special Rapporteur on Contemporary Forms of Slavery, including its Causes and Consequences, Urmila Bhoola: Thematic Report on Child Slavery (July 10, 2019), UN DOC A/74/48045. Bellagio-Harvard Guideline on the Legal Parameters of Slavery, Research Network on the Legal Parameters of Slavery, accessed October 13, 2017, http://glc.yale.edu/sites/default/files/pdf/the_bellagio-_harvard_guidelines_on_the_legal_parameters_of_slavery.pdf.

[14] Jean Allain and Kevin Bales, "Slavery and Its Definition," *Global Dialogue* 14, no. 2 (2012): 1–15, 5.

[15] See Report of the Special Rapporteur on Contemporary Forms of Slavery, including its Causes and Consequences, Gulnara Shahinian: Thematic Report on Servile Marriage (July 10, 2012), UN DOC A/HRC/21/41; and Anna Mae Duane, "Does Dependence Create Ownership? The Problem of Defining a Child Slave," Beyond Trafficking and Slavery, openDemocracy, November 17, 2015, accessed May 18, 2020, www.opendemocracy.net/en/beyond-trafficking-and-slavery/does-dependence-create-ownership-problem-of-defining-child-slave/.

[16] Thematic Report on Servile Marriage, 2019.

marriage narratives, the picture becomes further complicated given international labor standards which allow for children to undertake varying levels of work. From a legal perspective, it follows that many marriages involving children will therefore not amount to slavery per se, but many married children will experience levels of coercion that meet national and international definitions of slavery, servitude, practices similar to slavery, child trafficking, and forced labor.

In assessing narratives that involved child and forced marriage to decide on their inclusion or exclusion as narratives by slavery survivors, it was not possible to select narratives for analysis based solely on the legal definition of slavery under the 1926 Slavery Convention.[17] To do so would require a judgment on the degree to which an individual was subject to control tantamount to possession. Some of the narratives were too brief to provide sufficient data for such a judgment. Nor was it sufficient to classify all child marriages as slavery. Conscious of differing views on the definition of slavery, we used the indicators provided by Anti-Slavery International (ASI) in a 2013 guide also heavily used in the 2014 report of the Office of the UN High Commissioner for Human Rights to the UN General Assembly, *Preventing and Eliminating Child, Early and Forced Marriage*. The ASI guide identifies child marriage as slavery when one or more of the following elements are present:

- if the child has not genuinely given their free and informed consent to enter the marriage;
- if the child is subjected to control and a sense of 'ownership' in the marriage itself, particularly through abuse and threats and is exploited by being forced to undertake domestic chores within the marital home or labor outside it, and/or engage in non-consensual sexual relations; and
- if the child cannot realistically leave or end the marriage, leading potentially to a lifetime of slavery.[18]

[17] Art.1 (1) Slavery is the status or condition of a person over whom any or all of the powers attaching to the right of ownership are exercised, 1927 Slavery Convention, accessed May 18, 2020, www.ohchr.org/EN/ProfessionalInterest/Pages/SlaveryConvention.aspx.

[18] See Catherine Turner, Out of the Shadows: Child Marriage and Slavery (Anti-Slavery International, 2013), accessed May 18, 2020, www.antislavery.org/wp-content/uploads/2017/01/child_marriage_final-1.pdf, which argues that child marriage can often operate as a shield behind which slavery occurs with apparent impunity. See also Anti-Slavery International, "Child Marriage," accessed May 18, 2020, www.antislavery.org/slavery-today/child-marriage/.

We included for analysis only narratives that featured one or more of these indicators, so as to ensure a sample by survivors of forced and child marriage that has sufficient evidence of potential enslavement.

10.3 CODING INDIA NARRATIVES AGAINST THE SDGS

The majority of the India narratives came from NGO research reports, and several from research institutes' studies. The VOICES database gives information on origin for each narrative. These NGO origins for the narratives presented challenges for analysis. We recognize that gathering testimony can be difficult and is often undertaken by NGO workers under complex field conditions. NGO workers who seek to document survivors' voices may face restrictions on resource and time for recording, translating, and transcribing lengthy narratives. The resulting brevity of some survivor narratives meant they only provided a snapshot of experiences. Some narratives' origins also meant they were likely defined by NGOs' agendas of explaining to their readers what a particular kind of exploitation or trafficking journey involved, which at times could have inhibited broader narration beyond key details. Where narratives were particularly brief, in some cases we did not know whether portions of narratives may have been lost as NGOs sought to present excerpts that illustrated the overall purpose of their report. The particular focus of NGOs may also have shaped their selection of individuals for narrative-gathering. For example, 70 percent of the narratives were by women and girls. In some cases this reflects the focus of particular NGO reports, which included women's migration and the experiences of married girls. Another data challenge was that, in some cases, we did not know what interview questions were asked to elicit the final narrative. Some narratives were likely collected through traditional semi-structured interviews, without presenting an opportunity for a full, free narration by survivors. The interview techniques used, and NGOs' particular aims in gathering these narratives, will have influenced the language, details, and overall arcs of narratives.

The fact that NGOs have particular focus areas for their reports need not conflict with the aim of listening to survivors' accounts and building a detailed understanding of the structural factors that underpin exploitation. Nonetheless, in analyzing the narratives, we sought to counterbalance these data limitations by combining short narratives sourced from NGO reports that did not provide interview questions or clarify any process of excepting, with longer-form accounts that we could check against audio or video recordings and/or read alongside interview questions. Our coding method then sought to further neutralize any narrative shaping and messaging by the NGOs. We conducted an initial fact-based coding of all narratives by type of exploitation: first into the two major categories of modern slavery identified by the GEMS (forced labor and forced marriage), then further into experiences of debt bondage, sexual exploitation, domestic labor, forced marriage, prison labor, and forced labor exploitation in economic activities. We also categorized forced labor into industries, including agriculture/fishing, construction, domestic work, and manufacturing. Many narratives indicate more than one form of exploitation. Our fact-based coding then covered age at enslavement, country of origin, country of enslavement, type and source of narrative, gender, religion, profession in survival, and means of escape. This was done to provide context to our analysis.

After this initial coding, we employed constant comparison and coded survivor narratives for risk factors that led to the initial experience of enslavement or perpetuated slavery once it had begun, including environmental disaster or destruction, gender, ethnic or cultural discrimination, family debt, lack of access to financial services, moderate or severe food insecurity, lack of birth registration, local corruption and organized crime, loss of family members due to poor health, lack of access to education, and poorly managed migration processes. We matched these risk factors with the 169 SDG targets, noting each target's frequency, the sequences and interactions of multiple targets, and any possible causal factors where one target issue led to another. Most narratives revealed at least three primary SDG targets and some as many as five. Our most common SDG codings against 8.7/5.3 for all India narratives were 1.2 (reduce poverty), 3.8 (achieve universal health coverage), 4.1 (provide free, equitable education), 4.5 (eliminate gender disparities in education), 5.1 (end discrimination against women), 5.2 (eliminate violence against women), 8.3 (support job creation), 8.8 (protect labor rights), 10.2 (promote social inclusion), and 11.1 (safe housing for all).

In then coding the subset of forced and child marriage narratives against the SDG targets, we identified that they share three main SDG target issues as drivers of enslavement through forced and child marriage: 1.2 (poverty), 4.5 (gender disparities in education), and 5.1 (discrimination against women). All 50 of the India narratives that are primarily accounts of forced and child marriage, rather than forced labor, feature one or more of these three SDG target issues as key drivers of their exploitation.[19] By contrast, the 112 India narratives that are primarily accounts of forced labor, rather than forced marriage, did not consistently combine these three issues, instead showing regular combinations of 1.2 (poverty), 3.8 (lack of universal health coverage), 4.1 (lack of free, equitable education), 5.2 (violence against women), 8.3 (lack of decent job creation), 8.8 (insufficient labor rights), 10.2 (lack of social inclusion), and 11.1 (lack of safe housing).[20]

The multi-SDG focus on gender discrimination, poverty, and education disparity in the narratives of forced and child marriage provides one route to understand why it persists in the country, in spite of long-running legislative and policy attempts to curb the practice. The three common SDG targets are in line with existing analyses of child and forced marriage in India, which tend to list poverty, lack of access to education, and gender inequality as among its root causes.[21] But most studies and reports gather data that is limited in terms of rich text and do not directly quote or analyze survivors' own accounts. This approach limits the possibilities for identifying nuanced approaches to tackling slavery's root causes and designing survivor-informed interventions. In addition, the NGO and government intervention programs aimed at forced marriage that we have identified and examined tend to tackle the issue through community awareness-raising or development around a single SDG target issue (e.g., girls' education). Survivor narratives state that enslavement stems from a multi-SDG vulnerability. They confirm that SDGs 8.7 and 5.3 cannot be achieved in isolation but require a multi-SDG approach that accounts for simultaneous vulnerability factors. If attempts to achieve SDGs 8.7 and 5.3 by 2030 do not take this multi-SDG approach, one that tackles modern slavery as a complex issue of sustainable development rather

---

[19] All the narratives of child and forced marriage also demonstrated consequences that can mapped onto other SDG targets, including 5.2 (violence against women including sexual and other forms of exploitation) and 16.2 (violence against children).

[20] The following targets also arose with less frequency across narratives of forced marriage and forced labor in India: 5.4 (undervalued domestic work), 5.a (lack of equal rights to economic resources), 5.c (lack of enforceable gender equality legislation), 8.5 (lack of employment for all genders), 10.7 (unsafe migration), and 11.2 (lack of access to safe transport systems).

[21] See for example the Nirantar Trust and the American Jewish World Service (AJWS), *Early and Child Marriage in India: A Landscape Analysis (2015)*, 5, accessed May 18, 2020, https://ajws.org/wp-content/uploads/2015/05/EarlyChildMarriageinIndia_LandscapeAnalysis_FULL.pdf.

than predominantly one of criminal justice or lack of awareness, progress will remain slow.

10.4 SLAVERY AND DISCRIMINATION AGAINST WOMEN (SDG 5.1)

The value of an intersectional SDG approach to tackling slavery is clear in the narrative of Papuram (2018). She was forced to end her studies early and marry a 26-year-old man. Her parents took loans to pay for her dowry. She recounts:

I often told my mother that I did not want to get married but she kept saying that she has two daughters and it was a heavy responsibility. There was a general fear that it was not safe for girls to remain unmarried and that we would fall in love and elope. My parents spoke about girls in the village who had inter-caste marriages and eloped. Thus my marriage was fixed to a boy who was 26, the only son of his parents and had property. I was only 17 and did not want to marry, but thought about my parents, their poverty and responsibility of settling my sister and educating my brother. So I agreed without much fuss. My parents took heavy loans to pay for dowry, gave cash and gold to the boy's family and got me married.

But when I reached my marital home, I felt unwanted and like a stranger. Nobody spoke to me. I was not given instructions regarding where to put my things and my husband and his mother objected to whatever I did. My mother-in-law would just not help. She was violent and demanded that I get soaps, toothpaste and other things from my mother's house. I was never given special food to eat ... My husband gave his salary to his mother and never asked me if I wanted anything. Even when I visit my mother's house, he demands cash from my parents for travel expenses.

They did not let me talk to the neighbors and would get suspicious. Soon, they started to beat me up on trivial issues and I began crumbling. My husband would not listen to my complaints and shut me up brutally. He would ask me to talk to him only when his mother is not around ...

For the first two years there was no consummation of marriage. My mother-in-law would accuse me of not having children and used that as an excuse to beat me up. I picked up courage one day, confronted and told her that she very well knew that there had been no sexual contact between me and my husband and how did she expect me to have children? She said that I could leave the house if I was so unhappy. Her son would find another girl. I was so enraged that I asked the *kulam panchayat* [a local governance organization that deals with disputes] to meet and settle the matter of my divorce. Then I made a public statement in front of the community about the marriage not being consummated and also about the violence from in-laws. The *kulam panchayat* agreed for a divorce and agreed to my parents' demand to return the dowry amount of Rs.3 lakh as compensation for divorce me. At this demand, my in-laws took me back home and two months later, I was pregnant ... At the time of delivery my husband refused to be with me. It was a breech baby and my husband finally came to the hospital when he was threatened with action if he did not sign the form. He came on the condition that the baby should not be dark like me and a girl. I delivered a baby girl and stayed in my mother's house for recuperation. My husband and his family did not visit me for three months. My parents sought the help of the *kulam panchayat*, which met again and threatened my husband and mother-in-law to take me and the child back.

Nothing has changed in my relationship with the in-laws and husband. If anything, it has worsened. My baby is so undernourished. When my parents celebrated the baby's first birthday, my mother-in-law refused to bless me or the child. She pushed me against the wall and I was so hurt that I sought refuge at my mother's place.

The *kulam panchayat* met again. They recommended that I go back and that I and my husband live separately from his mother. They threatened to withdraw support if I did not take their advice. I have no strength to tolerate this cycle of violence, come home to parents, have a panchayat, go back to the husband and face domestic violence again and again. My parents hope that the situation will improve. I am isolated completely, doing all the work in the house and have no [contact] with anybody in my mother's house.[22]

Papuram's narrative reveals a key SDG target issue that underpinned her exploitation: discrimination against women (SDG 5.1). Her narrative points to patriarchal control of female sexuality, "a general fear that it was not safe for girls to remain unmarried and that we would fall in love and elope," and the son preference that meant she was married in order that her parents could continue "educating my brother."[23] It also illustrates the use of gender inequality via child marriage to maintain class, caste, and religious divides: "my parents spoke about girls in the village who had inter-caste marriages and eloped." Control of female bodies and the preservation of the caste system come together in Papuram's narrative through the fear she describes of inter-caste elopement. The anxiety around her being "not safe" stems not only from the fear of *kharab mahaul* (a dangerous external environment that includes the risk of sexual assault) but also from fears of disruption to the caste hierarchy.[24]

SDG 5.1 continues to underpin Papuram's narrative. Beyond the control of women's bodies to maintain a social hierarchy, the narrative illustrates the impact of undervaluing female economic contributions. Papuram must

---

[22] Papuram Prasanna, "VOICES: Narratives by Survivors of Modern Slavery," 2018, Antislavery Usable Past, accessed May 18, 2020, www.antislavery.ac.uk/items/show/1966.

[23] See Fred Arnold et al., "Son Preference, the Family-Building Process and Child Mortality in India," *Population Studies* 52:3 (1998): 301–315.

[24] Nirantar Trust and AJWS, *Early and Child Marriage in India*, 36.

marry because daughters are a "heavy responsibility." Importantly, her new husband's parents "had property." Pulled from education, she is a financial burden on her parents, then on her husband's family. Her parents pay a dowry to her husband's family to ease the ongoing burden of her unwaged status. After years of violence, confinement, and isolation, she tries to escape. But the dowry was so important that the prospect of repaying it is the key blockage to the possibility of being allowed to leave her husband's family: "At this demand, my in-laws took me back home and two months later, I was pregnant." The marriage continues, and involves violence and unpaid domestic labor: "I am isolated completely, doing all the work in the house." She experiences alienation and othering through derogatory references to the "dark skin" that her child might inherit from her.[25] When the *kulam panchayat* intervenes, its focus is preserving the marriage, not addressing her exploitation.

The practice of dowry has existed in India for centuries and can be traced to the Hindu succession laws that pre-date the Hindu law reforms of the 1950s. Under the *Mitakshara* system, a daughter was not entitled to a share of parental wealth until marriage, unlike male children who were entitled to a share of family wealth from birth. Upon marriage, a bride would be given a pre-mortem inheritance to assist with her financial security.[26] The practice evolved out of this notion of dowry as *stridhanam* (a wedding settlement) to become a narrative of female economic burden and lack of labor value. Today the practice of dowry is a monetary transfer to the groom's family that secures her marriage and relieves her natal family's financial responsibility. The Dowry Prohibition Act of 1961 has failed to prevent its practice or punish offenders.

The notion of economic burden recurs frequently in survivor narratives. For example, Sujatha's narrative (2018) echoes Papuram's account of parents' "heavy responsibility." Sujatha explains that the prompt for her marriage was "the burden of three girls in the family":

> I have an elder sister and a younger sister. My parents keep talking about how they have to bear the burden of three girls in the family. My elder sister was married off very early. I had no interest in studies and was severely punished at school one day. I discontinued studies and joined my mother to go for work. The issue of my marriage was brought up daily at home and I resisted it, but finally had to agree when I was 15 years old.

[25] Ibid., 4, 8.
[26] Sonia Dalmia and Pareena G Lawrence, "The Institution of Dowry in India: Why It Continues to Prevail," *Journal of Developing Areas* 38, no. 2 (2005): 71–93, 72–73.

I live with my in-laws, do all the work at home and also work as a casual laborer. I had a normal delivery and went to my mother's house to deliver. My son is one year old. I am back in my mother's house and full term pregnant again.[27]

Occupying a lower social status than men, with their labor devalued against a dowry system, girls and women have reduced negotiating power around the institution of marriage. There is a notable correlation between female autonomy and the prevalence of child marriage, where autonomy is measured by the ability of females to make household decisions (regarding their health, purchases, and savings), exercise physical mobility (visit friends and family, and travel unaccompanied), and access economic resources (owning land ownership or holding a bank account).[28] Sujatha and Papuram, along with nearly all of the other forty-eight Indian forced marriage narratives, describe this vulnerability factor of gender inequality as a key driver of their exploitation.

10.5 SLAVERY AND POVERTY (SDG 1.2)

The relationship between child marriage as a form of labor exploitation, and the exploitative labor practices that can occur in the context of a culture that enables child marriage, is even more complex than these narratives already reveal with their accounts of the dowry system and domestic labor. Girls can be exploited as a commodity once married, but the false or real promise of marriage is also a means by which girls are initially extracted from their families for the purpose of labor and/or commercial and conjugal sexual exploitation. Ruma was trafficked to Mumbai at the age of 11 by her cousin. After spending months working in her house, Ruma's cousin then sold her to a woman from Kolkata for sex work. Her narrative (2002) explains how an attempt at child marriage led to her forced sexual exploitation for commercial purposes (as opposed to the domestic sexual exploitation evident in most cases):

My father was a *richshawallah* [rikshaw driver] in Khulna. We were very poor. I was the eldest of 3 sisters and 1 brother. One day my cousin offered to take me to Mumbai. My parents agreed. This was in 1981–82. I was 11 years old.

---

[27] Sujatha, "VOICES: Narratives by Survivors of Modern Slavery," 2018, Antislavery Usable Past, accessed May 18, 2020, www.antislavery.ac.uk/items/show/1958.

[28] Shelah S. Bloom, David Wypij, and Monica das Gupta, "Dimensions of Women's Autonomy and the Influence on Maternal Health Care Utilization in a North Indian City," *Demography* 38, no. 1 (2001): 67–78.

I was supposed to work in her house for 1 or 2 years, then she would arrange my marriage if she found a suitable boy. I worked in her house for 7 to 8 months and, when I understood the language, the bitch sold me to a woman from Kolkata for sex work.

I worked and I cried every day. I was like a parrot in a cage. I was taught the language, I was fed when I pleased my keeper and I had no possibility to go out. The work was not the worst. I missed my family terribly. My cousin sometimes came to collect the money. When I asked her about my income she would reply:

'You are a child, yet you speak like a grown up. Your money is there. When you go home, you can take it with you.'

After one year I was freed. Then I myself decided to work in a bar. I understood that my cousin intended to sell me off as a wife to a man in Uttar Pradesh. One Bangladeshi woman helped me to escape and introduced me to bar work. Later, I paid her 10,000 rupees.

Two years after going to Mumbai, I recovered my freedom. I then renewed contact with my family and started sending them money through people. If I had been married, this would not have been possible ... One day, I met Ali Hussain. We agreed on a contract and I married him. I had learned a lot by then and I did not trust people easily. I made conditions very clear. After marriage, I would split my income in two: half to my family and half to my husband.[29]

The fact that Ruma could be sold and transferred as if property and without impunity is a strong indicator of what the 1926 Slavery Convention calls the powers attaching to the right of ownership. In her case, the practice of child marriage was employed for another's economic benefit, first via her sale to a brothel, then in the failed attempt to sell her into marriage to a man in Uttar Pradesh. It was by escaping from the intended sale into marriage that Ruma gained economic independence and was able to send money home to her family, eventually marrying as an adult and on her own terms. She notes that if she had been married earlier, "this would not have been possible."

Like the narratives by Sujatha and Papuram, Ruma's narrative frames her vulnerability in terms of gender inequality: her parents have the same economic burden as Sujatha's and Papuram's of two or three daughters. Her narrative also emphasizes the intersection of SDG 5.1 (discrimination against women) with SDG 1.2 (poverty): "We were very poor." Papuram touches on the same issue. The "heavy responsibility" of having two daughters is exacerbated by "their poverty." Anumaraju's narrative (2018) makes the same connection. Her narrative explains that her

---

[29] Ruma, "VOICES: Narratives by Survivors of Modern Slavery," 2002, Antislavery Usable Past, accessed May 18, 2020, www.antislavery.ac.uk/items/show/1929.

parents had three daughters, "were poor," and could not afford to delay her marriage past the age of 14:

My marriage was fixed when I was 14 years old to my aunt's son who is a truck driver. I did not want to marry, tried hard to stop it but my parents forced it on me saying that we were poor. I have 2 younger sisters and they could ill afford delaying [my] marriage. I had two miscarriages and my health is poor, I have aches and pains and am always fatigued. With difficulty my husband took me to a doctor who said there is some problem with my uterus and that I need treatment. There is so much violence from my mother-in law and father-in-law for not bearing a child – they pull my hair, bang my head against the wall, push me and knock my head with their knuckles. I shout back and scream but it has no effect on them. They are so angry and disappointed that I do not have children.[30]

Anumaraju's narrative points to the wider economic imperative behind child marriage. The economic repercussions of delaying marriage are exacerbated in families with more than one daughter, and in poorer families. Younger sisters are often unable to marry before their elder sisters, rendering earlier marriage an economic imperative. In addition, the dowry system renders earlier marriages economically advantageous because increased age attracts higher dowries. Younger, less educated girls are seen as easier to discipline and train for housework and childcare, requiring less of a financial contribution from their parents. Dowry is the most commonly cited reason for parents marrying their daughters at a young age, and poorer families are more likely to seek earlier marriages in order to minimize cost.[31] For both reasons, then—her age and the presence of younger sisters—Anumaraju's parents "could ill afford delaying."

While the majority of the fifty forced and child marriage narratives from India indicate that poverty is a driver for marriage, several also indicate that, in turn, marriage exacerbates poverty. Padmamma's narrative (2018) reveals this economic impact:

I have two elder sisters and one brother who didn't go to school and one younger sister who has completed Class X. I studied up to class XI and my marriage was fixed when I was 16 years old. As we had no money for the dowry, my wedding was delayed by nine months to raise the money. Another condition was that all dowry demands had to be met before the marriage. The boy's family began to put pressure to give them the dowry quickly. My father took credit with heavy interest. In the meantime, I also learnt tailoring.

[30] Anumaraju Rajeshwari, "VOICES: Narratives by Survivors of Modern Slavery," 2018, Antislavery Usable Past, accessed May 18, 2020, www.antislavery.ac.uk/items/show/1948.

[31] Nirantar Trust and AJWS, *Early and Child Marriage in India*, 34.

My husband has studied up to Class X and we spoke to each other after the engagement. He has one married older brother and they live together with their parents in a house with two rooms, which is 50 km from my parents' house. Immediately after marriage, I became pregnant. My mother-in-law wanted me to abort saying that I was educated and did not work. They complained that I had not learnt to do household work and my husband supported his mother. I did not like the idea of abortion and could no longer accept their taunts about me being educated and being lazy. I told my father about this and he warned them against such a move and said he could take care of the baby. To prove that I could work, I worked hard till the end of my term but never received a good word, not even from my husband. He treated me well only in the first two months of marriage after which he turned violent and sided with his mother.

I went to my mother's for my delivery and had a normal delivery. The in-laws were happy that I delivered a baby boy and my husband took me home after three months. I soon got pregnant again and delivered a second boy. On the advice of the nurse, I was sterilized. After my second delivery, I strongly protested against the workload and my mother-in-law's behavior with me. As I was weak and had two children, she asked us to set up a separate establishment.

Now we live separately. My workload has increased with taking care of two sons. I work as a coolie and my husband takes away all my earnings. He gives me nothing but at least he is all right with the children. I have a sewing machine and take some orders. This gives me some extra amount that I can spend on the children and on myself.[32]

Like Papuram's parents, Padmamma's took on a loan to enable her dowry. Her family had to delay her marriage while they raised money and her father eventually took a high-interest loan. The marriage also impacted her own earning capacity. Educated to the 11th grade—within a year of a full secondary education and three years beyond the compulsory education system—she was positioned for skilled labor and her own earning potential. She had also learnt tailoring. But the marriage ended her education, required heavy unpaid domestic labor in her husband's family home, and eventually led to work as a 'coolie' (an unskilled laborer). Her husband is violent and takes her earnings. Prompted by the gendered economics of being one of three sisters, the child marriage then perpetuated gendered poverty.

10.6 SLAVERY AND EDUCATION (SDG 4.5)

Forced and child marriage as a practice appears in survivor narratives as a fusion of the issues behind SDGs 1.2 (poverty) and 5.1 (gender

---

[32] Padmamma, "VOICES: Narratives by Survivors of Modern Slavery," 2018, Antislavery Usable Past, accessed May 18, 2020, www.antislavery.ac.uk/items/show/1957.

discrimination): families attempt to relieve the financial burden of daughters via child marriage and this both responds to and perpetuates gendered poverty. But the narratives also reveal a third interrelated SDG target issue: the marriages cut off further education—"how can I [continue with further studies]?" notes Sujatha. In many of the narratives, education is prioritized for the families' sons; for example, Papuram's marriage had the context of her parents' "poverty and responsibility of . . . educating my brother." Padmamma's relatively high level of secondary education even reduced her perceived value: "I became pregnant. My mother-in-law wanted me to abort saying that I was educated and did not work. They complained that I had not learnt to do household work . . . . [I] could no longer accept their taunts about me being educated and being lazy." In fact, the theme of gender disparities in education (SDG 4.5) is evident in 63 percent of the India forced and child marriage narratives – fusing with poverty and wider societal discrimination against women and girls as one of the three key SDG target issues that creates their vulnerability to forced marriage enslavement. This echoes several studies that find a strong correlation between levels of development, reductions in gender bias, and women's levels of literacy, agency, and labor participation in India.[33] With both their labor and education devalued, poor girls are instead assigned value through marriage.

There is consensus across the development community that the single most effective way to stem the flow of school-aged children into child marriage is to improve access to and quality of education. Education promotes children's rights, helps to break intergenerational cycles of poverty, and appears to reduce child marriage. Results from several large education programs in India suggest that girls' access to education reduces their vulnerability to child marriage, and that child marriage rates decline when girls can access education and dowry practices are challenged.[34] But secondary education remains limited and costly in rural areas and the barriers to accessing secondary education are further

[33] Amartya Sen, *Development as Freedom* (Oxford: Oxford University Press, 1999), 196–197; Mamta Murthi, Anne-Catherine Guio, and Jean Dreze, "Mortality, Fertility, and Gender Bias in India: A District-Level Analysis," *Population and Development Review* 21, no. 4 (1995): 745–782; Jean Dreze and Amartya Sen, eds., *Indian Development: Selected Regional Perspectives* (Oxford: Oxford University Press, 1996).

[34] The same pattern has been observed in Guatemala, Thailand, and Mali. See, World Vision, *Before She's Ready: 15 Places Girls Marry by 15 (2008)*, accessed May 18, 2020, https://resourcecentre.savethechildren.net/node/13827/pdf/publications_before_shes_ready.pdf; and Plan International, Breaking Vows.

compounded by gender norms.[35] Educational access is more gender-balanced at the primary level, where education is free, but sons are given priority at the secondary level when families are required to cover costs.[36] The inability to access education has long-term impacts for India's girls. It has been linked to food security and under-nutrition, with effects on child growth and cognition, as well as on future earning capacity, financial independence, and child marriage rates.[37]

A disruption to education is frequently cited in the narratives as a starting point for child marriage, including in Papuram's account the sudden lack of transport to school prompting a decision to have her married. In other narratives, the child marriage itself disrupts education. For example, Mardannapalle's narrative (2018) explains that she wanted to study but was threatened with homelessness if she did not get married instead. Married at 13, she was pregnant within a year and forced to labor in her husband's family home and fields:

I did not want to get married. I was in Class VII and wanted to study more. My parents threatened me and said that I could leave the house if I did not listen to them. I pleaded with them. I told them that I would stop school and work to earn wages and help them. They did not pay heed. I was just about 13 when I was married to a 22-year-old man .... After a year of marriage, I delivered a baby boy ... I stopped frequenting my mother's house because it was difficult with my child. I started doing all the work in the house, going to the fields to work, returning home and working again. There was no rest. ... He started to abuse me physically. His mother too joined in beating me up and silencing me. When I questioned him, he threatened to remarry and send me to my mother's house.[38]

Responding to this link between access to education and child marriage, both government and NGO efforts to prevent child marriage have used education as an anti-marriage solution. In one intervention, local *angan-wadi* (health) workers and the police work with the child rights

---

[35] Keith M. Lewin, "Expanding Access to Secondary Education: Can India Catch Up?" *International Journal of Educational Development* 31, no. 4 (2011): 382–393.

[36] Mehtabul Aza and Geeta Gandhi Kingdon, "Are Girls the Fairer Sex in India? Revisiting Intra-Household Allocation of Education Expenditure," *World Development* 42 (2013): 143–164.

[37] Adolfo Chávez et al., "The Effect of Malnutrition on Human Development: A 24 Year Study of Well-Nourished and Malnourished Children Living in a Poor Mexican Village," in *Community-Based Longitudinal Nutrition and Health Studies: Classical Examples from Guatemala, Haiti and Mexico*, ed. Nevin Scrimshaw (Boston: International Nutrition Foundation for Developing Countries, 1995), 79–124.

[38] Mardannapalle Pallavi, "VOICES: Narratives by Survivors of Modern Slavery," 2018, Antislavery Usable Past, accessed May 18, 2020, www.antislavery.ac.uk/items/show/1963.

organization M Venkatarangaiya Foundation (MVF) to enforce the Child Marriage Restraint Act by fining families and placing girls in government-run residential girls' secondary schools. Kotapalli's narrative (2018) explains that the plans for her marriage became known to the local *anganwadi* worker, who alerted the police and MVF (via Childline). Her parents tried to carry out the ceremony in secret, but the marriage was prevented:

When I was in Class X, my marriage was fixed to a 25-year-old relative. I was 15 at the time. The *anganwadi* worker called Childline one day before the marriage. Childline contacted MV Foundation (MVF) and also the police. The next morning MVF volunteers and the police came home. By then, my family knew that my marriage was going to be stopped and decided not to make any public preparations. There were no signs of a wedding being held ... We went to the nearby temple to perform the marriage. In the meantime, the police came to the temple and—all of us—the families, bridegroom, me and everyone else attending the wedding were rounded up and taken to the police station. The police tried to negotiate, persuade and threaten. They told us about the child marriage law and that the marriage was illegal. I was tutored by my parents to say that I was willing and wanted the marriage. My family would just not relent and said that they had made all arrangements for the marriage. The bridegroom's parents announced that my marriage was already over and they would take me to their house.

The police felt we were being adamant and took us to the Collector's office. The Collector ordered that I be admitted into the KGBV [residential school] and counselled my family, saying that she would immediately transfer Rs.10,000 to me and support my education. She did not allow my mother to take me home. I completed Class X in KGBV and was allowed to take the exam in the village, escorted by constables with strict instructions from the Collector that my family would not be allowed to meet me. I am now studying Class XI in Sadashivpet Junior College ... The Collector has said that all children who are 5–18 years of age have to study. If there is a child marriage, the teacher and *anganwadi* worker will be suspended.[39]

Placing her in school instead of a marriage, the intervention introduced the idea that education was compulsory up to the age of 18 – beyond the guarantees of the national Right of Children to Free and Compulsory Education Act (which guarantees free education up to the age of 14). It took the existing reality of girls' secondary education rendering them more expensive in dowry terms for their own parents and less valuable in domestic labor terms for their husband's parents – of education being disrupted by child marriage and educational disruption prompting

[39] Kotapalli Sandhya, "VOICES: Narratives by Survivors of Modern Slavery," 2018 Antislavery Usable Past, accessed May 18, 2020, www.antislavery.ac.uk/items/show/ 1975.

marriage plans – and instead turned compulsory education into a tool for blocking child marriage.

10.7 A MULTI-SDG APPROACH TO TACKLING MODERN SLAVERY

Kotapalli's narrative and the MVP intervention show a focus on education as a critical component in ending child marriage. But the intervention also relied on Kotapalli's marriage being reported in the first place. The embedded belief in females as *paraya dhan* (someone else's wealth) may mean it is unlikely for members of a girls' family or community to reliably report plans for a child marriage. As an intervention, it therefore lacked a long-term process of tackling structural factors that lead to high child marriage rates: the fusion of gender discrimination, poverty, and gender disparities in education that survivors reveal in their narratives. Although clear correlations exist between higher levels of education and lower rates of child marriage, eliminating child marriage will require interventions that tackle poverty, gender norms, and educational access as deeply intertwined factors: what scholar Vasanthi Raman has called "the complex social matrix within which child labor is embedded, reproduced and sustained" and which "the strategy of compulsory education as the core of policy initiatives ... obfuscates."[40]

The practice of child marriage in India is deeply embedded in gender norms, exacerbated by poverty, and perpetuated by a devaluation of female education. Survivors' own narratives reveal that gender disparities in education are a key vulnerability factor but cannot be addressed in isolation without tackling the gender-based and economic inequalities that lead to reduced education access in the first place. The limitations of a single SDG approach to the prevention of child marriage are perhaps most evident in the narrative of Byagari (2018):

I regret being married. I was the only child and studying in class VII. My father was terminally ill and my family decided to marry me to a boy from the same village. I wanted to study. MVF got to know about this and filed a case. The police and officials met with both families and all agreed not to get us married and abide by the law. But three days after the actual date of wedding, they got me married in a secret ceremony, in a temple in another village. I was asked to give a statement at the police station, that the decision to marry was my personal choice and I was not forced into the marriage.

---

[40] Vasanthi Raman, "Politics of Childhood: Perspectives from the South," *Economic and Political Weekly* 35, no. 46 (2000): 4055–4064, 4058.

My mother-in-law tortured and hit me for not getting enough dowry. The condition in the house was unbearable. I worked a lot through my pregnancy and never had enough food to eat. My husband too did not care to support me. He would come home drunk and beat me.[41]

Like most of the India forced marriage narratives, her marriage was prompted by financial necessity. The size of the dowry was important and so was the domestic labor she performed in the home. However, unlike in Kotapalli's case, the MVF intervention did not work. Bribery and a secret ceremony circumvented the attempt to intervene. Without addressing the gender norms surrounding female labor and education, and their exacerbation by poverty, the MVF technique of replacing marriage with education could not overcome her parents' persistence.

This narrative is one of many child marriage accounts in our database, including those by Papuram, Sujatha, Ruma, Anumaraju, Padmamma, Mardannapalle, and Kotapalli, as well as Byagari, that reveal how multiple SDG target issues work simultaneously to create vulnerability to slavery. This subset of a broader collection of India survivor narratives, itself a subset of a collection of narratives from dozens of countries, reveals where key SDG target issues have underpinned enslavement and therefore where development interventions could focus in the design and delivery. Survivors highlight the multidirectional relationships between gender discrimination (SDG 5.1), poverty (SDG 1.2), and unequal education access (SDG 4.5) that led to their exploitation. As an approach, this multi-SDG coding of narratives suggests that survivors' own voices could be more central to the global antislavery and development agendas. In the detail of individuals' unique lived experiences, we can identify the interrelated causal factors for vulnerability to exploitation. A survivor-informed approach of determining which development challenges make slavery resistant to eradication can enable governments and civil society to better design, deliver, and evaluate new antislavery interventions that tackle particular and interrelated SDG targets.

Such a multi-SDG approach would be a step-change for the delivery of SDGs 8.7 (end forced labor, modern slavery, and human trafficking) and 5.3 (end child, early, and forced marriage). Currently, development interventions remain siloed. If in-country multi-SDG collaborations exist, they are rarely systemic or long-term. But as our multi-SDG analysis of

---

[41] Byagari Anitha, "VOICES: Narratives by Survivors of Modern Slavery," 2018, Antislavery Usable Past, accessed May 18, 2020, www.antislavery.ac.uk/items/show/1943.

survivor narratives shows, the antislavery community needs to tackle the socio-economic, cultural, and political drivers for slavery that are embodied in a range of other SDG target combinations – rather than tackling 8.7 and 5.3 in isolation from the wider development agenda. Survivors' narratives suggest the imperative of designing, testing, and evidencing the effectiveness of community-based strategies that tackle the development issues currently enabling slavery to thrive.

Slavery emerges from our narrative mapping as a multidimensional development challenge, with indivisible causes and consequences across the SDGs. Our conclusion is that antislavery development must be not only bidirectional but intersectional in its design. This multi-SDG approach may prove central to making slavery a tractable development issue, and ultimately may demonstrate that just as slavery exerts a disproportionate drag in developing countries, inhibiting social and economic development for free people as well as the enslaved, so reducing slavery will mean a better world for everyone: safer, more sustainable, more prosperous, and more equal.

AFTERWORD

If There Is No Struggle, There Is No Progress[1]

Ambassador (ret.) Luis C. deBaca

No one shall be held in slavery or servitude; slavery and the slave trade shall be prohibited in all their forms.[2]

Neither slavery nor involuntary servitude, except as a punishment for crime whereof the party shall have been duly convicted, shall exist within the United States, or any place subject to their jurisdiction.[3]

Article IV of the Universal Declaration of Human Rights and the 13th Amendment to the United States Constitution are unequivocal in their declaration that there is no place in the modern world for slavery in all of its manifestations. But of what relevance are these human rights instruments to the modern practitioner or academic? Are they simply reminders of something that once existed but are no more, or are they ongoing guarantees of rights that too often go unused, even by those who work for human rights? What is modern slavery and why should we fight it? Why should we fight about it?

In this Afterword, I will reflect not just on Fighting Modern Slavery, but on some of the ongoing questions and issues that are worth fighting for and fighting about, whether in the academy, in political and policy arenas, within the organizing mission, or in cultural spaces. While the Introduction – and for that matter the entire volume – addresses the

---

[1] Frederick Douglass, "West India Emancipation," speech delivered at Canandaigua, NY, August 4, 1857, located in *Two Speeches by Frederick Douglass* (Rochester, NY: C.P. Dewey, 1857), 22, accessed May 18, 2020, www.loc.gov/resource/mfd.21039/?sp=1.
[2] Universal Declaration of Human Rights, G.A. Res. 217A (III), U.N. Doc. A/810, at Art. 4 (1948).
[3] U.S. Constitution, Amdt. XIII (1865).

question "what is modern slavery?" I will start with two corresponding questions: when is modern slavery, and what is the modern slavery movement?

Knowing that there are as many starting points as there are terms to describe it, for the purposes of this Afterword, I locate the rough beginning of the modern antislavery movement – at least in the United States – to 1995, when the conviction of crew-leader Miguel Flores provided a model for a victim-centered, multidisciplinary approach, the then First Lady Hilary Clinton raised the issue at the United Nations Conference on Women in Beijing, and the discovery of the El Monte sweatshop started the policy process that would lead to the formulation of the "3P Paradigm" of Prevention, Protection, and Prosecution, the formation of the Worker Exploitation Task Force, and the passing of the US Trafficking Victims Protection Act (TVPA). That timeframe comports to what many think of as the modern slavery or modern anti-trafficking movement, though it necessarily needs to be understood as part of a modern antislavery era reaching back to the abolition of chattel slavery.

It might also be helpful to interrogate what we label the modern slavery movement. The groups and actors working on this issue are not homogenous, are often oppositional, and have at times approached internal fights as existential. Even labels are tricky. Some scholars, accepting the moniker that they gave themselves, call the vocal Bush-era coalition of evangelicals and feminists "abolitionists" or variations thereon. I am unwilling to cede that term to any particular wing of the modern slavery movement, or to assign membership in that group to people merely because of their use of slavery or abolitionist referents. Rather, I will adopt Nicole Bromfield's description of them in her study of the legislative battles around the TVPA as the right/left "mega-coalition."[4] That group not only successfully claimed credit for passage of the bill despite having failed to achieve their goals for the legislation (such as focusing only on sex trafficking to the exclusion of labor and legally defining all prostitution as per se coercive), but then dominated the rhetoric of the early years of implementation. As the loudest voice and supported by at least parts of the Bush Administration, the mega-coalition was given such primacy in the movement by observers and critics that their policy positions and combativeness have at times been attributed to everyone fighting modern slavery – even their opponents. That tendency is itself a compelling

---

[4] Nicole F. Bromfield, *The Hijacking of Human Trafficking Law During its Creation: A US Public Policy Study* (Saarbrücken: VDM Verlag Dr. Müller, 2010), 109.

rationale for rigorous modern slavery scholarship: social movement theory, historical analysis, and use of such tools as the Advocacy Coalition Framework can hopefully lead toward a more nuanced understanding of the many differing parts of the ecosystem as we ask "what is the modern slavery movement?"

WHY – AND HOW – WE FIGHT

Over the last twenty-five years, I investigated and prosecuted cases, worked to create avenues through which victims were eligible for immigration and social benefits, and helped to rewrite US slavery laws dating back to the Civil War in an attempt to better address power dynamics and the understanding of psychological coercion gained through the feminist-led legal revolution in America in the late twentieth century around domestic violence and sexual abuse. Internationally, I not only assessed other countries' activities, but through bilateral and multilateral diplomacy sought to get them to adopt laws and policies that focus on workers' rights, migrants' rights, and the ability of vulnerable and excluded minority communities to access justice.

So, I have done my share of fighting slavery.

I have also seen my share of fighting about slavery.

I have seen companies fighting to characterize labor abuses as something less than slavery, whether to escape criminal liability or to route exploitation into light-touch multi-stakeholder initiatives or into administrative labor regimes under which an occasional fine was an absorbable cost of doing business.

I have seen government officials fighting to keep anti-trafficking diplomacy and policy confined to sex trafficking, so as not to challenge a bilateral relationship, an economic status quo, rent-seeking opportunities, or corruption profit centers.

I have seen countries fighting to maintain the old definitions of trafficking that would relegate migrant women – especially in the sex industry – to detention and removal regimes rather than seeing them as rights-holders.

I have seen workers in agriculture, garment, fishing, mining, and the sex industry harness the tools of antislavery, choosing what is appropriate to their context to advance their organizing and to bring new allies and actors into their movements.

I have seen opposing advocacy communities use slavery concepts and rhetoric in the service of their long-standing fights about prostitution and how it should be regulated (criminally, administratively, or not at all).

I have seen institutions that held bureaucratic responsibility for a myriad of unused or defanged international instruments and domestic laws react to the energy of the modern anti-trafficking movement, unsure of whether to wait out a passing fad, to fight it off as a threat to budgets and power, or to make common cause and use the political moment.

I have seen the modern movement brashly and ahistorically enter into ongoing policy conversations and processes, sometimes as a positive disrupter and sometimes as a clumsy interloper. I have seen bitter ideological battles hinder the development of a community of interest and have seen observers assign the positions of the most aggressive combatants to the entire movement.

But as the modern slavery field matures, I have also seen disparate and even oppositional actors reach for commonalities. I have seen collaboration and partnerships, organizing and advocacy, and the long-overdue inclusion of affected communities in solutions both practical and structural.

So too, I have seen the welcome growth of academic interest in the field. As with the adversarial nature of litigation, academic inquiry often is most effective in advancing understanding when there is the healthy testing and clash of ideas, developing insights and arguments through rigorous research and thought. A new area is often at its most exciting when through its complexity it challenges existing structures and disciplines (much as the modern antislavery movement has challenged institutions and legal instruments that had for a host of reasons unrelated to the passion and commitment of the people involved not materially improved the lot of workers or migrants over the late twentieth century).

The incorporation of a new issue can be a heady time. Who "owns" it in the academy – in what discipline does it belong and what means of analysis are most effective in addressing it? Are those who come to it initially does the work of activists or academics? What is the right mix of practical application, accurate description and measuring, and critique? As Senior Fellow in Modern Slavery at Yale's Gilder Lehrman Center for the study of Slavery, Resistance, and Abolition – the Center that convenes the Working Group from which this volume flows – I am blessed with the "best seat in the house" at this exciting time.

For, as a practitioner in an academic setting, I am eager to incorporate and actualize the insights that come from rigorous research and productive debate. As a lawyer who worked in a jurisprudence based on case law and precedent, the historical is not just interesting, it is part of the work of the courtroom as my colleagues and I sought to apply the protections of antislavery laws to their fullest extent, putting the power of the state behind abused workers in an attempt to advance the "largely impossible yet imperative effort to retrieve some trace of the countless lives that slavery consumed."[5]

That is why this volume is so important. It brings together key thinkers, from multiple disciplines, to explore just a few of the many aspects that we today find clustered under the concept of modern slavery. They don't always agree on methods, responses, or even whether there is such a thing as modern slavery, but they agree that these issues demand study.

IF SLAVERY IS WORTH FIGHTING, IT IS WORTH FIGHTING ABOUT

That the study of modern slavery could lead to passionate debate should be no surprise – the study of prior slaveries has not been a staid exercise either, but the push and pull of academic discourse has made it a dynamic and interesting field. To effectively study slavery, historians and economists of past slave systems have moved past the hegemony of the English-speaking Atlantic experience, broadening their inquiry to address slaveries across time and space. Scholars of historic slavery are examining social and economic systems and the lives of the enslaved alike, as well as rethinking how the laws and politics of slavery are studied. The geographies of slavery studies have gone global, with important historical work being done in the Indian Ocean, the Levant, and Russia as well as in the Caribbean Basin. The time horizon of current slavery studies does not just reach back to ancient slaveries, but allows us to see Roman Law influences that cast light on differences among the various colonizers' New World slaveries.

That expansive time horizon forces us to the modern day as well. As the University of Michigan's Earl Lewis recently framed it,[6] study of the First (ancient) and Second (transatlantic) Slaveries require us to examine the continued legacies and practices of compelled service – a Third Slavery in a time of official freedom that reaches from the post-Emancipation era to today. For practitioners and policy-makers, understanding slaveries

---

[5] Andrew Delbanco, "A Vengeful Fury: Review of Greg Grandin's The Empire of Necessity," *New York Times*, January 10, 2014.

[6] Earl Lewis, "What Our World Needs Now: Undoing the Third Slavery," (Rice University Campbell Lecture, Houston, TX, November 12, 2019). This lecture is not yet available online.

across time and space can help us recognize and confront the troubling persistence of slavery-based legal and social regimes long after the slave system that gave them logic and life was abolished. Sex trafficking in the Balkans, forced labor in Uzbekistan, and prison labor and discriminatory policing are given context when understood in light of the Ottoman Black Sea slave trade, Soviet mobilization practices, and the use of violence by antebellum US slaveholding communities.

FIGHTING (ABOUT) SLAVERY IS NOT A MODERN PHENOMENON

Studying slavery across time and space also reveals that the events and fights of the last twenty-five years are not as exceptional as both supporters and critics of the modern slavery movement may think. People, and their interests and motivations and jealousies and competition for status and control, have remained fairly constant, much as racial and economic systems predicated on extraction of value from marginalizable communities and individuals have remained constant even after the formal abolition of chattel slavery.

In the rear-view mirror of how we characterize historical slavery in contrast to modern manifestations, we often don't recognize the definitional fights of the past. Historical slavery seems so clear-cut, and modern slavery seems so messy and contested. The nature and definitions of antebellum slave systems in the United States or transatlantic slavery in England's American possessions might seem obvious at a casual observer, but history indicates otherwise. Ancient slaveries aside, I would suggest that all who study or fight (or fight about) slavery are engaged in a 500-year-old project of defining slavery, labor, race, and their boundaries. Ideas of compelled service seem to have been contested throughout that time, starting with initial attempts of colonizers to define various gradations of freedom and the types of labor and social systems that would flow therefrom. This project intensified after Emancipation, continues to this day, and in some ways permeates current controversies around modern slavery.

The answers might change throughout the years but the questions remain the same. If there is a concept of unfree labor, the possibility of a status attached thereto, and a legal regime that regulates it across all possible spectra (practicing, allowing, protecting, tolerating, abolishing, criminalizing), then even apart from recognizing and impacting the operation of such systems one must determine who is included in – and who is excluded from – that concept. In short, to whom do slavery concepts apply and when they are applied, what (and whose) rights do they strip or protect? Sometimes those questions have been answered in favor of enslavers or employers. Sometimes the answers advance the interests of enslaved communities or individuals or groups subjected to post-Emancipation forms of exploitation. Often, those answers have spill-over effects on inseparable issues of decent labor, women's rights, and migration that affect many more people than those held in compulsory service.

A LONG-TERM PROJECT IN SCOPING OUT THE BOUNDARIES OF COMPELLED SERVICE

Through recognizing the limitations of an Atlantic-centric approach, I will nevertheless concentrate on New World slaveries to work through the claim that this is a centuries-old project, given how much of my work comes from an American legal and historical context. From the early 1500s, policy-makers and courts in the Western Hemisphere set up dividing lines of types of unfreedom ranging from short-term duration to outright ownership and inheritability. Pre-emancipation policy and jurisprudence seem to have focused on regulating the roles, duties, and rights of masters and the enslaved, and the extent to which government would support and subsidize slaveowners. In the United States, enslavers were advantaged by the privatization to them of the state's judicial and penological functions and monopoly on violence, and were publicly supported by the power of the state when private action was insufficient to prevent escape or resistance.

Under this regulatory phase of the definitional experiment, binaries of freedom and unfreedom that we think of when we casually characterize historical slavery developed. But the meanings and practice of slavery were not so cut-and-dried. For instance, even as legally supported race-based chattel slavery continued, American policy-makers and judges had to wrestle with how to address those who might hold someone in compulsory service without state sanction, whether through contracts or violence. Accordingly, the Northwest Ordinance of 1787, bringing into the new country frontier regions from Ohio to Minnesota, not only prohibited the system of chattel slavery, but involuntary servitude as well. Attempts by slaveholders to bind people in the Territory through contracts of indenture were rejected in cases such as that of Mary Clark, who gained her freedom in Indiana in 1821 through a habeas corpus action.[7] So too, kidnappings of free people in the South and border states tested legal systems in antebellum America in ways that anticipated modern analysis by forcing them to focus on the extra-legal actions of employers claiming ownership of another.

Much of the last 150 or so years has been an even more intense exercise in delineating the gradations of types of compelled service, because in a post-Emancipation world where slavery is illegal, enslavement is no longer a status, but a crime. Pre-Emancipation, the abuser's task was to convince the court that a person seeking remedy was a slave: and thus, not a rights-holder. But post-Emancipation, the inquiry was turned on its head. Since then the abusive employer's legal argument must be that an aggrieved worker was not subjected to slavery practices and is thus not able to access the remedies that flow from violations of the anti-slavery right.[8]

The defining project was active in the early years after the creation of the antislavery right in 13th Amendment as workers and employers contested its reach. US Courts and Congress clarified that the 13th Amendment covered vulnerable Latino peons in the colonized Southwest, Native Americans in Alaska, and European immigrant street children in the cities of the Northeast. Strategic litigation prosecutions in the American South sought to fight back against retrenchment and re-enslavement. Employers' and defendants' strategies of that time are redolent of today's business interests: using law and politics to exclude as many people and activities as possible from the reach of the slavery concept so as to remove them from the reach of constitutional and criminal law, in order to relegate their experiences of worker abuse to administrative and regulatory regimes that can be watered down and circumvented in the name of business-friendly policies.

Unlike the consistency of the business community and racial/social elites over the last 150 years in evading and rolling back any extension of slavery protections or workers' rights laws, the forces acting on behalf of workers and vulnerable communities have been less constant in their course of action, often putting down the tools of antislavery and moving to other issues after achieving particular victories, in no small part because of the need to fight multifaceted political battles against the many

---

[7] The case of Mary Clark, a Woman of Color, Supreme Court of Judicature of the State of Indiana, 1 Blackf. 122 (Ind. 1821).

[8] Rebecca J. Scott, "Social Facts, Legal Fictions, and the Attribution of Slave Status: The Puzzle of Prescription," *Law & History Review*, vol. 35 (2017): 9–30.

problems stemming from endemic racism and economic marginalization. As a result, short-term wins on the slavery front are not built upon as part of a progressive, pro-worker agenda, but appear throughout the decades in peaks and valleys. For instance, at the turn of the last century, a secret litigation strategy from Booker T. Washington's Tuskegee circle and Progressive Era reformers pushed hard to characterize African Americans arrested for petty offenses and rented out to Southern employers as being covered by the 13th Amendment and the anti-peonage statutes enacted under its aegis. But, even successful peonage prosecutions and victories in the Supreme Court did not usher in a new day for African American labor in the South, as the Wilson Administration abandoned federal antislavery enforcement and allowed evasion and racial violence free rein to maintain a racialized economic and social status quo.[9]

In the New Deal era, working closely with labor unions, Civil Rights groups, and leftist activists in "anti-peonage societies," government attorneys in the Justice Department's newly formed Civil Rights Section not only ramped up efforts in agriculture and other traditional sectors but also brought cases involving domestic servants and bargirls, breaking the stereotype that to the extent slavery still existed in America it was a problem being faced only by men in agriculture or convict leasing schemes. Renaming the enforcement program as Involuntary Servitude and Slavery removed an artificial barrier to justice – whether because of legal timidity or cultural evasion on the part of federal attorneys in southern states, the prior label of peonage had artificially narrowed enforcement to only those cases in which a debt was present. Civil Rights Section prosecutors even sought to use anti-slavery tools to preserve not just the right to be free from forced labor, but the right to organize as well.[10]

Some of those prosecutors took the US approach with them to Nuremburg, bringing the concepts into international law as they had to delineate the scope of the War Crimes charges against those who used slave labor. In the 1950s, the ultimate success of the post-War years in ending the Southern convict leasing system in the Supreme Court gave way to an abandonment of the 13th Amendment as the driver of Civil Rights enforcement, in favor of cases brought under the anti-discrimination aspect of the 14th Amendment. It might seem like progress

---

[9] Pete Daniels, *The Shadow of Slavery: Peonage in the South, 1901–1969* (Urbana-Champaign: University of Illinois, 1990).

[10] Resa L. Goluboff, *The Lost Promise of Civil Rights* (Cambridge: Harvard University Press, 2010).

that the United States was seemingly ready to fight for access to education, jobs, and public accommodations instead of having to fight against slavery and lynching, until one realizes that it had been almost 100 years since Emancipation.

Starting in the 1960s, when changes in immigration law and Civil Rights gains in the African American population started to shift the profile of workers in the most dirty, dangerous, and demeaning jobs, decisions as to the boundaries of slavery often turned on the type and amount of objectively observable coercion in a case. Some cases exempted those who were threatened with deportation from the protection of the 13th Amendment, while others recognized the psychological coercion of living and working in a climate of fear. Especially during the Carter and early Reagan Administrations, enforcement of the Involuntary Servitude and Slavery statutes was done hand-in-glove with anti-poverty and migrant-serving organizations, especially Legal Aid.

One need only to look at the sign-on letter sent from the Workers' Defense League to President Reagan in the early 1980s to see how anti-slavery continued to be part and parcel of a progressive agenda – Civil Rights groups, farmworker advocates, old-school leftist activists, and other social justice players successfully prevailed upon the Reagan Administration to have the Immigration and Naturalization Service and the Department of Labor join forces with the Justice Department to protect migrant workers. This is an example in recent history of a coalition using antislavery tools to address structural issues within the US labor economy. But it is also an example of the resilience of slavery systems and the ability of the business community to evade and coopt attempts at regulation, just as they had done after the activist enforcement of the Roosevelt and Taft administrations two generations before. In the wake of several high-profile farmworker cases in North Carolina and Florida, the North Carolina Farm Bureau placed its lobbying might behind guestworker legislation, creating temporary worker programs that undercut the farmworkers' ability to organize and achieve better conditions in the fields.

I use these examples to respond in some little way to the controversies identified in the Introduction: does the antislavery movement cannibalize more effective, more established movements? Does an antislavery lens detract from structural change? Is the use of slavery terms and slavery histories inappropriate?

Those controversies are bigger questions that can be addressed in a short Afterword, which is why this volume and the ongoing project are so critical. They are the important questions that should be asked. But they need to be answered openly and with rigor lest they simply become anti-antislavery talking points built on nihilistic critiques or – at worst – play into the hands of those who gain when abused workers and communities' lack access to justice.

To the extent that such critiques are aimed at getting the antislavery movement to go away and let the established groups and established frames "get back to work" on issues such as wage theft, housing conditions, and structural inequities in globalized labor markets, they must confront the presence of antislavery activities and rhetoric in labor and social justice groups and frames over the last fifty years. An eviction strategy that seeks a return to a perceived pre-2000s status quo not only assumes that the prior approaches were working, but also fails to allow for the harnessing of antislavery energy or thought for the ongoing project of improving workers' lives by creating political and cultural change. In so doing, one risks ignoring the worst manifestations of abuse – physical injury, threats, rapes, and compulsion – thereby creating a zone of impunity in which the most unscrupulous employers do not face consequences beyond administrative fines and directives that can be absorbed as a cost of doing business.

If we assume that workers are not enslaved because we do not like the term or we do not like our colleagues or if we insist that workers' rights be pursued only through tools of enforcement that are not carceral or based on a right to be free from slavery, we are leaving the most abused to their fate, because we then don't have a way to recognize them or vindicate their rights. We exclude them from not only the concept, but we also cut off the potential for antislavery rights guarantees to be real and powerful and linked to other structural issues. By confining those rights to simply a historical echo or a rhetorical flourish, or siloing the issue into the prostitution debate, we are in a way doing the job of the enslaver by denying people access to those rights. If we do that, we will have again ceded the field to power structures eager for yet another employer-friendly backlash and retrenchment.

DEFINITIONS

While the extraction of value from people through both structural and individualized coercion continues on a global scale, much energy has been given to fighting about slavery, even to the level of bitter disputes about whether the use of that term is valid, much less useful. As a prosecutor and a diplomat, I spent decades as a practitioner on the front lines of something that over the course of twenty years in the United States was called Involuntary Servitude and Slavery, came to be known as Human Trafficking, and is now again with increasing frequency being called slavery (under the label "Modern Slavery"). No matter the job and no matter the label used to describe my practice area, I was responsible for the same chapter in the US Criminal Code, partnered with the same community groups and victims' rights organizations, worked to meet the same needs of survivors, confronted the same inequities in vulnerable workplaces, and fought the same political and diplomatic battles.

Given my experiences, I take terminology arguments with a bit of a grain of salt. I worked on an effort that started as a Worker Exploitation Task Force under a liberal President and activist First Lady. I helped that project survive a conservative administration that gave public priority to sex trafficking but eventually settled on a more pragmatic approach. During that time, attacks on the term slavery came from the mega-coalition as it pursued its anti-prostitution agenda – they felt "trafficking" kept the attention on prostitution fight whereas "slavery" was too focused on labor rights and could even lead to acceptance of non-coerced prostitution as a valid form of labor. I served in a subsequent government that tried to rebalance to more fully focus on all forms of exploitation and the structural underpinnings of agricultural, extractive, and manufacturing supply chains and government procurement policies.

Though I should be used to it, critiques that the anti-trafficking movement as being brash, presumptuous, or expansionist by using slavery language have always rung a bit dissonant. For those of us in the Involuntary Servitude and Slavery program in the Clinton Administration, the term "trafficking" was a price we were willing to pay to obtain domestic and international legal improvements to focus not just on prosecution but also on victim protections and prevention efforts. That the term "slavery" or "modern slavery" has renewed currency in the last decade or that anti-trafficking work reincorporated a labor lens after the initial dust of implementation settled feels less like a rhetorical appropriation or mission creep than it does a reversion to the norm after only a few short years.

But my experiences are not everyone's experiences, and the modern anti-trafficking movement has not spoken with a shared voice or a shared set of assumptions. Accordingly, it may be helpful to explore how some of those differing perspectives and the resulting controversies were almost "baked in" to the modern movement as it combined activisms and histories that for over a century had separately addressed forced labor and forced prostitution.

A MULTIDISCIPLINARY APPROACH FOR A HYBRID ISSUE

Twenty-five years in, modern slavery as a field – and even as a term – is ripe with areas of inquiry. For one, it would be helpful to look not just at the strengths and limitations of slavery language, but at the controversy itself. What are the underlying considerations that fuel this controversy? Movement rhetoric and coalition competition and enmities aside, to what extent does the controversy reflect organizational and political power, often manifested around organizational lines and often with someone's "turf" having been bumped up against. The possibilities for examination of turf fights alone are almost endless: different disciplines competing for where the issue should be located in the academy; United Nations convention regimes (and the agencies who "keep" them and the processes and civil society ecosystems that have built up around them) adjusting to new instruments and new interest groups impatient with the perceived limitations of the "talk shop" model of multilateral diplomacy; and old-line Protestant and Catholic refugee-serving organizations confronted with evangelical communities engaging the issue on faith and enthusiasm rather than established systems and professionalism. Even within national governments, offices and bureaus addressing slavery or other business and human rights concerns not only by practice but also through their very existence will challenge the unquestioned assumptions of the security state or a country's longstanding economic and political arrangements.

But not every controversy is about organizational power. Sometimes controversies are about ideology, about access, or even about personal experiences or relationships. But some of the controversies in the modern slavery arena may also be about cultural and historic differences within the movement, often unseen or unidentified and thus themselves worthy of study. This emerging field may also be characterized as an emerging subfield within many different disciplines, each of which has differing modes of research and analysis. Just as critiques of slavery language can be dissonant to me as someone who came to the issue from prosecuting slavery in the Civil Rights Division, the slavery focus of some actors can be jarring to those who place the origin of this movement in the migrant prostitution issue that used slavery as a rhetorical frame rather than as a rights-enforcing mechanism.

The Working Group had to confront a divide that didn't start with the members, but dates back to the late 1800s, when for a host of reasons, countries attacked migrant prostitution under the rubric of "White Slave Trafficking Acts" (WSTAs), so named even though such laws were based on countries' borders and international commerce rather than on human rights guarantees such as the US 13th Amendment. As a result, those who come to human trafficking or modern slavery from the WSTA branch of the field's "family tree" interpret state action through a historic lens not in which the law is used to vindicate violations of human or civil rights, but one in which migrant women have been suspect, border controls have been used to enforce morality and strengthen national policing bureaucracies, and women's agency has been ignored. Those who come to human trafficking/modern slavery from a civil or human rights angle seem more likely to cite the concepts in international law, the 13th Amendment, or international slavery and forced labor conventions, and to see state action taken in defense of those rights to be a valid and improvable alternative. From a Civil Rights perspective, placing people involuntarily held in prostitution in a separate category from other workers left them unprotected and resulted in them being treated as co-conspirators with their abusers. From a WSTA perspective, where expanding the reach of antislavery laws to this population echoes the rhetorical use of slavery terms, bringing yet another carceral solution and negating the agency of those who are not coerced.

The definitional project that I identify has also taken place in the study of the WSTA throughout the years. Robust scholarship since the 1970s seems to have landed on a consensus characterization (and to some degree dismissal) of the effort as a "moral panic." In seeking to preserve agency for women, this interpretation risked suggesting that no-one in prostitution during that time period was brought into or held in service through force, fraud, or coercion. More recent scholarship is unpacking the issue: placing it in the contexts of urban and progressive reform, border security, and sexuality; tracking the cross-pollination of the issue with suffrage movements; contextualizing women in the workforce; assessing diplomatic and bureaucratic responses; highlighting gender and racial exclusions, and even beginning to address the violence and compulsion that at least some women suffered at the time.

The modern regime's bringing together of the rights-based slavery approach and the commerce-based sex trafficking approach created a field with multiple origin stories, which do not necessarily hold the entire community together with a shared understanding of a Golden Era or a legacy worth drawing from.[11] Emancipation can be a world historical success to be celebrated and emulated, or it can be cast as a dream betrayed in re-enslavement, persistent racism, and diminishing of workers' rights. Historical efforts to curb the trafficking of women and girls – a battle that was not seemingly "won" as was the initial abolitionist fight and is thus more likely to be mirrored than evoked by modern activists – is often accurately seen as having been a gateway for securitized borders, an excuse for anti-immigrant policymaking, and control of women's sexuality and movement. Depending on one's starting point, modern slavery is either a continuation of a long-standing freedom struggle, or a cloaking device for morality enforcement by the security state.

Until recently, just as scholars or historical and modern slaveries were largely working in siloes, slavery scholars and those who study the WSTA were not in a shared field, did not speak a shared language, and may not even have known of each others' work much less admitted its application to their subjects. The Working Group is an important effort to bridge that divide and develop a common understanding.

Just as the Working Group had to confront the fact that there is not one "origin story" of modern slavery as currently conceived, they also have had to deal with a different manifestation of hybridity – the institutional and professional issues particular to an emerging interdisciplinary field.

Unlike fields such as human rights, gender, or labor, there is not yet an accepted way of learning, teaching, or turning knowledge into practice. So sometimes, to an academy-adjacent practitioner, some of the debates can sound like colleagues talking past one another rather than discussing the same phenomenon. Why and how are we talking past each other? This emerging field, to capture the full breadth of experiences and mechanisms that create and sustain and are affected by modern slavery, necessarily draws in multiple disciplines, with not only differing modes of research

---

[11] In reviewing again the Congressional findings in the TVPA, I am struck how Congress did not reference the US version of the WSTA or the international instruments pertaining to prostitution or "White Slavery," but specifically rooted the law as a response to the Supreme Court slavery jurisprudence as well as such United Nations documents as the Universal Declaration of Human Rights; the 1956 Supplementary Convention on the Abolition of Slavery, the Slave Trade, and Institutions and Practices Similar to Slavery; the 1948 American Declaration on the Rights and Duties of Man; the 1957 Abolition of Forced Labor Convention; the International Covenant on Civil and Political Rights; the Convention Against Torture and Other Cruel, Inhuman or Degrading Treatment or Punishment; and the Fourth World Conference on Women (Beijing, 1995), among others. TRAFFICKING VICTIMS PROTECTION ACT OF 2000, P.L. 106-386, sec. 102 (October 28, 2000).

and analysis but also differing systems of recognition and advancement, journals and conferences. For some, their first exposure to a different discipline might be in the modern slavery work.

Lacking an infrastructure, not yet having a canon and shared values and techniques, scholars who wanted to work on modern slavery in its many forms come to it on their own. Unlike related fields such as labor, there are not entire schools (such as at Cornell's School of Industrial and Labor Relations or the City University of New York's School of Labor and Urban Studies), much less departments, or sub-fields within different disciplines. Until recently, young scholars had few opportunities for mentorship or graduate work in the new field on its own terms, as opposed to coming to it from another specialty.

In these early years, the energy of activism drove much of the output, dominated by descriptive accounts, awareness raising, and assessments of policies that were changing almost faster than they could be critiqued, often in service of the author's personal activism or social cohort. Given the focus on task forces and training, traditional federal research funding under established channels with safeguards of peer review and oversight was slow to be set up. At its worst, rigor was abandoned for instrumental goals – research and reports were as likely to have been commissioned or pushed by the "ideas industry" as the academy. Anti-prostitution donors eager for point-of-view support funded initial social science work, and members of the Bush Era mega-coalition published articles designed for use by their allies in government or by the conservative think tank that managed their activities.

This tendency in itself raises an interesting aspect of the emerging and maturing field that the Working Group wrestled with – the interplay of academic work and activism. Not everyone needs to be an activist, and not all academic work needs to be in furtherance of activism, but all academic work certainly needs to be rigorous. Questions and insights need to be judged by the broader community on their merits, rather than simply for their instrumental value as ammunition in policy and cultural battles. The way thinktanks and lobbyists create and use scholarship and pseudo-scholarship make it much harder for bad ideas to exit the public sphere,[12] a tendency on full display in the leadership and tactics of the Bush Era mega-coalition. The centrality of advocacy industry actors in the

---

[12] Daniel W. Drezner, *The Ideas Industry: How Pessimists, Partisans, and Plutocrats are Transforming the Marketplace of Ideas* (New York: Oxford University Press, 2019).

early years of the modern movement has thankfully given way to more traditional academic inquiry, peer review, and the use of social science.

DEFINITIONS, REVISITED

But let's get back to definitions, since that is one of the things that seems to trigger so many disputes, and ask a baseline question: why do we keep feeling that we need to define slavery? So that there is a legal definition for lawyers and policy-makers and judges to use? Or an academic definition so we can critique? Or so we can measure and analyze?

Are we looking for a social definition, so we can name things that we feel are familiar and assess slavery-related claims of aggrieved populations that use it as a frame of reference or an organizing tool? Because not only did slavery provide a good rhetorical and organizing basis for prisoners' rights movements in the 1970s, allow for the expansion of federal hate crimes legislation to LGBT communities, and fuel the current prison abolition movement, but as of this writing we have also seen meatpacking workers in the state of Georgia equate their employers' callousness in the face of COVID-19 deaths as a form of "modern day slavery." Clearly, aggrieved populations see slavery language as a powerful tool with which to name the injustice they are experiencing.

Are we looking for a definition so that we can exclude from the coverage of the Universal Declaration and the 13th Amendment's guarantees of freedom those who do not know or think to say the "magic words" that identify the exact aspect of slavery or worker exploitation set forth in the law? Or are we looking for definitions that protect people from compelled service, allow access to social and migration benefits, and challenge information and power differentials that maintain corrupt status quos? If the second, are we working to make those outcomes meaningful and available?

Are we looking for a definition that does not challenge any pre-existing formulation or bureaucratic structures? One that not only vindicates individual rights violations, but also encompasses root causes and structural coercions such as guest-worker programs and gender exclusion? Or one that conversely goes away and lets us work only on root causes without the distraction of using slavery tools to catch and punish the worst employers and pimps, who profit from a captive workforce?

How does the use of slavery lenses impact the disparate approaches of the last century? From my perspective on the front lines as a lawyer and diplomat, the modern approaches seemed to have breathed new life into moribund institutional responses. Even while criticizing the modern slavery movement as not sufficiently rights-based, dependent on the American unilateral reposting mechanism, or seemingly focused on individual interventions over systemic solutions, skeptics have in recent years recognized that the slavery frame and the modern anti-trafficking movement have advanced or contributed to policy agendas around transparency, human rights due diligence, worker-led social responsibility, and government procurement practices. We even see new players coming to gridlocked prostitution debates, hopefully bringing new insights that might better include and protect people rather than just using them as anecdotal evidence for one's preferred regulatory regime. Are these changes generational? Are new ways of movement-building changing the contours of old debates? Is change happening because people are fighting slavery, or because pushing back against a slavery frame demands new action and revised assumptions? Or are all of those things happening simultaneously, both collaboratively and contradictorily?

These are tough questions, and I fear that the answer to all of them might simultaneously be "yes." But that is exciting in and of itself. It demonstrates to me that this nascent field of interdisciplinary study has a lot to offer, and a lot to say.

THE MODERN SLAVERY WORKING GROUP'S WORK – MORE THAN JUST THIS VOLUME

The Gilder Lehrman Center's Modern Slavery Working Group at Yale University and the authors of this book are confronting all of these questions and controversies that I have set out and many more, bringing their various disciplines, experience, and insights to bear. The Working Group was born out recognition that the hard questions have to be confronted head-on. That it would be useful to break out of a cycle in which the traditional academic back and forth in articles or monographs was not leading to mutual understanding and learning, but only hardening everyone's assumptions about their subject and their colleagues. A well-crafted critique or dismissal of others' work might win one status within their cohort or school of thought, but likely will not change any minds or be useful in the community of practice; the Working Group dared to come together in person across disciplinary lines and even prior disagreements, in order to wrestle with these key themes.

Through the Gilder Lehrman Center's annual conference in 2018, the Working Group members were also exposed to the community of interest and community of practice, whose day-to-day experience with this issue is often very different than that of the academicians. This was invaluable, as it shone the light on blind spots and unquestioned assumptions of present-ers and attendees alike. I recall hearing representatives of a faith-based sex trafficking organization in the audience recognize the need to interrogate the images that they were using in their fundraising. I also recall hearing an academic participant realizing that the Coalition of Immokalee Workers was not using slavery just as a rhetorical or political tool: they use the term proudly, their representative said, because they had successfully brought their abuser to justice under the American slavery statutes. I have wit-nessed and participated in other such moments because of the Working Group and its members, such as the 2019 Texas State University confer-ence Chasing Slavery: The Persistence of Forced Labor in the Southwest, co-hosted by Working Group co-chair Jessica R. Pliley.[13]

I have also been able to hear the members of the Working Group learning from one another and sharpening their analysis not just in this book, but on the Gilder Lehrman Center's podcast series Slavery and Its Legacies. On this platform, Yale's Thomas Thurston and members of the Working Group discuss such issues as narrative construction, impacts of terminology, how memories of race, empire, and history influence modern anti-trafficking campaigns, forced labor, sex work, border control, and the efficacy and limitation of contemporary solutions. In other words, the full range of the controversies and issues that the group tackled by coming together throughout this process. Since most of the podcasts pair members of the group, the cross-cutting discussions are a particularly helpful way to place this work in dialogue. I highly encourage you to listen along; episodes are available online at https://slaveryanditslegacies.yale.edu/.

SOME PARTING QUESTIONS FOR THE READER AND THE AUTHORS

It should be apparent by now that I am an eager consumer of the work that has come out of the Working Group in conferences and presentations. I listen to the podcast on the train and in the car, and look forward to being able to assign this volume in my classes. In other words, I am an

---

[13] For video of the Chasing Slavery conference see "Chasing Slavery: The Persistence of Forced Labor in the Southwest," Center for the Study of the Southwest, Texas State University (2019), accessed May 18, 2020, www.txstate.edu/cssw/projects/chasing-slavery.html.

unabashed fan of the group and its members, whether long-time acquaint-ances, those who I only knew through their work, or those who I have recently met. But I was not part of the Working Group, having arrived at Yale just as it was winding up its convenings.

It might therefore be presumptuous as an outsider to offer my own set of questions now that this important project is winding to a close, but I want to set forth some additional controversies/queries that might sup-plement those set forth in the Introduction:

How do we best assist people in claiming and defending their core human rights? Should we be defining unfair and coercive work in or out of this concept? What are the boundaries? What are the follow-on effects of that decision? If some people aren't covered by the spectrum of coerced service and rights that attach, how do we fight for their ability to never-theless have a job that is safe, empowering, well-paid, and protected by organizing and effective regulation?

What is the proper balance between addressing root causes and the exigency of the crime against the person and society? Does everyone in the field need to be an advocate or activist? Is being an advocate or activist bad if one's scholarship is good? Does everyone in the field need to participate in the structural work of challenging power dynamics and global capital-ism, or should the field include those working on discrete but important issues such as trauma response or the efficacy of reporting mechanisms? Or even people whose activist goals are different?

Are all targeted or personalized interventions distracting from a larger struggle or better more established approaches? Are they themselves little parts of such a struggle or a continuation/sharpening of moribund processes and talk shops? Are the discrete tasks of establishing hotlines or other avenues through which vulnerable communities can make their voices heard in themselves a challenge to the status quo? If workers' freedom of information and expectation of remediation isn't a dangerous challenge to current power dynamics, why are so many policy-makers in so many countries so loath to adopt baseline worker protections? Why do workers get punished when they stand up for themselves?

How efficacious are/were the established approaches from which mod-ern slavery is said to be distracting? What and how did the 1957 Convention end forced labor? How successful have the Harkin Engel Protocol or anti-sweatshop multi-stakeholder initiatives been? Why did the United Nations site the Trafficking Protocol at the Office of Drugs and Crime rather than in the Human Rights Council? How best can Business and Human Rights instruments and the trafficking/slavery focus of Supplemental Development Goal 8.7 interact? How can treaty language, reporting mechanisms, and multilateral processes move past being "talk shops" to be actualized on behalf of workers and other communities who have little access to them?

How do we credit and anticipate that moment of decision in which abused workers decide that it is time to stand up to the boss or to leave, despite whatever coercion they may be under? How to prepare ourselves to walk supportively with the survivor when they do get out? Most people self-emancipate, but the anti-trafficking movement is properly criticized when it exhibits a rescue mentality – how do we square that? What groups are actually rescue groups, what groups have moved beyond that model, and what is the difference between rescue and victim identification or legal service provision? Is the anti-trafficking movement really a rescue operation, or are some vocal parts of it amplified not only by their own supporters but by their critics, elevating them so as to characterize the entire movement by their actions?

How do we address compelled service in mixed populations, where structural inequalities or designed labor migration systems place everyone in a coercive baseline but only some are subjected to force, fraud, or coercion? How can the modern slavery movement add to our understanding of migration routes, opportunities for organizing among migrant workers, and the economic and racial milieu surrounding migrant labor?

What tools of literary analysis, history, and social movement theory can best be deployed to assess antislavery rhetoric and the stories told by survivors, governments, and activists?

What makes an intervention stop being credited as an antislavery intervention and start being something else? When it looks like a proto-union? When it is successful? The El Monte Thai garment worker case of the mid-1990s (which with the *Flores* farmworker case in Florida could serve as a historical starting point of the modern slavery movement) is claimed by the anti-sweatshop movement and the business and human rights community in language that elides the fact that the workers were enslaved, participated in the slavery prosecution of their bosses, and were instrumental in founding one of the most effective organizations in the anti-slavery space, Los Angeles' Coalition to Abolish Slavery and Trafficking (CAST).[14] The Coalition of Immokalee Workers is claimed

---

[14] For the El Monte case see Leslie Berestein Rojas, "El Monte Sweatshop Slavery Case Still Resonates 20 Years Later," *KPCC*, July 31, 2915, accessed May 18, 2020, http://www.scpr.org/news/2015/07/31/53458/el-monte-sweatshop-slavery-case-still-resonates-20/

as a success story by many in the workers' rights community, but they are also a founding member of the national trafficking victim services group, the Freedom Network, and themselves attribute part of their organizing success to their ongoing antislavery program – the specter of renewed federal enforcement is one of the many incentives that they leverage to bring farmers to the table.

How do we place the energy and access of the modern slavery movement in the hands not just of identified survivors, but in service of the most socially excluded? How do we credit the survival needs of LGBTQ people and the communities that they so often find in sex work? How can we incorporate hard-won understandings of power differentials, endemic sexual harassment, and sexual violence, so that everyone, no matter their gender, age, or nationality, are protected from such abuse and able to access remedies?

To what extent is the movement shifting toward social science, and what are the best practices for project design? Is the best use of social science the study of affected populations? Of workers' conditions? As a tool for monitoring and evaluation? A prevalence measure? To test whether multi-stakeholder or task force approaches do and don't make a difference? How do we capture the efficacy of various psychological, medical, or victim service interventions that might flow from different conceptual frames and legal regimes?

Who is served by calls to reject the terms of the movement or the protections or rights because they are imperfect, watered-down, or subject to evasion or corruption? As we have seen in the antislavery fight for over 200 years, anything worth doing that changes power structures will not just be resisted but will be immediately subjected to a backlash, especially because "winning" coalitions often move on to other issues while losing coalitions dedicate themselves to undercutting the hard-fought change. How do we sustain the energy of antislavery activism as to prevent that this time around?

And finally, in the study of the recent history of modern slavery policy, how can we move beyond the loudest actors and their claimed victories to assess policy outcomes, as opposed to political noise? How do we elevate the pragmatic and change-making actors? How do we uncover the entire modern history of antislavery legislation and policy, when government sources might not be accessible for years? How do we not reify claims of

---

for more on the Flores case see Steven Greenhouse, "3 Plead Guilty to Enslaving Migrant Workers in South Carolina," *New York Times*, May 8, 1997.

particular segments of the anti-trafficking movement by assigning their approaches to everyone working on the issue?

DIGGING DEEPER – THE NAME GAME

I ask this last question because sometimes academic descriptions or critiques of policy or political activities do not reflect the diversity of went on "in the room where it happened."[15] An example: some observers focus in on the US Congress's choice to name some of the reauthorizing legislation amending the TVPA for abolitionists such as William Wilberforce (the 2008 Reauthorization) or Frederick Douglass (the 2018 Reauthorization).[16] Simply assigning the use of abolitionist name choices as virtue signaling or state triumphalism is a stand-off analysis that fails to capture all of the nuances of what was happening around those bills.

For some in Congress, such names signaled bipartisanship. For others, it kept the reauthorizing language focused on the stated antislavery purpose of the original Trafficking Victims Protection Act, as opposed to drifting into prostitution debates through the trafficking lens. But for still others, it is more personal and tied in with the actions and causes that the abolitionists worked toward. For instance, in the 2018 Reauthorization Frederick Douglass's descendants, who through their family foundation have worked against human trafficking for over a decade, lobbied hard to have a piece of antislavery legislation named after their ancestor in the 200th Anniversary of his birth. Douglass's historical membership in the Republican party of the mid-1800s seemingly allowed modern conservatives to overlook Douglass's radical social justice agenda of racial equality, women's rights, and free labor – aspects that appealed to Congressional Democrats as they sought to commemorate his legacy on his bicentennial.

In 2008, the Wilberforce dedication was also a popular naming choice for both political parties, who had to work in tandem to pass legislation across the two chambers of Congress. Evangelicals and neo-conservatives

---

[15] Apologies to Lin Manuel Miranda.

[16] For context, those choices were seen at the time as an improvement over Congress's penchant for tortured titles in service of a contrived characterizing acronym (for instance, the "Prosecutorial Remedies and Other Tools to end the Exploitation of Children Today" Act was named such in order to craft the contrived acronym of the PROTECT Act, telegraphing to the public how they should feel about the law). While TVPA reauthorizations may be named for abolitionists, they have thankfully not devolved into the hyperbolic acronyms that characterize much post-9/11 legislation.

in the Bush-era right/left coalition supported it, seeing Wilberforce as an example of evangelical moral activism that transcended his membership in another country's legislature. But also enthusiastic were key African American legislators, especially my boss at the time, Judiciary Committee Chairman John Conyers.

For Chairman Conyers and other senior members of the Congressional Black Caucus, the Wilberforce title not only was a way to note the 200th Anniversary of the legislation in both the United States and Britain ending the transatlantic slave trade by honoring the great British abolitionist, but reflected his deep historical significance in the African American community. The reauthorization was redolent of how Wilberforce and other British abolitionists like Thomas Clarkson were not just known about but celebrated in free Black antebellum communities each year on the anniversary of West Indian abolition – such as the celebration in 1857 at which Frederick Douglass not only challenged those who tolerated slavery with the words that serve as the title of this Afterword but also lauded Wilberforce and his colleagues as examples to be emulated. And, the reauthorization title was redolent also of Wilberforce University: the first African American college in the United States, a beacon of hope for Black education before the Civil War, and an important incubator of Black educational and political leadership following Emancipation.

Doggedly pursuing long-overdue reparations for chattel slavery while at the same time advancing the 2008 trafficking reauthorization, Chairman Conyers characterized Emancipation not as a one-time event, but instead as a living promise written in the blood of all who served in bondage. For the Chairman and for other members of the Black Caucus like Representative Alcee Hastings, who testified to his colleagues about his own childhood experiences in the fields of South Florida, modern slavery was inseparable not only from past slaveries but also from their pro-worker agenda and ongoing struggles against the continuing badges and incidents of slavery. With such a strong Civil Rights focus and awareness of history, it should be no surprise that the 2008 Reauthorization was notable for expanding civil liability, loosening the knowledge requirement for businesses who turn a blind eye to their suppliers' abuses, expanding family unification, and setting up programs for unaccompanied children.

CONCLUSION

So, where do all of these questions and commentary leave us? What is fighting slavery today, and what is fighting about slavery today?

As a practitioner desperate for useful research, a policy-maker calling for the field to no longer be a "rigor-free zone,"[17] and now in the academy, I have seen colleagues fight slavery in all the ways possible. Unlike in the years immediately following the passage of the Trafficking Victims Protection Act and the promulgation of the United Nations Protocol (when most academic work was either descriptive of the problem, designed to advance a particular prostitution agenda, or critical of the Bush Administration's response), academic engagement on this issue has matured with the field. We see colleagues whose output ranges all the way from contesting whether modern slavery exists to exploring "what works" (and doesn't) to address it. From assessing how anti-trafficking groups and survivors use metaphor and imagery to researching the efficacy of post-trauma counseling interventions. From estimating prevalence to tracing shipping manifests and financial data. From reclaiming individual narratives of enslavement to assessing how best to harness class action and multi-district litigation to bring workers together for a unified legal effort.

As inquiry into the myriad slaveries of the modern era blossoms, we will no doubt see not only insights and breakthroughs, but also the sparks, jealousies, competition, and warring camps that accompany any academic pursuit worth doing. But we will also see innovative thinking, pushed out of its comfort zones. We will see a generation of graduate students and young scholars pushing past old controversies and uncovering new aspects of issues that had frozen in gridlock. We will see the development of a new slavery studies that reaches into the criminal Third Slavery of the modern era as well as the legal slavery systems of antiquity and the transatlantic world, becoming even more universal across time and space as it wrestles with the many different forms that unfree labor takes on in a globalized marketplace. In doing so, we will bump up against those who study migration, labor, gender, race, class, economics, public health, law, social work, management, supply chains, and industrial operations, all of whom have existing funding streams, foundation myths, professional assumptions, and guild requirements. And so we can expect that, with the growth of a modern slavery studies, there will be no shortage of opportunities to fight (about) slavery.

We can also expect that our students will come to us with prior experience in the field, even as survivors. Some of them will make

---

[17] Martina Vandenberg & E. Benjamin Skinner, "Preface," *Journal of Human Trafficking* 1, no. 1 (2015): 6–7.

a career in fighting on the frontlines as service providers, organizers, activists, attorneys, and policy-makers in antislavery offices. Many of us will undertake not just study, but activism and advisory roles with non-governmental organizations, businesses, and governments. There will be no shortage of opportunities to fight (against) slavery.

Too often in the last 150 years – whether because of other priorities, changes in government, crises, or other reasons – a burst of antislavery practice has withered away, leaving those in compelled service unrecognized and unremediated until a new generation "discovers" that forms of slavery still exist. Only in the last 25 years have we seen a sustained, vigorous, growing field that seems to have broken out of its cyclical nature.

My fear is not that we currently are fighting both against and about slavery, it is that we might stop. May the legacy of the Modern Slavery Working Group in this volume serve as fuel for those fights for years to come.

Index

CPSIA information can be obtained
at www.ICGtesting.com
Printed in the USA
LVHW010558240222
711889LV00002B/280